Age Discrimination and Children's Rights

INTERNATIONAL STUDIES IN HUMAN RIGHTS

VOLUME 86

The latest titles published in this series are listed at the end of this volume.

Age Discrimination and Children's Rights

Ensuring Equality and Acknowledging Difference

by

Claire Breen

MARTINUS NIJHOFF PUBLISHERS
LEIDEN • BOSTON
2006

This book is printed on acid-free paper.

Library of Congress Cataloging-in-Publication Data

Breen, Claire.
  Age discrimination and children's rights : ensuring equality and acknowledging difference
/ Claire Breen.
    p. cm. – (International studies in human rights ; v. 86)
  Includes bibliographical references and index.
  ISBN 90-04-14827-2 (alk. paper)
    1. Children's rights. 2. Age discrimination. I. Title. II. Series.

HQ789.B74 2005
323.3'52–dc22

                                                                2005054040

ISBN 90-04-14827-2

© 2006 Koninklijke Brill NV, Leiden, The Netherlands.
Koninklijke Brill NV incorporates the imprints Brill Academic Publishers, Martinus
Nijhoff Publishers and VSP.

PRINTED IN THE NETHERLANDS

For my husband, Al.

CONTENTS

CHAPTER ONE

'Difference' or Discrimination? Exploring the Concepts Underpinning Children's Rights, Discrimination and the Need to Acknowledge Difference

CHAPTER TWO

Children's Rights and Medical Treatment: Issues of Capacity, Choice and Consent

CHAPTER THREE

Human-Assisted Reproduction and the Child's Right to Identity

CHAPTER SIX

Age Discrimination and the Rights
of Irish-Born Children of Asylum Seekers

INTRODUCTION

"during the period for which any living being is said to live and to retain his identity . . . he does not in fact retain the same attributes, although he is called the same person; he is always becoming a new being and undergoing a process of loss and reparation, . . ."[1]

This book starts from the philosophical premise that children are rights-holders. Implicit in this assertion is the recognition that, although rights are accorded to the child, a lack of capacity may inhibit the child from exercising his or her rights. Accordingly, the notion of paternalism is an inherent part of any discussion regarding the exercise or practical effect of the accordance of rights to the child, with much of the analysis surrounding children's rights being imbued with discussions regarding the welfare of the child and determinations of what is in his or her best interests. However, equally implicit in any discussion of children's rights is the gradual replacement of paternalism with autonomy as the guiding principle as to the exercise by the child of his or her rights. Thus, the child matures and evolves towards full capacity and the ensuing autonomy to exercise his or her rights that is generally accorded to adults.

These philosophical premises are echoed in national and international law. The philosophy underpinning rights has found particular legal expression in international human rights law. This body of law consists of the identification of a wide variety of rights which are expressed in broad terms in various human rights instruments and which stipulate that the rights contained therein are to be accorded to all members of the human family, including children. At the level of international law, States may agree to adhere to the rights contained in these instruments and to ensure that such rights are extended to their own citizens. Thus, human rights may become enshrined in domestic legislation as a consequence of the State's legal undertakings in the international sphere. However, in spite of the fact that domestic law may echo provisions of international human rights law, any such echoes may be quite independent, and in fact they often pre-date, any international legal obligations that the State may undertake. Thus, the notion of human rights has found expression, to varying degrees, in domestic law.

---

[1] Plato, *The Symposium* (W Hamilton (trans)), London, Penguin Classics, 1959 at paras 207D-208A.

Central to international human rights law are the concepts of equality and non-discrimination, whereby rights and the legal protection that they afford are to be accorded to all without any discrimination, particularly with regards certain enumerated grounds of which race and gender are two of the more common examples. Discrimination law does not seek to treat all persons equally. Rather, recognition of difference and differential treatment are implicit aspects of those measures that seek to ensure equality in society. Differential treatment only becomes discriminatory treatment once the difference in treatment cannot be justified by virtue of being a legitimate measure whose object and effect are rational and proportionate to the aim of the measure. The distinction to be drawn between discrimination and differential treatment is also a necessary corollary to the notion of human rights, with its emphasis on the rights of the individual. The autonomous nature of human rights is tempered by the fact that such rights are, with only a few exceptions, not absolute. Human rights law recognises and encompasses the need for limitations, limitations that also must be justifiable in order to avoid claims that they are discriminatory. The prohibition of discrimination finds expression at State level with varying degrees of success. National legislation may prohibit conduct or practices that are directly discriminatory or which have the effect of indirectly discriminating against a particular group in society such as women or individuals of a particular ethnicity.

Anti-discrimination law has evolved more recently to include discrimination on the basis of age. Age discrimination legislation derived initially from successful measures to combat the negative differential treatment that was being accorded to older members of society particularly in the area of employment law. The ambit of age discrimination has extended beyond rights issues associated with employment and is increasingly being used to consider the rights of the more mature members of society in areas of law such as health and social welfare. Nor is the expansion of age-related equality legislation limited to the rights protection accorded to this particular societal group. In many jurisdictions, claims of age-based discrimination are being pursued by people of all ages, a basis for discrimination that is arguably infinite. Some States, such as New Zealand and Ireland, have sought to make the bases of age discrimination claims more finite by limiting the categories of individuals that can bring claims of age-based discrimination, namely children and young people under the age of 16 and 18 years respectively. As a consequence, this particularly vulnerable group of rights-holders is prohibited from bringing actions for discrimination on a basis that is particularly pertinent to it without any clear justification for such a limitation on its rights. However, as some of the ensuing chapters of this book demonstrate, such clear legislative measures excluding children and young persons from bringing claims of age-based discrimination are not the only examples of age-based discrimination to affect this group. Limitations on children's rights that, at first glance, may be legitimised by paternalistic notions of securing the welfare and best interests of the child, may not stand up to closer scrutiny. What is perhaps of greater concern is the fact that such limitations, which may also be based upon the need to balance children's rights with those of other rights-holders in general, and parents in particular, have not been subject to the type of scrutiny required by the principles of equality and non-discrimination. This lack of scrutiny lends further support to the argument that the child rights-holder may be the subject of discrimination based on age.

To that end, Chapter 1 explores some of the theories surrounding the implementation of children's rights ranging from historical perceptions with their emphasis upon the philosophies of paternalism and paternal authority through to the more modern conception of children's rights, which focus on children as rights-holders endowed with an evolving capacity to exercise their rights with full autonomy. The exploration of the philosophical bases for children's rights is complimented by an exploration of the legal bases for regarding children as rights-holders within the context of international human rights law, in order to determine whether the bases for the differentiation in the limits imposed upon children's rights satisfy the basic human rights principles of equality and non-discrimination and can, therefore, be regarded as legitimate differentiation. Such exploration encompasses an analysis of theories underpinning discrimination law and its role in distinguishing between legitimate and illegitimate differentiation, or discrimination. Both national and international human rights law provide that differential treatment may be justifiable, and thus non-discriminatory, if it can be established that the limitation is legitimate, proportionate, and necessary. An alternative expression of this test is whether the limitation has an important and significant object, and whether the measures employed to obtain this objective and effects of the objective are rational and proportionate. Accordingly, Chapter 1 will provide the theoretical backdrop against which the issues raised in the ensuing chapters may be considered.

Chapter 2 considers the child's right to medical treatment, or more particularly, whether this right can be refused by either the parents on behalf of their child or by the young person themselves. The issue of medical treatment illustrates vividly the potential for conflict between the core principles underpinning children's rights that are paternalism and autonomy. Not only that, this issue illustrates the need to strike the appropriate balance between the rights of the child and those of the parent or the State, exercising its *parens patriae* jurisdiction, a balance that may mean life or death for the child in question. Chapter 2 seeks to strike such a balance by contending that the legitimacy of any limitations that may be imposed upon the child's right to refuse medical treatment must take into account the obligation to protect and provide for children, which is to regarded as an important and significant objective. Thus, any limitations on the rights of the child in the context of medical treatment – whether such limitations arise from the child, parents or the courts, must satisfy not only that objective but they must also satisfy the further requirements of rationality and proportionality.

Chapter 3 deals with the issue of human-assisted reproduction as an illustration of the often difficult relationship between law and technology. This chapter focuses on one particular issue affecting the human rights of children born of assisted human reproduction (AHR), that is, the right to identity. Encompassed in the child's right to identity is the right of the child to access information regarding his or her genetic identity. Chapter 3 considers whether current New Zealand legislation compromises this right as the law provides for a number of limitations governing if, when, and what type of information may be accessed. In particular, this chapter considers the legitimacy of such limitations as they allow for differential treatment as between various groups of New Zealand children due to the fact that the current legislation, which seeks to regularise the relationship between the adults and children concerned, provides no means of signalling to donor-conceived children that they are not genetically related to either one or both of their birth parents. Moreover, where such children become aware that their genetic parentage may be different to their birth parentage, access to information regarding their genetic parents is also subject to limitations, the justifications for which are also considered in Chapter 3.

The role of the State in balancing children's rights and parental rights is further considered in Chapter 4, which deals with corporal punishment in New Zealand. The defence of domestic discipline highlights the conflict inherent in New Zealand legislation between the comparatively recently-recognised concept of children's rights and the much older concept of parental rights. However, the results of attempts to balance the rights of children and parents have been inconsistent in relation to corporal punishment in terms of the level of protection against assault that has been accorded to children. The courts have not only had to consider what is reasonable punishment, they have also had to try to reconcile the lower level of protection flowing from the defence of domestic discipline with other legislation which is aimed at providing for and protecting children both generally and, more specifically, from domestic violence. Thus, Chapter 4 considers whether the statutory defence to corporal punishment of children encompasses age discrimination, both in light of the fact that it permits differential treatment as between children and adults, but also because it allows the courts to make determinations as to the reasonableness of force used are which based, *inter alia*, upon the age of the child in question.

Chapter 5 examines the protection accorded to the rights of at-risk children in Ireland who are the subjects of the State's exercise of its *parens patriae* jurisdiction.

In Ireland, the right of State intervention to secure the welfare of non-offending children at risk has not been adequately supported by the Government because of it failure to implement policy and to put in place appropriate secure units to ensure their welfare. Rather, in some instances, children have been confined in penal institutions. It is these instances that raise issues of age discrimination as both national and international law prohibit the detention of individuals in penal institutions where such detention is not as a consequence of the committing of a criminal act. However, the lack of care facilities for at-risk children has left the Irish courts with no option but to order such detentions. This chapter considers the State's obligation to secure the welfare and best interests of the child and the extent to which this obligation may be, and has been, used to justify differential treatment. In so doing, it considers whether the principle of the best interests of the child should trump the principle of non-discrimination and equality. Although the protection of and provision for the child may be regarded as being an important and significant objective, Chapter 5 focuses on whether the means used to achieve this objective were rational and proportionate in order to justify such differential treatment.

Chapter 6 examines the rights accorded to Irish-born children of asylum-seekers. Recent changes to the Constitution, which were accompanied by legislative change, have removed the automatic right to citizenship and any Constitutional protection that might ensue. However, the recent change in legislation is not retrospective and, consequently, the Supreme Court decision in *Lobe v Minister for Justice, Equality and Law Reform*,[2] continues to affect those children born before the automatic right to citizenship was removed. The decision has the effect of limiting the citizenship rights of such children since it may give rise to the *de facto* deportation of Irish children as a consequence of the deportation of their non-national parents. In this chapter, the paternalistic aspect of children's rights is considered as the extent to which the children in question may be able to exercise their rights is dependent on upon the ability of their parents to exercise their parental rights. In the context of children born of asylum-seekers, any actions that limit parental rights have to be weighed against the impact of such limitations on the rights of their children in order to determine whether limitations on the rights of the latter are justifiable and amount to no more than legitimate differentiation. Failure to assess such an impact presents issues of age discrimination in its broader sense because such failure does not factor in the extent to which (extreme) youth may act to curtail the capacity to exercise one's rights.

---

[2] *Lobe v Minister for Justice, Equality and Law Reform* [2003] IESC 3 (23 January 2003) http://www.bailii.org.ezproxy.waikato.ac.nz:2048/ie/cases/IESC/2003/3.html, as viewed 27 April 2005.

The ensuing chapters of this text seek to demonstrate that it is not only possible to consider violations of children's rights within the framework of non-
discrimination and equality, but that such a consideration is necessary in order
for States to satisfy their obligations, derived from both national and international law, to prohibit discrimination. The differential treatment accorded to
children, treatment that is normally related to their perceived lack of capacity,
in the context of age-based discrimination should be subjected to closer scrutiny,
so that the same tests of legitimacy, proportionality and necessity that underpin discrimination law in general will provide a further level of protection to
the rights of the child.

CHAPTER ONE

'DIFFERENCE' OR DISCRIMINATION? EXPLORING THE CONCEPTS UNDERPINNING CHILDREN'S RIGHTS, DISCRIMINATION AND THE NEED TO ACKNOWLEDGE DIFFERENCE

The law relating to parent and child is concerned with the problems of the growth and maturity of the human personality. If the law should impose on the process of "growing up" fixed limits where nature knows only a continuous process, the price would be artificiality and a lack of realism in an area where the law must be sensitive to change.[1]

1. Introduction

As the ensuing chapters of this book demonstrate, many jurisdictions, as well as international human rights law, recognise that children are rights-holders. Such recognition obviates the need for this book to re-engage in much of the philosophical enquiries surrounding the issue of whether children are rights-holders. Rather, this chapter will (re)consider the complex nature of children's rights, which stems from the limits on a child's capacity to exercise his or her rights. Although these limits may derive from many sources, they ultimately find expression in legal limitations on whether and to what extent children may exercise their rights. Limitations on the manner and extent to which an individual may put his or her rights into effect is well recognised nationally and internationally. Although human rights law primarily identifies with the autonomous individual, the practicalities of human rights protection, on the whole, requires a balancing of rights between individual rights-holders, be they adults or children. With regard to human rights law in general, the need for balance in determining whether and to what extent an individual's rights may be limited is illustrated by the fundamental principles of equality and non-discrimination. However, much of the analysis surrounding children's rights, in addition to any limitations upon these rights, focuses quite rightly on the welfare of the child and determining what is in the best interests of the child.

---

[1] *Gillick v West Norfolk and Wisbech Area Health Authority* [1986] AC 112, 186, per Lord Scarman.

The limitations imposed upon children's rights by the need to balance these rights with those of other rights-holders in general, and parents in particular, have not been subject to the type of scrutiny required by the principles of equality and non-discrimination. This lack of scrutiny gives rise to the argument that a child rights-holder may be the subject of discrimination based on age.

This chapter will explore some of the theories surrounding the implementation of children's rights in an attempt to determine whether the bases for the differentiation in the limits imposed upon children's rights satisfy the basic human rights principles of equality and non-discrimination and are therefore legitimate. It will also explore some of the theories underpinning discrimination law and its role in distinguishing between legitimate and illegitimate differentiation or discrimination. In so doing, this chapter will provide the theoretical backdrop against which the issues raised in the ensuing chapters may be considered.

2. *Children's Rights: Liberation, Protection or (Il)Legitimate Differentiation?*

The law has always acknowledged that there are differences between children and adults and, accordingly, it has differentiated in its treatment of children and adults. This differentiation in legal treatment was a reflection of varying societal views that, historically, included the notion that children were simply the property of their parents. This view of children was used as the basis for parental, and in actuality paternal, decision-making. Children – who, over time, came to be regarded as something more than simply the property of their parents/father – remained in the firm control of adult decision-makers as, in classic liberal political theory, they were regarded as being as irrational beings[2] dependent on the care of others, normally their parents and, in some cases, the State.

Early discussions about the nature of rights also identified the capacity for rationality and autonomy as being a pre-requisite to having and exercising rights. Although theories of rights have expanded beyond these basic parameters[3] to the

---

[2] See, C Breen, "Traditions of the Western Child: The Social and Legal Constructions of Innocence and the Standard of the Best Interests of the Child" in C Breen, *The Standard of the Best Interests of the Child: A Western Tradition in International and Comparative Law*, Dordrecht, Martinus Nijhoff, 2002, 27, 29–42.

[3] See, e.g., J Rawls, *A Theory of Justice*, Massachusetts, Harvard University Press, 1971; J Feinberg, "The Nature and Value of Rights" in J Feinberg, *Rights, Justice and the Bounds of Liberty: Essays in Social Philosophy*, Princeton, Princeton University Press, 1980, 143; M Freeman, *Rights and Wrongs of Children*, London, Pinter, 1983; R Franklin, "The Case for Children's Rights: A Progress Report" in R Franklin (ed), *The Handbook of Children's Rights: Comparative Policy and Practice*, Routledge, London, 1995, 3.

extent that children are now regarded as rights-holders[4] and notions of rights have become embedded to varying degrees in the laws of many jurisdictions, the initial pre-requisites of rationality and autonomy – repackaged as the issue of capacity – still have currency as they continue to form the basis for the differential treatment between child and adult, particularly with regard to analyses concerning the extent to which children may put their rights into effect. Accordingly, those national and international laws which concern children recognise the 'evolving capacities' of children. They acknowledge that, on the whole, a child's capacity to exercise his or her rights increases with age as the child becomes increasingly independent and able to reason. Thus, the law reflects the changing attributes of individuals as they progress from childhood to adulthood. It is these changing attributes that continue to form the analytical and legal bases for the differential treatment between child and adult.

2.1. Child Protectionism

Child protectionists, who are regarded as being more concerned with the welfare rather than the autonomy of the child, continue to draw on the Lockean notion that children are born as blank slates, slates that are gradually filled in during the process of the physical and mental development of the child. According to Locke, children's natures could be moulded by education, which was to be concerned with the 'best' and fastest ways to produce 'rational' adult men out of immature children.[5] However, Locke was also of the opinion that parents did not have "an authority to make laws and dispose as they please of their [children's] lives and liberties".[6] According to Locke, children and adults alike had natural rights that needed to be protected.[7] He believed that children were destined to take their place in the moral and social order as individuals and that parents were obliged to bring their children to a state where they were capable of independence.[8] As such, Locke's view of paternalism was one whereby paternal authority curbed parental dominance.[9] This recognition of

---

[4] See, e.g., Rawls, ibid, at 506, 509–510; S Wolfson, "Children's Rights: The Theoretical Underpinning of the 'Best Interests of the Child'" in M Freeman and P Veerman (eds), *The Ideologies of Children's Rights*, Dordrecht, Martinus Nijhoff, 1992, 7, at 23; J Kleinig, "Crime and the Concept of Harm" (1978) 15 American Philosophical Quarterly, 27.

[5] J Locke, "Some Thoughts Concerning Education" in J Adamson (ed), *The Educational Writings of John Locke*, London, Edward Arnold, 1912.

[6] J Locke, *Two Treatises of Government*, (P Laslett (ed)), Cambridge, Cambridge University Press, 1960 (originally published in 1690), para 67.

[7] Ibid, paras 56–76.

[8] Ibid.

[9] Ibid.

the difference between child and adult has also been expressed much more recently. According to Goldstein, Freud and Solnit, children differed from adults in their mental nature, their functioning, their understanding of events and their reaction to them. In addition, children also differed amongst themselves in the course of their individual growth and development as a family member.[10] As such, children were not to be regarded as adults in miniature, rather they were to be regarded as beings in their own right. Child protectionists, such as Goldstein, Freud and Solnit, regarded families, on the whole, as being the fundamental unit responsible for, and capable of, providing a child with an environment which served his or her numerous physical and mental needs on a continuing basis during immaturity:[11]

> where the family exerts its influence benevolently, with consideration, understanding, and compassion for each individual child member, the balanced opportunities for a unique development and for social adaptation are maximised.[12]

Child protection theorists, therefore, adhere to paternalism,[13] an already well-established legal approach to decision-making, whereby rational autonomous adults make decisions on behalf of those irrational and dependent individuals on the basis that:

> Interference with a person's liberty of action . . . [is justifiable] by reasons, referring exclusively to the welfare, good, happiness, needs, interests or values of the person being coerced.[14]

Such theories have found legal expression in the concept of *parens patriae*.[15] In the case of children, such decision-making has been formulated in terms of the standard of the best interests of the child or the paramountcy principle with regard to the welfare of the child. As previously mentioned, paternalistic decision-making by adults on behalf of children is justified by virtue of the fact

---

[10] J Goldstein, A Freud and A Solnit, *Beyond the Best Interests of the Child*, London, Burnett Books, 1980; New York, The Free Press, 1973, at 10.

[11] Ibid.

[12] Ibid, at 16.

[13] See, e.g., J Kleinig, *Paternalism*, Totowa, Rowman & Allenheld, 1942; G Dworkin, "Paternalism" in R Wasserstrom (ed), *Morality and the Law*, California, Wadsworth Publishing, 1971, at 107; R Sartorius, *Paternalism*, Minneapolis, University of Minnesota Press, 1983.

[14] Dworkin, ibid, at 108.

[15] The doctrine of *parens patriae*, literally translated as "parents of the country", may be traced back to the early English Court of Chancery where Esher MR, in *R v Gyngall* [1893] 2 QB 232, 239, described it as:

> a paternal power, a judicially administrative jurisdiction, in virtue of which the Chancery Court was put to act on behalf of the Crown, as being the guardian of all infants, in the place of the parent, and, as if it were the parent, of a child, thus superseding the natural guardianship of the parent.

that, according to classical liberal theory, a child is deemed to have an irrational and dependent nature. Such decisions are made on the basis of what is in the latter's best interests or welfare. Although the standard of the best interests of the child or the welfare of the child forms the basis of much of the decision-making, both at national and international levels, it has also been the subject of numerous interpretations and criticisms thereof,[16] as "the flaw is that what is best for any child or even children in general is often indeterminate and speculative and requires a highly individualised choice between alternatives".[17] Furthermore, Jon Elster maintains that the principle of the best interests of the child is "indeterminate, unjust, self-defeating and liable to be overridden by more general policy considerations".[18]

2.2. Child Liberation

Although the nature of children and the nature of the legal protection that was afforded to children can be traced back for millennia, it was only in the early 1970s that the notion of children's rights began to be the subject of any significant academic analysis. The newly emergent discourse on children's rights echoed advances made in both the civil rights movements and women's movement in many jurisdictions in the West. The children's rights movement was also yet another facet of the long history of the relationship between children and the law, a relationship that had evolved from (dis)regarding children as being nothing more than the property of their parents to recognising the need for decision-makers to take the best interests of the child into account.[19] Comparisons were drawn by children's liberationists who sought to emancipate children in much the same way that minorities and women had previously been emancipated.[20] Liberationist writers such as Foster and Freed argued that the law failed to recognise that children were persons and that "The status of minority is the last relic of feudalism. . .".[21] The exclusion or 'segregation' – to use the words of the liberationists – of children from the

---

[16] See, Breen, supra note 2, at 43–63.

[17] R Mnookin and E Szwed, "The Best Interests Syndrome and the Allocation of Power in Child Care" in H Geach and E Szwed (eds), *Providing Civil Justice for Children*, London, Edward Arnold, 1983, at 8.

[18] J Elster, *Solomonic Judgements: Studies in the Limitations of Rationality*, Cambridge, Cambridge University Press, 1989; J Elster, "Solomonic Judgements: Against the Best Interests of the Child" (1987) 54 University of Chicago Law Review, 1–45, at 7.

[19] Breen, supra note 2, at 22–42.

[20] See D Archard, *Children: Rights and Childhood*, London, Routledge, 1993, at 45–46.

[21] H Foster and D Freed, "A Bill of Rights for Children" (1972) 6 Family Law Quarterly, 343, at 345.

adult world was a form of oppressive and unwarranted discrimination based upon a false ideology of 'childhood' which had only recently been invented by Western society. According to John Holt, there was little reason to exclude children from the freedoms granted by the State to adults.[22] Rather, children were to be entitled to all the rights and privileges possessed by adults.[23] The segregation of children and the denial from them of adult rights, such as the rights to travel, work, own property, vote and take control their own sexual lives, inhibited the child's right to self-determination or to make choices as to how to live his or her own life. It was this interference with the child's right to self-determination that most concerned the children's liberationists:

> the issue of self-determination is at the heart of children's liberation. It is, in fact, the only issue, a definition of the entire concept. The acceptance of the child's right to self-determination is fundamental to all the rights to which children are entitled.[24]

Whilst the writings of Holt and Farson may be particularly memorable for their radical views on children's rights, the basis for such views lay in Farson and Holt's criticisms; first, of age as an arbitrary criterion for the possession or otherwise of rights, and second, of children's lack of competence which disqualified them from being rights-holders. It is these criticisms that continue to inform much of the discussion on children's rights.

Later advocates of child liberation asserted that lack of competency on the part of a child should not constitute a sufficient reason to deny the child rights and maintained that children do in fact display a competence for rational thought and that they can make informed choices.[25] They further argued that children should be allowed to make decisions, even incorrect ones, because they would never gain experience in such matters otherwise and that children should not be prevented from making decisions simply because they might make the wrong ones.[26] In Dworkian terms, the right to do some thing should not be confused with doing the right thing.[27] Any lack of competency in decision-making on the part of children was not a sufficient reason to exclude children from participation in decision-making, on the grounds that adults may also be

---

[22] See, J Holt, *Escape from Childhood: The Needs and Rights of Children*, Harmondsworth, Penguin, 1975.

[23] Ibid, 18.

[24] R Farson, *Birthrights*, London/New York, Macmillan, 1974, at 27.

[25] C.f. MDA Freeman, *Rights and Wrongs of Children*, London, Pinter, 1983.

[26] J Harris, "The Political Status of Children", in K Graham (ed), *Contemporary Political Philosophy*, Cambridge, Cambridge University Press, 1982; R Franklin, "The Case For Children's Rights: A Progress Report" in R Franklin (ed), *The Handbook of Children's Rights: Comparative Policy and Practice*, London, Routledge, 1995.

[27] R Dworkin, *Taking Rights Seriously*, London, Duckworth, 1977, at 188.

lacking in such competency to a similar degree and that exclusion on this basis could amount to a double standard.

The right to self-determination, or freedom to choose, is certainly a fundamental tenet to the concept of rights. In politico-philosophical terms, Archard describes modern liberal theory as being based on the contention that:

> all adult human beings are capable of making rational autonomous decisions. In view of this they should be left to lead their own lives as they see fit. The one constraint on this freedom is that its exercise should not interfere with a similar freedom of others.[28]

The basis for this capacity is derived from Locke's reasoning that individuals are usually the best judges of what is in their interests and acting on the contrary assumption, that others may know better, is likely to lead to far worse outcomes. But such observations should also be weighed against Locke's comments regarding children, as identified above. Although the child liberationists may trace their theories back to Lockean notions of liberal theory, Locke himself did not regard children as being autonomous rational beings and thus the Lockean liberal theories as a basis for theories of child liberation are somewhat flawed. A similar analogy may be drawn between the theories of child liberation and child protection, which may serve as counter-weights in decision-making, as such decision-making is undertaken both by and for children.

More recently, the debate between child protection and child liberation has been recast in the mould of rights wherein a distinction has been drawn between welfare rights – rights to protection – on the one hand, and liberty rights – rights to participation – on the other.[29] Welfare rights have been considered to be concerned with the protection of children, whereas liberty rights have been described as being geared towards a child's self-determination.[30] Farson described this distinction as being one where welfare rights protected children whilst liberty rights protected children's rights.[31] According to Freeman, welfare rights or protection rights merely required that the individual possessed interests which could be protected and promoted, as in the doctrine of the best interests of the child. In contrast, the hypothesis that lay behind participation rights was based on the requirement that, in order for the individual to be recognised as a right-holder, he or she was to be capable of making and exercising choices. Freeman asserted that those persons who sought to accord protection rights to children also sought to deny children

---

[28] Archard, supra note 20, at 52.
[29] Freeman, supra note 25, at 40–43.
[30] Ibid, at 43–45.
[31] Farson, supra note 24, at 9.

their participation rights. As such, these individuals argued, first, that children were not rational and were incapable of making reasonable and informed decisions and that lack of maturity was sufficient reason to deny autonomy to children. Secondly, they maintained that children were prone to make mistakes because they lacked the wisdom that came with the experience of life and that children should be protected from their own incompetence.[32]

Irrespective of the potential merits of such arguments, mid-adolescence has now been identified as the period when a child's cognitive processes have been regarded as being developed enough to allow the majority of children to become autonomous and capable of exercising their right to self-determination.[33] Consequently, discussions regarding the autonomy of younger children and their right to self-determination may not be as pertinent and there is a degree of consensus regarding the need to protect children, from themselves and others[34] that is reflected in domestic legislation and international children's rights law.

3. Children's Rights, Interests, and the Law

At the level of international law, at least, the conflict between paternalism and autonomy has been resolved somewhat by the approach adopted in the United Nations Convention on the Rights of the Child 1989. Not only is the best interests standard one of the governing General Principles of the Convention, it may also be regarded as being a general overall theme given that it appears eight times in the fifty-four article Convention. Although the ideology of welfarism may have permeated the Convention, it is the language of rights which dominates as is apparent from the Convention's title. Accordingly, the basis for the interrelationship between the rights and the protection to be granted to the child would appear to be enshrined in the provisions of the Convention, which are to be interpreted in accordance with the best interests of the child.

The balance between autonomy and paternalism is also to be found in the Preamble to the Convention, which recognises that "the family is the fundamental group in society and the natural environment for the growth and

---

[32] Freeman, supra note 25, at 40–60.

[33] See, J Fortin, *Children's Rights and the Developing Law*, London, Butterworths, 2003, at 26–28.

[34] See, L Fox Harding, *Perspectives in Child Care Policy*, London, Longman (1997), ch 5; Archard, supra note 20, chs 4 and 5.

well-being . . . of children"[35] and that the child "should grow up in a family environment".[36] However, Article 3(1) recognises the concept of special protection for children with its express provision for decisions regarding the child to be made by persons external to the family unit who may act on behalf of, or in the place of parents:

> In all actions concerning children, whether undertaken by public or private social welfare institutions, courts of law, administrative authorities or legislative bodies, the best interests of the child shall be a primary consideration.[37]

The child's best interests are to be "a primary consideration", which means that the interests of the child are not to be the overriding, paramount consideration in every case. This recognises that other parties might have equal or even superior legal interests in some cases (e.g., medical emergencies during childbirth). However, the drafters intended this provision to establish the principle that official decisions affecting a child must be taken with primary consideration for the child's best interests, and that neither the interests of the parents nor the interests of the State should be the most important consideration.[38] More specifically, whilst Article 3(2) recognises that parents have rights and duties, it also charges "States Parties to undertake to ensure to the child such protection and care as is necessary for his well-being" and they are charged to undertake all legislative and administrative measures to do so. The duties placed upon States by Article 3 were expanded upon by the Committee on the Rights of the Child in its General Comment 5:

> Every legislative, administrative and judicial body or institution is required to apply the best interests principle by systematically considering how children's rights and interests are or will be affected by their decisions and actions – by, for example, a proposed or existing law or policy or administrative action or court decision, including those that are not directly concerned with children, but indirectly affect children.[39]

The interrelationship between parental rights and those of the child is further recognised in Article 5 of the Convention, which states that:

> States Parties shall respect the responsibilities, rights and duties of parents . . . to provide, in a manner consistent with the evolving capacities of the child,

---

[35] Preamble, United Nations Convention on the Rights of the Child, UN Doc. A/44/736, (1989), UNGA Doc. A/Res/44/25 of 5 December, (1989) 28 I.L.M., 1448, (1989), at para 5.

[36] Ibid, para 6.

[37] UN Doc. E/CN.4/1989/WG.1/WP.2; See also E/CN.4/1989/29/Rev.1, 5.

[38] UN Doc. E/CN.4/L.1575, at 3–5; UN Doc. E/CN.4/1989/WG.1/WP.2, at para 118–125.

[39] Committee on the Rights of the Child (2003), General Comment *No. 5: General measures of implementation for the Convention on the Rights of the Child*, at para 12.

appropriate direction and guidance in the exercise of the rights recognised in the . . . Convention.

The concept of the 'evolving capacities of the child' and the weighting of children's rights against those of his or her parents is echoed in Article 12's recognition of the right of the child to express an opinion and to have that opinion taken into account:

1. States Parties shall assure to the child who is capable of forming his or her own views the right to express those views freely in all matters affecting the child, the views of the child being given due weight in accordance with the age and maturity of the child.
2. For this purpose, the child shall in particular be provided the opportunity to be heard in any judicial and administrative proceedings affecting the child, either directly, or through a representative or an appropriate body, in a manner consistent with the procedural rules of national law.

Therefore, the obligations imposed upon decision-makers by Article 3 are amplified by the requirements of Article 12 of the Convention. Whilst the Convention itself does not specify whose rights are to prevail, the spirit and purpose of the Convention would indicate that the rights of the child are to trump those of the parents. Even if the Convention is not equivocal on this matter, the Committee on the Rights of the Child, in relation to the issue of corporal punishment, has stated that:

A way should . . . be found of striking the balance between the responsibilities of the parents and the rights and evolving capacities of the child that was implied in article 5 of the Convention.[40]

At the level of regional human rights protection, Europe provides probably the most comprehensive system of protection.[41] Under the auspices of the Council of Europe, three human rights treaties seek to protect children's rights. Various Articles of the European Convention on Human Rights have been interpreted to protect the (civil and political) rights and interests of children[42] whilst greater emphasis upon protecting the economic and social rights

---

[40] Summary Record of the 205th Meeting, U.N. GAOR, Comm. on the Rts. of the Child, 8th Sess., 205th mtg., U.N. Doc. CRC/C/SR.205 (1995) at 17.

[41] C.f. the African Charter on the Rights and Welfare of the Child 1990 OAU Doc. CAB/LEG/24.9/49 (1990), which expands upon the sole reference to the rights of the child contained in the African [Banjul] Charter on Human and Peoples' Rights 1981, OAU Doc. CAB/LEG/67/3 rev. 5, 21 I.L.M. 58 (1982) Article 18.

[42] For example, the prohibition on inhuman and degrading punishment in Article 3, the right to liberty and security in Article 5 and protection of the right to respect for private and family life in Article 8. The protection afforded by these rights to children and young persons is more fully considered in the ensuing chapters.

of children is to be found in the European Social Charter.[43] The European Convention on the Exercise of Children's Rights,[44] which is aimed at securing the rights of children in family proceedings, describes its object and purpose as:

> in the best interests of children, to promote their rights, to grant them procedural rights and to facilitate the exercise of these rights by ensuring that children are, themselves or through other persons or bodies, informed and allowed to participate in proceedings affecting them before a judicial authority.[45]

To that end, the Convention's provisions include procedural measures to promote the exercise of children's rights and outline the roles of the judiciary and legal representatives which are underpinned by the best interests standard.

Finally, a further level of protection is accorded to European children by Article 24 of the Charter of Fundamental Rights of the European Union (the European Charter),[46] which states:

1. Children shall have the right to such protection and care as is necessary for their well-being.
2. In all actions relating to children, whether taken by public authorities or private institutions, the child's best interests must be a primary consideration.
3. Every child shall have the right to maintain on a regular basis a personal relationship and direct contact with both his or her parents, unless that is contrary to his or her interests.

These treaties are a valuable tool in determining the balance to be achieved between protection and autonomy when securing children's rights at the level of international law. The jurisprudence generated by the treaties, perhaps most especially with regard to the balance between parental rights and children's rights stemming from the European Court of Human Rights,[47] is a useful indicator of how international standards are to be applied within the domestic context. Finally, given that European Union law forms part of the law of Union members, increased recognition of the international rights of the child will become inevitable.

---

[43] European Social Charter CETS No.: 035. For example, Part 1(7) states that children and young persons have the right to a special protection against the physical and moral hazards to which they are exposed, Article 7 secures the right of children and young persons to protection in employment, and Article 17 provides the right of mothers and children to social and economic protection.

[44] European Treaty Series – No. 160, 25.I.1996.

[45] Article 1(2).

[46] (2000/C 364/01).

[47] See, Breen, "The Emerging Tradition of the Best Interests of the Child in the European Convention on Human Rights" in C Breen, supra note 2, at 241.

4. Equality and Non-Discrimination in International and
National Human Rights Law

The recasting of the debate between child protection and child liberation into
the language of rights is also useful from a human rights perspective because
it draws on the recognition that not all rights are absolute and that, in the
implementation and protection of human rights, a balance needs to be struck.
Effective protection against discrimination ultimately relies upon the recognition of difference. This recognition of difference extends equally to children and
there are a number of reasons as to why children are treated differently when it
comes to the extent to which they can exercise their rights. Consequently, children often are not in a position to assert their rights or challenge those decisions that may be made of their behalf. The legitimacy of limits on the rights
of the child have traditionally been measured by the standard of the best interests or welfare of the child and have been justified by reference to the argument that decisions that are made in the best interests of the child best protect
the rights of the child. Non-discrimination and equality legislation does not
extend, on the whole, to protecting the rights of the child.[48] However, it is
important to ensure that anti-discrimination legislation is in place and that it
constitutes an effective mechanism to respond to potentially illegitimate limits
on rights, irrespective of whether they are held by children or by adults. That
said, the achievement of equality in rights protection between children and
adults will have to recognise the difference between children and adults where
such difference is based on the drawing of valid distinctions between the two
groups. The actual appropriate response is a question of balance in every case
whereby the appropriate administrative or judicial decision-makers assess the
legitimacy, proportionality and necessity of the limitation in question.

4.1. Equality and Non-Discrimination in International Human Rights Law

The principles of non-discrimination and equality constitute the cornerstone
of international human rights treaties, which enshrine the notion that dignity
and equality is to be accorded to *all* human beings. The underlying theme of
all international human rights treaties is that the rights that they seek to protect apply to everyone without distinction, whether the rights are contained in
the more 'historical', 'bedrock' instruments such as the Universal Declaration
of Human Rights,[49] the International Covenant on Civil and Political Rights[50]

---

[48] For example s 21(1)(e) of the New Zealand Human Rights Act 1991.
[49] Universal Declaration of Human Rights, G.A. Res. 217A, (III) U.N. Doc. A1810 (1948).
[50] International Covenant on Civil and Political Rights, U.N. G.A. Res. 2200 (XXI), 21 UN
GAOR, Supp. (No. 16) 52, U.N. Doc. A16316 (1966).

and the International Covenant on Economic, Social and Cultural Rights,[51] or whether they are to be found in more specialised treaties such as the United Nations Convention on the Rights of the Child.[52]

The Universal Declaration of Human Rights (the Declaration) states that all human beings are "born free and equal in dignity and rights . . ."[53] Moreover, Article 1 of the Declaration provides that "All human beings are born . . . equal in dignity and rights" whilst Article 2 states that "Everyone is entitled to all the rights and freedoms set forth in this Declaration, without distinction of any kind such as . . . birth or other status." These principles and rights were given a legally binding nature in the International Covenant on Civil and Political Rights (ICCPR) and the International Covenant on Economic, Social and Cultural Rights (ICESCR). The Preambles to both Covenants also state that their rights are to be extended to "everyone" as well as recognising "the inherent dignity"[54] and "the equal and inalienable rights of all members of the human family"[55] where such rights "derive from the inherent dignity of the human person".[56] Similarly, Article 2(1) of the ICCPR, echoing the principles of the Declaration, states that:

> Each State Party to the present Covenant undertakes to respect and to ensure to all individuals within its territory and subject to its jurisdiction the rights recognised in the present Covenant, without distinction of any kind, such as . . . birth or other status.[57]

Furthermore, Article 2(2) requires that:

> Where not already provided for by existing legislative or other measures, each State Party to the present Covenant undertakes to take the necessary steps, in accordance with its constitutional processes and with the provisions of the present Covenant, to adopt such legislative or other measures as may be necessary to give effect to the rights recognised in the present Covenant.[58]

In terms of the rights of the child, the notions of dignity and equality are enhanced by the recognition of the special protection accorded by international

---

[51] International Covenant on Economic, Social and Cultural Rights, G.A. Res. (XXI), U.N. GAOR 21st SESS., (Supp. No. 16), at 49, U.N. Doc. A/6316 (1966).
[52] United Nations Convention on the Rights of the Child, supra note 30.
[53] Universal Declaration, supra note 49, at Article 1.
[54] ICCPR, supra note 50, Preamble, para 1. ICESCR, supra note 51, Preamble, para 1.
[55] Ibid.
[56] Ibid, at para 2.
[57] ICCPR, supra note 50.
[58] Ibid.

human rights instruments to the rights of the child which can be traced back to Article 24(1) of the ICCPR, which states:

> Every child shall have, without any discrimination as to race, colour, sex, language, religion, national or social origin, property or birth, the right to such measures of protection as are required by his status as a minor, *on the part of his family, society and the State*.[59]

More recent treaties have been aimed at the protection of the rights of more vulnerable members of society and reiterate these fundamental principles.[60] The Preamble to the Convention on the Rights of the Child reiterates the recognition by the United Nations Charter of the inherent dignity of all members of the human family as well as its recognition of the dignity and worth of the human person. It also recognises that the fundamental rights and freedoms contained in the Declaration and the International Covenants should be extended to all individuals without "distinction of any kind", and considers that the child should be brought up in the spirit of the ideals proclaimed in the Charter including dignity and equality. Article 2 of the Convention contains the Convention's principle of non-discrimination whereby all rights contained in the Convention are to be extended to all children "without discrimination of any kind".[61]

These provisions have been expanded upon by the Committee on Human Rights which has drafted a number of General Comments pertaining to equality and non-discrimination.[62] The Preamble to the Convention on the Rights of the Child reiterates the recognition by the UN Charter of the inherent dignity of all members of the human family as well as its recognition of the dignity and worth of the human person. The Preamble also states that the fundamental rights and freedoms contained in the Declaration and the International

---

[59] See also, ICCPR, GENERAL COMMENT 17: *Rights of the child (Art. 24): 07/04/8.*

[60] See, e.g., International Convention on the Elimination of All Forms of Racial Discrimination 1965, 660 U.N.T.S. 195; Convention against Torture and Other Cruel, Inhuman or Degrading Treatment or Punishment 1984, G.A. res. 39/46, annex, 39 U.N. GAOR Supp. (No. 51) at 197, U.N. Doc. A/39/51 (1984); Convention on the Elimination of All Forms of Discrimination against Women 1979, G.A. res 34/180, 1249 U.N.T.S. 13 (1979).

[61] Convention on the Rights of the Child, supra note 30.

[62] CCPR, GENERAL COMMENT 3: *Implementation at the national level (Art. 2): 29/07/81;* CCPR, GENERAL COMMENT *4: Equality between the sexes (Art. 3) 30/07/81;* CCPR, GENERAL COMMENT 13: *Equality before the courts and the right to a fair and public hearing by an independent court established by law (Art. 14) 13/04/84;* CCPR, GENERAL COMMENT 15: *The position of aliens under the Covenant 11/04/86;* CCPR, GENERAL COMMENT 18: *Non-discrimination 10/11/89;* GENERAL COMMENT 27: *Freedom of movement (Art.12), CCPR/C/21/Rev.1/Add.9, 02/11/99;* CPPR, GENERAL COMMENT 28: *Equality of rights between men and women (article 3), CCPR/C/21/Rev.1/Add.10. 29/03/2000.*

Covenants should be extended to all individuals without "distinction of any kind" and that the child should also be brought up in the spirit of the ideals proclaimed in the Charter including dignity and equality. In terms of non-discrimination and equality, Article 2 of the Convention on the Rights of the Child states:

1. States Parties shall respect and ensure the rights set forth in the present Convention to each child within their jurisdiction without discrimination of any kind, *irrespective of the child's or his or her parent's . . . status.*
2. States Parties shall take all appropriate measures to ensure that the child is protected against all forms of discrimination or punishment on the basis of the *status . . .* of the child's parents . . .[63] [emphasis added]

Regional examples of the prohibition on discrimination include the American Convention, which specifies that its rights are to be extended to every human being[64] whilst also declaring that "everyone has the right to have . . . his dignity respected."[65] Article 1 of the European Convention on Human Rights and Fundamental Freedoms (the European Convention) reiterates the language of the United Nations treaties with its guarantee that the rights contained in the Convention are to be secured to "everyone".[66] Equally, Article 14 repeats the theme of non-discrimination with its statement that "the rights and freedoms set forth in this Convention shall be secured without discrimination on any ground . . .". The Charter of Fundamental Rights of the European Union (the European Charter)[67] goes further that the European Convention, as the Preamble to the European Charter states that the European Union "is founded on the indivisible, universal values of human dignity, freedom, [and] equality . . .".[68] Furthermore, Article 21(1) of the European Charter states:

Any discrimination based on any ground such as sex, race, colour, ethnic or social origin, genetic features, language, religion or belief, political or any other opinion, membership of a national minority, property, birth, disability, age or sexual orientation shall be prohibited.

Moreover, the Preamble notes that "Enjoyment of these rights entails responsibilities and duties with regard to other persons, to the human community

---

[63] Convention on the Rights of the Child, supra note 30.
[64] American Convention on Human Rights, O.A.S. Treaty Series No. 36, Article 1(2).
[65] Ibid, Article 11(1).
[66] *European Convention for the Protection of Human Rights and Fundamental Freedoms*, 213 U.N.T.S., p. 221, no. 2889; Council of Europe, European Treaty Series, 4 November 1950, no. 5; Council of Europe, Collected Texts, Strasbourg (1987), 3–21.
[67] Charter of Fundamental Rights of the European Union, 2000/c 364/01 (2000).
[68] Preamble, European Charter, ibid, at para 2.

and to future generations."[69] Not only are fundamental human rights principles given an update, they are also given a rights basis. As such, the significance of human dignity is highlighted in Article 1 which states that "Human
dignity is inviolable. It must be respected and protected."

Given the legally binding nature of treaties, in addition to the status of the
Declaration as part of customary international law, each of the above instruments impose legally binding obligations on States Parties, albeit within the
sphere of international law only.

4.2. Limits to Non-Discrimination

The fact that human rights treaties accord rights to all without distinction
should not be confused with the fact that not all of these rights are accorded
absolutely and their exercise is subject to varying degrees of limitation. Thus, in
determining the extent to which these rights may be exercised, a balance must
be struck to reflect the tension in the relationship between the rights-holder and
the State, and as between rights-holders themselves. Human rights law recognises the need for such flexibility in the exercise of rights to reflect that tension.
This flexibility finds expression in the proviso that rights may be limited.

Limitations on rights may be achieved in a number of ways. First, rights
may be categorised as positive and negative rights. Thus, in human rights language, the accordance of negative rights to individuals means that States are
obliged to refrain from certain actions which would otherwise be a violation
of those (negative) rights. Second, the language used to frame the right is a further means by which it may be limited. The extent of the obligation to refrain
may vary from being absolute to permitting some interference in or limitation
on the right, depending on the circumstances. For example, Article 2(1) of the
ICCPR places an obligation on States Parties "to respect . . .," which means that
States Parties must not restrict the exercise of any of the rights contained in the
Covenant, unless such a restriction is allowed by the provisions of the Covenant.[70]

---

[69] Ibid, at para 6.

[70] The first example of the limitation of ICCPR rights is to be found in Article 4(1) of the
Covenant, with its provision that:

> In time of public emergency which threatens the life of the nation and the existence of which is officially
> proclaimed, the States Parties to the present Covenant may take measures derogating from their obliga-
> tions under the present Covenant to the extent strictly required by the exigencies of the situation, provided
> that such measures are not inconsistent with their other obligations under international law and do not
> involve discrimination solely on the ground of race, colour, sex, language, religion or social origin.

Article 7 of the ICCPR is an example of an absolute right with its prohibition on torture in
all circumstances. Other provisions permit a degree of restriction so that only arbitrary interference is prohibited, for example, with respect to the right to life as provided for in Article 6(1).

The law also places obligations upon the State to take certain actions. This concept also finds expression in human rights law, which speaks in terms of positive rights requiring a State to undertake some action. Such rights are known as positive rights or programmatic rights and are perhaps best exemplified by the ICESCR.[71] Like the rights contained in the ICCPR, these rights are also subject to limitations, although language-based limitations are used to a lesser degree in the ICESCR. Rather, 'blanket' limitations are used to a greater degree such as that contained in Article 4 of the ICESCR, which states that the rights contained therein are subject to limitations "as are determined by law only in so far as this may be compatible with the nature of these rights and solely for the purpose of promoting the general welfare in a democratic society". Furthermore, Article 5(1) states:

> Nothing in the present Covenant may be interpreted as implying for any State, group or person any right to engage in any activity or to perform any act aimed at the destruction of any of the rights or freedoms recognized herein, or at their limitation to a greater extent than is provided for in the present Covenant.

However, the extent of the obligations imposed upon States Parties to put programmes in place to secure such rights is limited to the extent to which they can afford to, as Article 2(1) is subject to the proviso "to the maximum of its available resources, with a view to achieving progressively the full realization

---

Finally, States Parties may impose certain restrictions on the rights contained in other articles of the ICCPR whereby, for example, the right to freedom of expression provided for in Article 19(2) is limited by the provisions of Article 19(3)(a) and (b) – which are aimed at protecting the rights and reputations of others and national security, public order, or of public health or morals respectively – and which is also subject to Article 20(2)'s prohibition on the advocacy of racial hatred.

[71] S Joseph, J Schulz and M Castan, M, *The International Covenant on Civil and Political Rights: Cases, Material and Commentary,* Oxford, OUP, 2000, at 21–22. Examples of such rights are to be found, inter alia, in the ICESCR, Article 10(3) of which seeks to protect the rights of children and young people by putting States Parties under the obligation to take "special measures of protection and assistance . . . on behalf of all children and young persons without any discrimination for reasons of parentage or other conditions." States Parties are obliged to protect children and young persons from economic and social exploitation. Accordingly, Article 10(3) makes reference to the need for States Parties to pass legislation whereby the employment of children and young people:

> in work harmful to their morals or health or dangerous to life or likely to hamper their normal development should be punishable by law. States should also set age limits below which the paid employment of child labour should be prohibited and punishable by law.

The ICESCR also includes the right to education, as provided for in Article 13(1), with its associated obligations contained in Article 13(2) which imposes on States Parties obligations such as to make primary education "compulsory and freely available to all" and the obligation to make secondary education "generally available and accessible to all by every appropriate means, and in particular by the progressive introduction of free education".

of the rights recognized in the present Covenant by all appropriate means, including particularly the adoption of legislative measures".[72]

Positive rights may also stem from those very same negative rights requiring the State to refrain from acting in a certain manner. As such, the positive character of civil and political rights, which were traditionally classified as negative rights,[73] can also be seen in Article 2(1) of the ICCPR with its obligation 'to ensure' all rights contained in the Covenant. This obligation requires States Parties to take positive steps to give effect to the ICCPR rights and to enable individuals to enjoy these rights.[74] This duty of performance implies the obligation to adopt the necessary legislative and other measures under Article 2(2), to provide an effective remedy to victims of human rights violations pursuant to Article 2(3), and to safeguard certain rights institutionally by way of procedural guarantees or the establishment of relevant legal institutions.[75] Similarly, the requirement of positive action may become apparent in other areas. For example, the prohibition on discrimination contained in Article 3 of the ICCPR has been interpreted to include all rights, which indicates that the enforcement of civil and political rights has been permeated by the positive language more commonly associated with economic, social and cultural rights.[76]

The role of human rights law is not confined to the vertical effect of regulating the relationship between the State and individuals by protecting the rights of the latter from interference by the State. It also extends to regulating relationships between individuals. With regard to the ICCPR, for example,

---

[72] The extent of the limitations on States Parties' obligations are spelt out in more detail in the Limburg Principles on the Implementation of the International Covenant on Economic, Social and Cultural Rights in UN Doc E/CN.4/1987/17, at paras 16–34.

[73] Joseph, supra note 71.

[74] See, General Comment 3(13), para.1 UN Doc. CCPR/C/21Rev.1, 3; UN Doc HRI/GEN/1/Rev.3, 4–5 as cited in M Nowak, "The Covenant on Civil and Political Rights" in R Hanski and M Suksi (eds), *An Introduction to the International Protection of Human Rights: A Textbook* (2nd ed), Turku/Abo: Institute for Human Rights, Abo Akademi University, 1999, at 87.

[75] A classic example of such a right is that regarding the prohibition of torture has some positive elements such as the obligation to take effective steps for the prevention of torture by implementing procedural guarantees to prevent the occurrence of torture and to investigate allegations of its occurrence: Nowak, ibid, at 87–88. This interpretation has been substantiated by the Human Rights Committee, which has stated that States Parties have duties to investigate alleged violations of the ICCPR, as well as to provide procedures and mechanisms to prevent breaches of the Covenant. See, e.g., Human Rights Committee General Comment 20, *Replaces general comment 7 concerning prohibition of torture and cruel treatment or punishment (Art. 7)*, 1992.

[76] *Broeks v Netherlands* (172/84) and *Zwaan-de-Vries v Netherlands* (182/84), cited in Joseph, supra note 71, at 17, 23.

Article 2(1)'s obligation 'to ensure' also implies a basic obligation to protect individuals against certain interferences with their civil and political rights by other private individuals, groups or entities. This horizontal effect operates similarly to the vertical effect by imposing requirements upon individuals to refrain from committing certain acts and by also placing obligations upon individuals to act in a certain way. Similarly to the vertical effects of State obligations, the protection offered by the horizontal effects of the Covenant's obligations depends upon the precise wording of the provision. Therefore, the general duty 'to ensure' implies a duty of a varying degree of strictness to protect violations of their rights under the Covenant by others. There are some provisions which will have primarily a horizontal effect such as the right to freedom of expression which must be balanced with the positive requirement placed upon the State to prohibit advocacy of racial hatred (Article 20). Others, such as the right to life (Article 6) indicate a special requirement to take positive measures to protect the right to life so that States must provide legal protection from homicides.

In summary, therefore, human rights law is made up of positive and negative human rights, which have a horizontal or vertical effect, and which may be subject to some limitation.[77]

Third, one of the clearest provisos regarding the limitations that may be put upon rights is to be found in the European Convention on Human Rights, with many Articles stating that the right is subject to limitation only:

> except such as is in accordance with the law and is necessary in a democratic society in the interests of national security, public safety or the economic well-being of the country, for the prevention of disorder or crime, for the protection of health or morals, or for the protection of the rights and freedoms of others.[78]

It is these limitations that form the bases of enquiries into whether the limitations in question are legitimate or illegitimate. To that end, the European Court of Human Rights stated that:

> A Difference in treatment is discriminatory if it has no reasonable justification: that is, if it does not pursue a legitimate aim, or there is not a reasonable relationship of proportionality between the means employed and the aim sought to be realised.[79]

As such, differential treatment will constitute discrimination if it places a disproportionate burden on the group in question unless this burden is justified.

---

[77] See further, Joseph, supra note 71, at 21–22.

[78] See, e.g., Article 8 (right to respect for private and family life) and Article 9 (right to freedom of thought, conscience and religion).

[79] *Belgian Linguistic Case (No.2)* Series A No 6 (1968) 1 EHRR 252, at para 10; *Marckx v Belgium* Series A No 31 91979) 2 EHRR 330, at para 33.

These international legal obligations also find expression in domestic law.[80] That leaves the courts with the issue of determining what is justifiable or legitimate. The court will have to determine whether there is no alternative but to adopt unequal treatment or alternatively it may choose to accept an (apparently) rational explanation for the unequal treatment.[81]

5. Equality and Age-Based Differentiation

Any analysis of the relationship between children and the law, whether that law operates at the national or international level, reveals the particular difficulties inherent in this relationship. Inasmuch as law in general has the dual purpose of emancipating and protecting its subjects, so too does the law regarding children. As the previous section demonstrates, this function of the law is particularly apparent in human rights law, which serves to emancipate individuals by according them rights against the State by both protecting them from undue interference by the State and by the right to make demands against the State. The manner in which the law operates must be equal and non-discriminatory. Both of these principles are well recognised and are underpinned by the principles of equality and non-discrimination, so that the necessity of balancing the extent and impact of human rights is not without scrutiny. Such scrutiny recognises that, although all human beings are rights-holders and that rights are inalienable and inherent, rights-holders nevertheless face a range of difficulties that may range from legitimate limitations to illegitimate limitations. Ultimately, however, the question of whether a person may legitimately demand a particular right may be answered by whether a decision not to accord that person that right would be discriminatory and would subject that person to unequal treatment by the law where such unequal treatment is measured in a variety of ways. At its most simple level, the aim of equality is that of treating like with like.[82] In response to the observation that such an approach may allow for individuals, in this case children, to be treated equally badly a number of other formulations of equality have

---

[80] See, e.g., s 5 New Zealand Bill of Rights Act 1990, s 19 Human Rights Act 1991 (New Zealand), s 1(1)(b) Race Relations Act 1976 (UK) and s 1(1) Sex Discrimination Act 1975, and s 3(1)(c)(iv) Equal Status Act 2000 (Ireland). Ireland's legislation is regrettably notable as s 3(3) provides that the treatment of a person who has not attained the age of 18 years less favourably or more favourably than another, whatever that other person's age, is not to be regarded as discrimination on the grounds of age.

[81] S Fredman, "The Age of Equality" in S Fredman and S Spencer (eds), *Age as an Equality Issue: Legal and Policy Perspectives,* Hart, Oxford, 2003, 21–69, at 60.

[82] Ibid, at 38.

been identified. However, the utility of such formulations has been under-mined by the fact that they tend to rely upon group-based stereotypical assumptions that overlook the capacity of the individual.[83] The use of stereo-types as a basis for equality may not be problematic and arguably it is inevitable because inasmuch as one's gender or ethnicity may serve as a trig-ger for differential treatment, so too does one's age.

Even a cursory glance across domestic legislation aimed at equality and non-discrimination will reveal that it is formulated in terms of direct and indi-rect discrimination. Thus, at this point, the distinction that is commonly drawn between direct and indirect discrimination should be referred to because of the particular difficulties that these forms of discrimination pose for age-based distinctions and children's rights. Direct discrimination is based on the principle that there will only be direct discrimination if there is inconsis-tent treatment as between the complainant and a similarly-situated person. Courts would be unlikely to regard an adult as a similarly-situated person and consequently the comparator would have to be another child. This outcome could prove somewhat problematic for the advancement of equality for chil-dren as direct discrimination may be difficult to prove if all children are treated equally badly,[84] for example, if all children are denied access to their biological parentage or all children have the potential to be subjected to phys-ical punishment. Fredman suggests that the adoption of legislation would pro-hibit the subjection of a person to a detriment simply on the grounds of age,[85] which would avoid the problem of all children being treated equally badly. However, such legislation would need to take into account the legitimacy of subjecting an individual to detriment by limiting their rights, once such a lim-itation was deemed to be legitimate, proportionate and necessary. Indirect discrimination – in terms of age – covers instances of apparently equal treat-ment which impacts more heavily on people of a certain age. The requirement of differential impact has proven difficult even in the more 'straightforward' categories of discrimination of race and sex. In terms of age discrimination, the difficulty lies in the need to find a fixed comparative group, which is more difficult in terms of age because it may be difficult to identify a specific age cat-egory or limit of quantify the degree of difference between comparators in terms of age – 6 days, or 6 months.[86] The difficulty in finding a fixed comparative

---

[83] Ibid, at 39.
[84] Ibid, at 55–56.
[85] Ibid, at 56.
[86] Ibid, at 56–57. Fredman explores numerous models of equality, all of which reveal them-selves as relying on stereotypes and being unable to avoid the criticism of being arbitrary. However, the inability to escape stereotypes and any consequent arbitrariness is not a problem in itself once those stereotypes are not demeaning and any ensuing arbitrariness can be justified.

group has led to age-based distinctions as a basis for legitimate differentiation, in spite of the apparent arbitrariness of such an approach which is contrary to the philosophy underpinning equality and non-discrimination, a philosophy which forms the cornerstone of international and national human rights law.

Moreover, even within the field of equality legislation there appears to be some discrepancy in the significance to be attached to the different forms of discrimination. In particular, age-based discrimination tends to be viewed in a different light to discrimination based on race or gender. Race discrimination is "aimed at redressing prejudice against discrete and insular minorities with little access to political or economic power" and gender discrimination, is seen as a means of overcoming "pervasive legal and social barriers faces by women over the centuries [and] has provided the impetus for policies and legislation to achieve gender equality".[87] However, of age-based discrimination it has been observed that, unlike race or gender, "age does not define a fixed delineated group".[88] From the point of view of equality and non-discrimination, the effect of such differentiation may be said to be lessened because it affects all members of society and only at particular points in their lives. If children are to be regarded as being discriminated against, they will eventually escape this category by growing up.[89] This point was reiterated in the UK by the Electoral Commission's Report, *Age of Electoral Majority*. With regard to the issues of minimum age limits and maturity, the Commission noted:

> Of course, some – perhaps many – will develop social and emotional maturity earlier than the age prescribed in law, and we recognise that the law can seem arbitrary in these circumstances. Parallels are sometimes drawn between the campaign for a lower voting age and historical struggles for the enfranchisement of the working classes, women, and ethnic minorities. However, contemporary law in those historical contexts presented a permanent bar to electoral participation for those groups of people, whereas by its very nature a statutory minimum age merely imposes a wait – albeit that some find that wait undesirable and feel it unjustified.[90]

Nevertheless, as Bastarche J observed in *Gosselin v Quebec (Attorney General)*, age is still the criterion for differential treatment and although this criterion may operate to affect all people at different stages in their lives, the basis of the differential treatment remains and, more particularly, a societal group continues to be

---

[87] Ibid, at 37.
[88] Ibid.
[89] O O'Neill, "Children's Rights and Children's Lives", in P Alston, S Parker and J Seymour (eds), *Children, Rights and the Law*, Oxford, Clarendon Press, 1992, at 38–39.
[90] Electoral Commission, "Minimum Age Limits and Maturity" in *Age of Electoral Majority: Report and Recommendations*, London, Electoral Commission, 2004, at 25.

treated differently even if the individual members of the group do not remain constant:

> While age is a ground that is experienced by all people, it is not necessarily experienced in the same way by all people at all times. Large cohorts may use age to discriminate against smaller, more vulnerable cohorts. A change in economic, historical or political circumstances may mean that presumptions and stereotypes about a certain age group no longer hold true. Moreover, the fact remains that, while one's age is constantly changing, it is a personal characteristic that at any given moment one can do nothing to alter. Accordingly, age falls squarely within the concern of the equality provision that people not be penalised for characteristics they either cannot change or should not be asked to change.[91]

Therefore, from the point of view of equality and non-discrimination, the effect of such differentiation may be said to be lessened because it affects all members of society and only at particular points in their lives.

According to Fredman:

> In the field of age discrimination, the courts have in practice been more deferent to policy-makers than in other areas, such as race discrimination. The danger then is that courts will be too ready to accept a proffered justification.[92]

This view was echoed by McLachlin CJ, speaking on behalf of the majority of the Canadian Supreme Court when she noted:

> Unlike race, religion, or gender, age is not strongly associated with discrimination and arbitrary denial of privilege. This does not mean that examples of age discrimination do not exist. But age-based distinctions are a common and necessary way of ordering our society. They do not automatically evoke a context of pre-existing disadvantage suggesting discrimination and marginalisation under this first contextual factor, in the way that other enumerated or analogous grounds might.[93]

She further noted that "Both as a general matter, and based on the evidence and our understanding of society, young adults as a class simply do not seem especially vulnerable or undervalued."[94] Although all age-based legislative distinctions had an element of this literal kind of "arbitrariness", that did not invalidate them.[95]

In terms of age-based distinctions and children's rights, demeaning stereotypes can be avoided by recognising that general age-based assumptions about

---

[91] *Gosselin v Quebec (Attorney General)* [2002] 4 SCR 429, 2002 SCC 84, http://www.canlii.org/ca/cas/scc/2002/2002scc84.html, as viewed on 5 July 2004, para 227, Bastarche J (dissenting).

[92] Fredman, supra note 81, at 60.

[93] *Gosselin*, supra note 91, at para 31.

[94] Ibid, at para 33.

[95] Ibid, at para 57.

the capabilities of group members to exercise their rights are a useful starting point for differential treatment but such assumptions should not prevent an inquiry as to an *individual's* capability to exercise his or her rights, because "age should not be mechanically related to decision-making capacity or maturity thereby denying equal rights to make decisions to those who are in fact able to do so".[96] The adoption of such an enquiry lends support to the assertion that such differential treatment cannot be based upon arbitrary or demeaning stereotypes that violate the rights of the child and negatively affect his or her human dignity.

A common sense approach to this issue has been advocated by the Canadian Supreme Court. CJ McLachlin in *Gosselin*, when referring to Iacobucci J's comments in *Law*,[97] stated that it should not be demanded "that legislation must always correspond perfectly with social reality in order to comply with s 15(1) of the [Canadian Charter of Rights and Freedoms]".[98] She added that:

> The fact that some people may fall through a program's cracks does not show that the law fails to consider the overall needs and circumstances of the group of individuals affected, or that distinctions contained in the law amount to discrimination in the substantive sense intended by s. 15(1).[99]

According to McLachlin CJ:

> The legislator is entitled to proceed on informed general assumptions without running afoul of s. 15, [of the Charter] . . . provided these assumptions are not based on arbitrary and demeaning stereotypes. The idea that younger people may have an easier time finding employment than older people is not such a stereotype.[100]

Two problems remain with this approach. First, the rights (or any restriction thereof) of the group trump the rights of the individual member of the group, which is especially problematic for those societies that appear to favour the autonomy of the rights-holder. Any discrimination suffered by an individual member of that group is rendered less visible rather than being highlighted by the fact such discrimination extends to a group. This trumping of the restriction of the rights of the individual by virtue of the restriction of the rights of all based on the age criterion leads to the second problem with differentiation based upon age, namely that although the differentiation is only temporary,

---

[96] Fredman, supra note 81, at 40.
[97] *Law v Canada (Minister of Employment and Immigration)* [1999] 1 SCR 497.
[98] *Gosselin*, supra note 91, at para 55.
[99] Ibid.
[100] Ibid, at para 56.

the effect of such differentiation is, nonetheless, total for that period. Age is still the criterion for differential treatment and although this criterion may operate to affect all people at different stages in their lives, the basis of the differential treatment remains and, more particularly, a societal group continues to be treated differently even if the individual members of the group do not remain constant. This problem is particularly relevant with regards to children. It has been commented that children do not suffer from discrimination because they will eventually escape that category by growing up.[101] However, this comment does not take into account that there will always be a category of children, this category will always be treated differently and their rights may always be restricted. As L'Heureux-Dubé J noted in his dissenting opinion in *Gosselin*:

> It may be argued that in the long view of history, young people have not suffered disadvantage, and therefore, for the purposes of an equality analysis, a court need not consider young people to suffer from pre-existing disadvantage. This is, however, inconsistent with a basic premise of discrimination law. In *Brooks*, . . . this Court held that a disadvantage need not be shared by all members of a group for there to be a finding of discrimination, if it can be shown that *only* members of that group suffered the disadvantage. This Court held that a distinction drawn on the basis of pregnancy could be found to discriminate against women, since although not all women would become pregnant, only women could.[102]

Although the decision of the majority of the Canadian Supreme Court implied that the Executive may refer to everyday experience and common sense in order to justify age-based distinction, in his dissenting opinion, L'Heureux-Dubé J cautioned against reliance on stereotypes (even those which were not demeaning). Accordingly, he quoted in full the manner in which the Supreme Court addressed the issue of stereotypes in *Law*:

> It may be said that the purpose of s. 15(1) is to prevent the violation of essential human dignity and freedom through the imposition of disadvantage, stereotyping, or political or social prejudice, and to promote a society in which all persons enjoy equal recognition at law as human beings or as members of Canadian society, equally capable and equally deserving of concern, respect and consideration. Legislation which effects differential treatment between individuals or groups will violate this fundamental purpose where those who are subject to differential treatment fall within one or more enumerated or analogous grounds, and *where the differential treatment reflects the stereotypical application of presumed group or personal characteristics, or otherwise has the effect of perpetuating or promoting the view that the individual is less capable, or less worthy of recognition or value as a human being or as a member of Canadian society.*[103] [emphasis added]

---

[101] O'Neill, supra note 89, at 38–39.
[102] Supra note 91, at para 138.
[103] Ibid, at para 51.

According to L'Heureux-Dubé J:

> This passage presents the application of stereotypical characteristics, and the "effect of perpetuating or promoting the view that the individual is less capable, or less worthy of recognition" as *alternative* bases for finding discrimination. The presence of a stereotype is therefore not a necessary condition for a finding of discrimination and support for this proposition can be found throughout this Court's equality jurisprudence.[104] [emphasis added]

In his opinion, discrimination could arise in circumstances other than in the presence of stereotypes and he based his opinion on the following portion of the judgment of the Court in *Law*:

> Human dignity means that an individual or group feels self-respect and self-worth. It is concerned with physical and psychological integrity and empowerment. Human dignity is harmed by unfair treatment premised upon personal traits or circumstances which do not relate to individual needs, capacities or merits. It is enhanced by laws which are sensitive to the needs, capacities, and merits of different individuals, taking into account the context underlying their differences. Human dignity is harmed when individuals and groups are marginalized, ignored, or devalued, and is enhanced when laws recognize the full place of all individuals and groups within Canadian society. Human dignity within the meaning of the equality guarantee does not relate to the status or position of an individual in society *per se*, but rather concerns the manner in which a person legitimately feels when confronted with a particular law. Does the law treat him or her unfairly, taking into account all of the circumstances regarding the individuals affected and excluded by the law?[105]

As the debate between the majority and dissenting judges of the Canadian Supreme Court indicates, careful consideration needs to be given to the bases of age-based distinctions. It is clear that justifiable limits may be imposed on rights, whether those of children or adults. It is also clear that distinctions may be drawn as between adults, young persons, and children, for the protection and provision for children or young persons. However, what is less clear is whether such obligations may be defined solely in terms of age. The role of law, both national and international, is to ensure that any restrictions on rights are justifiable. There are a variety of methods by which differential treatment may be determined to be legitimate or illegitimate. Such a determination calls for the identification and critique of a number of different concepts of equality, particularly those that may seek to justify age discrimination.

---

[104] Ibid, at para 116.
[105] Ibid, at para 121.

6. Assessing Age-Based Distinctions

Although the appropriateness of differential treatment as between children and adults is to be recognised, a legislative distinction solely based upon age, and without consideration of other factors, should not be justifiable under equality and anti-discrimination law. Age should be regarded a general predictor of capacity, especially with regard to the exercise of their rights by young persons as it is indicative of the general attributes of a given age group. However, age should not be used as the sole measure of the capacities of every individual in that group. To do so would be to promote stereotypical behaviour, which has the potential to degenerate into demeaning stereotypes and which could serve to limit the rights of the individual who does not conform to that stereotype. The result of such behaviour could be a disproportionate limitation upon the rights of that individual and the sidestepping of the autonomous nature of human rights. Consequently, the requirements of legitimacy, proportionality and necessity must be met in conjunction with the obligation to protect and provide for young persons imposed by both international and national law.

At the level of international law, the Convention on the Rights of the Child acknowledges this obligation to protect and provide for young persons in its Preamble, which states:

> Recalling that, in the Universal Declaration of Human Rights, the United Nations has proclaimed that childhood is entitled to special care and assistance, . . .

> Bearing in mind that the need to extend particular care to the child has been stated in the Geneva Declaration of the Rights of the Child of 1924 and in the Declaration of the Rights of the Child adopted by the General Assembly on 20 November 1959 and recognized in the Universal Declaration of Human Rights, in the International Covenant on Civil and Political Rights (in particular in articles 23 and 24), in the International Covenant on Economic, Social and Cultural Rights (in particular in article 10) and in the statutes and relevant instruments of specialized agencies and international organizations concerned with the welfare of children . . .

> Bearing in mind that, as indicated in the Declaration of the Rights of the Child, "the child, by reason of his physical and mental immaturity, needs special safeguards and care, including appropriate legal protection, before as well as after birth, . . .

According to the Committee, the development of a children's rights perspective was required for effective implementation of the whole Convention and, in particular, in the light of those Convention articles identified by the Committee as General Principles.[106]

---

[106] Committee on the Rights of the Child, (2003), General Comment No. 5: supra note 39, at para 12.

In terms of the Convention on the Rights of the Child, there are two distinctions regarding age contained in the Convention. Article 1 states:

> For the purposes of the present Convention, a child means every human being below the age of eighteen years unless under the law applicable to the child, majority is attained earlier.

The significance of the objectives of the protection of and provision for children may also be seen in Article 38's prohibition on the participation of children under the age of 15 years in armed conflict. Accordingly, limitation of children's rights and protection of their interests are inextricably linked with age-based distinctions[107] and the obligation to protect and provide for young persons can function effectively only if these distinctions are drawn in a manner that recognises the evolving capacities of the child. This tension is evidenced by Articles 3, 5, and 12 of the Convention which allow for paternalistic decision-making to secure the best interests of the child whilst recognising the evolving capacities of the child as evidenced by the latter Article's provision for the recognition of the right of the voice of the child to be heard. However, inherent in this approach is latitude for paternalistic decision-making that overlooks the capacity to exercise rights of the individual child. Thus, the drawing of distinctions based upon age should only be regarded as the starting point of such an analysis. According to the New Zealand Court of Appeal in *Moonen v Film and Literature Board of Review (Moonen No. 1),*[108] the determination of whether age-based limitations are necessary and justifiable for the provision of such protection remained to be considered:

> In determining whether an abrogation or limitation of a right or freedom can be justified in terms of s 5, it is desirable first to identify the objective which the legislature was endeavouring to achieve by the provision in question. The importance and significance of that objective must then be assessed. The way in which the objective is statutorily achieved must be in reasonable proportion to the importance of the objective. A sledge hammer should not be used to crack a nut. The means used must also have a rational relationship with the objective, and in achieving the objective there must be as little interference as possible with the right or freedom affected. Furthermore the limitation involved must be justifiable in the light of the objective. Of necessity value judgments will be involved. In this case it is the value to society of freedom of expression, against the value society places on protecting children and young persons from exploitation for sexual purposes, and on protecting society generally, or sections of it, from being exposed to the various kinds of conduct referred to in s 3 of the Act.[109]

---

[107] A comprehensive analysis of the tension between children's rights and protectionism may be found in Fortin supra note 33, at 3–32.

[108] [2000] 2 NZLR 9.

[109] Ibid, at para 18. In that case, the right to freedom of expression as provided for in s 14 of the Bill of Rights Act was to be restricted with regard to the s 3 definition of objectionable contained in the Films, Videos and Publications Classification Act 1993, which provides:

Some of the difficulty attached to definitions of children and young persons based solely upon age were further considered by the New Zealand Court of Appeal in *Moonen v Film and Literature Board of Review (Moonen No. 2)*,[110] which was a sequel to the earlier *Moonen* case. Moonen had appealed the Board of Review's conclusion regarding a book containing objectionable material on the basis, *inter alia*, that the Films Video and Publications Classification Act 1993 failed to define children and young persons. It was submitted that that the 1993 Act was deficient in not defining the crucial terms "children" and "young persons"; that the consequence was unacceptable vagueness and uncertainty, breaching natural justice and s 27 of the New Zealand Bill of Rights Act 1990; and that the Court should fill in the gap by providing a definition or should make a declaration of incompatibility with Bill of Rights standards. However, the Court of Appeal took a broader view than that of solely age-based definition as a means by which the legislation could provide and protect for young persons. The Court stated that the legislation was concerned with the vulnerability of young people and with the corrosive injury to the public good of depicting persons perceived to be children or young people as subjects for exploitation and that a s 3 inquiry as to whether material was objectionable or not did not require the ascertainment of the precise age of the person photographed. Thus, according to the Court of Appeal, differentiations based solely upon age may not constitute the important and significant objective of protecting and providing for children.[111]

As a consequence, a more holistic approach may be required with broader considerations being taken into account. Recognition of the utility of a broader approach can be seen in the Committee on the Rights of the Child's General Comment No. 5 on the implementation of the Convention, in which the Committee advised States Parties to have regard to the General Principles of the Convention when seeking to protect and provide for children.[112] In particular, the Committee had regard to the justiciability of children's rights and

---

(2) A publication shall be deemed to be objectionable for the purposes of this Act if the publication promotes or supports, or tends to promote or support,—

(a) The exploitation of children, or young persons, or both, for sexual purposes;

The Court of Appeal concluded that the limitations on the right to freedom of expression of an adult were deemed to have an important and significant objective for the purposes of protecting and providing for children.

[110] [2002] 2 NZLR 754.

[111] Ibid, at para 40.

[112] General Comment No. 5, supra note 39. See also, Human Rights Committee, General Comment No. 18 (1989), HRI/GEN/1/Rev.6. To that end, the Human Rights Committee has stated:

1. Non-discrimination, together with equality before the law and equal protection of the law without any discrimination, constitutes a basic and general principle relating to the protection of human rights. Thus, article 2, paragraph 1, of the International Covenant on Civil and Political rights obligates each

noted that for rights to have meaning, effective remedies had to be available to redress violations:

> Children's special and dependent status creates real difficulties for them in pursuing remedies for breaches of their rights. States need to give particular attention to ensuring that there are effective, child-sensitive procedures available to children and their representatives. These should include the provision of child-friendly information, advice, advocacy, including support for self-advocacy, and access to independent complaints procedures and to the courts with necessary legal and other assistance. Where rights are found to have been breached, there should be appropriate reparation, including compensation, and, where needed, measures to promote physical and psychological recovery, rehabilitation and reintegration, as required by article 39.[113]

The comments of the Committee are significant because they identify the broad framework of issues that States Parties need to take into account, particularly in this context of legislative drafting. However, in order for violations to be redressed they first have to be identifiable. First, current and prospective legislative age-based distinctions often operate to prevent identification of such legislation as being in violation of children's rights, thus rendering redress for age-based discrimination unavailable. Second, legislation that forms the basis for decision-making that impacts upon children's rights may not contain any reference to age-based distinctions. Nevertheless, such legislation is equally open to an interpretation that breaches the requirements of reasonable limitations and justification and has resulted in decision-making that is discriminatory to children and young people. In relation to both avenues of potential discrimination, the test formulated by Supreme Court of

---

state party to respect and ensure to all persons within its territory and subject to its jurisdiction the rights recognized in the covenant without distinction of any kind, such as race, colour, sex, language, religion, political or other opinion, national or social origin, property, birth or other status. Article 26 not only entitles all persons to equality before the law as well as equal protection of the law but also prohibits any discrimination under the law and guarantees to all persons equal and effective protection against discrimination on any ground such as race, colour, sex, language, religion, political or other opinion, national or social origin, property, birth or *other status*. [emphasis added]

In the view of the Committee, Article 26 went further than Article 2, as it prohibited discrimination in law or in fact in any field regulated and protected by public authorities. Article 26 was therefore to be concerned with the obligations imposed on States Parties in regard to their legislation and the application thereof. The Committee stated that when legislation was adopted by a State Party, it would have to comply with the prohibition of discrimination contained in Article 26. However, the Human Rights Committee also observed that not every differentiation of treatment would constitute discrimination, if it could be established that the criteria for such differentiation were reasonable and objective and if the aim was to achieve a purpose which was legitimate under the Covenant.

[113] General Comment No. 5, supra note 39, at para 24.

Canada's decision in *R v Oakes* is a useful point of departure. According to Dickson CJ:[114]

> To establish that a limit is reasonable and demonstrably justified in a free and democratic society, two central criteria must be satisfied. First, the objective, which the measures responsible for a limit on a . . . right or freedom are designed to serve, must be "of sufficient importance to warrant overriding a . . . protected right or freedom" . . . The standard must be high in order to ensure that objectives which are trivial or discordant with the principles integral to a free and democratic society do not gain . . . protection. It is necessary, at a minimum, that an objective relate to concerns which are pressing and substantial in a free and democratic society before it can be characterized as sufficiently important.

> Second, once a sufficiently significant objective is recognized, then the party invoking [the limitation] must show that the means chosen are reasonable and demonstrably justified. This involves "a form of proportionality test" . . . Although the nature of the proportionality test will vary depending on the circumstances, in each case courts will be required to balance the interests of society with those of individuals and groups. There are . . . three important components of a proportionality test. First, the measures adopted must be carefully designed to achieve the objective in question. They must not be arbitrary, unfair or based on irrational considerations. In short, they must be rationally connected to the objective. Second, the means, even if rationally connected to the objective in this first sense, should impair "as little as possible" the right or freedom in question . . . Third, there must be a proportionality between the *effects* of the measures which are responsible for limiting the . . . right or freedom, and the objective which has been identified as of "sufficient importance".[115]

This test can be adopted to determine the legitimacy of age-based distinctions in order to both link one's capacity and the ability to exercise one's rights and further to ensure that a child's age (and presumed lack of capacity) should not be the basis for failing to protect fully his or her rights.

With regard to determining the legitimacy of age-based distinctions, a series of further questions can be raised. In terms of the *Oakes* test, therefore, the first question to be asked is whether the age-based distinction serves an important and significant objective. As both this chapter and ensuing chapters demonstrate, national and international law imposes obligations upon the State to protect and provide for children and young persons. Juvenile justice legislation provides a good example of where age-based distinctions may be used positively to protect and provide for children and young persons. To that end, the provisions relating to the principles of youth justice as contained in s 208 of (New Zealand's) Children, Young Persons and Their Families Act are

---

[114] [1986] 1 SCR 103; 1986 CanLII 46 (SCC), http://www.canlii.org.ezproxy. waikato.ac.nz:2048/ca/cas/scc/1986/1986scc7.html as viewed on 7 February 2005.

[115] Ibid, at paras 69–70.

a clear example of age-based distinctions having an important and significant objective where such objectives/principles include:

- The principle of keeping young children and young persons out of the criminal justice system;
- The principle of protecting the child or young person from excessive use of the court system;
- The principle of a child or young person's age; and
- The principle of the child or young person's umbrella of special protection during investigations.[116]

This obligation can be regarded as an important and significant objective for the purposes of the *Oakes* test where such obligation is can initially be defined solely in terms of age. However, in situations where capacity is not at issue, age-based distinctions may not be an appropriate means of ensuring that State obligations are met. In some instances, the obligation to protect and provide for young persons can function effectively only if these distinctions are drawn so that, for example, age-based distinctions may be imposed to ensure that young persons do not act to limit their opportunities that they have in later in life. Thus, in New Zealand and the UK, for example, 16 years is the age at which young persons are deemed to have sufficient capacity to consent to or to refuse medical treatment. The imposition of an age-based distinction takes on added significance when such consent relates to life-saving treatment. A corollary of this issue is the State obligation to ensure that third party decision-making also should not limit the opportunities that young persons have later in life.[117]

Once it has been established that there is an important and significant objective arising from the imposition of age-based distinctions, a series of further questions must be asked in order to determine whether the means chosen are reasonable and demonstrably justified – the formulation of a proportionality test in which three further requirements must be satisfied. First, the measures adopted must be rationally connected to the objective. Consequently, where distinctions are adopted, whether in regard to children of a particular age or children in general, such measures must be carefully designed to achieve the objective in question. They must not be arbitrary, unfair or based on irrational considerations. Thus, the threshold for determining the justifiability of an age-based distinction should be no different to that applied to other prohibited

---

[116] See, further, PHR Web, and PJ Treadwell, *Family Law in New Zealand* (11th ed), Wellington, LexisNexis, 2003, at para 6.652.

[117] See, e.g., Breen, "Death Row Kids and Philosopher Kids: The Best Interests Standard and the Constitutionality of the Juvenile Death Penalty in the United States" in C Breen, supra note 2, 195.

grounds of discrimination. Any suggestions that a lower threshold of justification may be appropriate not only because of the transitory effect of age-based distinctions on any one individual but also because of the lesser scope for stigma associated with distinctions based upon age as opposed to those based on other proscribed characteristics such as race or gender may themselves be regarded as being arbitrary, unfair or irrational. With regards to the second and third requirements of proportionality, the effects of the age-based distinctions adopted should impair "as little as possible" the right or freedom in question. Again, these requirements are to be linked back to the need for carefully-designed measures where rights and freedoms may be impaired but only to the extent to which such impairment satisfies the important and significant objective of provision and protection for young people. Age-based distinctions may provide predictable and objectively applicable standards but they are only to be regarded as a starting point for analyses, because young persons develop at different rates. Age, therefore, is only an approximate reflection of their developing capacities or needs. As a result, analyses involving age-based distinctions should, in the first instance, be guided by appropriate legislation and policy with each case being examined on its own merits.

6.1. Assessing Age-Based Distinctions – the Case of New Zealand

New Zealand has a statutory framework that has rendered age discrimination unlawful in both the public and private spheres since the early 1990s.[118] Specifically, s 19(1) of the New Zealand Bill of Rights Act (NZBORA) 1990 provides that "everyone has the right to freedom from discrimination on the grounds of discrimination in the Human Rights Act 1993." Section 21(1) of the Human Rights Act (HRA) sets out the prohibited grounds of discrimination and age is included as one of these grounds. However, s 21(1)(i) provides that age discrimination only commences "with the age of 16 years". In 2004, there were 497 provisions in New Zealand legislation that contained an age-based distinction. These distinctions ranged from such issues as the ability to gamble and purchase alcohol, access to education and social assistance benefits, contractual maturity, criminal responsibility, electoral rights, marital rights, parental obligations and responsibilities, and participation in certain professional activities.

---

[118] The Human Rights Commission Amendment Act 1992 outlawed age discrimination in relation to private activities such as employment and the provision of goods and services. Age discrimination has been prohibited on the part of Government under the New Zealand Bill of Rights Act with the enactment of the Human Rights Act 1993.

The inclusion of age as a ground of discrimination gives rise to the possibility of legal challenge to any government policy, programme or practice that contains an age-based distinction. The HRA provides an individual, who alleges that they have been discriminated against on the basis of their age, recourse to an independent publicly-funded complaints mechanism whereby their complaint may be heard and redress provided. This process has exposed the Government to risks of complaints to the Human Rights Commission, with cases having been brought before the Human Rights Review Tribunal or litigation in the courts.[119] The introduction of a Bill containing an aged-based distinction before Parliament activates s 7 of the NZBORA, which requires the Attorney-General to report to Parliament where a Bill appears to be inconsistent with Bill of Rights. In terms of age-based distinctions, this seems to be an ad hoc approach with each piece of proposed legislation being examined on its own merits for compatibility with s 19 of the Bill of Rights Act.[120]

In its report, *Consistency 2000*, the New Zealand Human Rights Commission acknowledged "that some minimum age restrictions are necessary to take into account the evolving capacity of children and young people".[121] The Commission further noted that a draft document had been prepared by the Ministry of Youth Affairs entitled "Legal Ages and Young People", which stated that "legal ages can be "an administratively convenient tool. However, they also stereotype young people, are inconsistent and lack a common rationale".[122] The Ministry's draft suggested that:

> while it is often justifiable to treat young people differently, this is seldom because of their age alone. There should be careful analysis of an issue before using age as a proxy to determine capability, entitlement or need for protection.[123]

More recently, the Ministry of Youth Affairs recognised that:

> Sometimes it makes good sense to use youth ages in New Zealand law and policy. It acknowledges the young person's vulnerability due to their age, with a method to:

---

[119] Cases have tended to be brought by older persons alleging age discrimination in terms of employment matters. See, e.g., *Fogelberg v Association of University Staff of New Zealand Inc* (2000) 6 HRNZ 206; [2000] 2 ERNZ 196.

[120] See further, Ministry of Justice website, http://www.justice.govt.nz/bill-of-rights, as viewed on 22 February 2005. Advice includes, e.g., *Report of the Attorney-General under the New Zealand Bill of Rights Act 1990 on the Care of Children Bill*; 5 September 2005; Crown Law Office, *Consistency with the New Zealand Bill Of Rights Act 1990: Civil Union Bill*, 29 April 2004; Ministry of Justice, *Consistency with the New Zealand Bill of Rights Act 1990: Identity (Citizenship and Travel Documents) Bill*, 11 March 2003.

[121] Human Rights Commission, "Generic Issues" in *Consistency 2000*, Wellington, Human Rights Commission, 1998.

[122] Ibid.

[123] Ibid.

- Protect them
- Empower them
- Determine their entitlements and define their responsibilities.[124]

The Ministry has favoured a movement away from sole reliance upon age-based distinctions with its recommendation to policy-makers that they first assume a youth age is not necessary. In the course of further analysis, the Ministry has further recommended that policy-makers consider: the purpose of using a youth age – to protect, empower, determine entitlements, or define responsibilities; alternative methods – other ways by which the desired results could be achieved without using age restrictions; and the best alternative – the most cost-effective and reasonable solution.[125]

If policy-makers did decide that an age-based distinction was appropriate, the Ministry then recommended that they identify the age group it would affect, taking into consideration to a number of questions, including:

- What age is most likely to achieve the desired purpose?
- Is the youth age likely to be in young people's 'best interests'? Why?
- Is the youth age consistent with other ages in similar laws and policies?
- Does the youth age fit with UNCROC?
- How will the youth age affect young people's ability to have a say in decisions that affect them?
- Will the youth age help or hinder young people's active participation in society?
- Does the youth age comply with the Human Rights Act 1993, the New Zealand Bill of Rights Act 1990 and New Zealand's international obligations?[126]

These recommendations are a useful guide to a more considered analysis of age-based distinctions. However, their focus on the rights of youth as a whole perpetuates the tendency to exclude an approach that takes account of the evolving capacities of each child and may also exclude considerations of what is in the best interests of the individual child.

---

[124] Ministry of Youth Affairs, *Does Your Policy Need An Age Limit? A Guide to Youth Ages from the Ministry of Youth Affairs,* Wellington, Ministry of Youth Affairs, at 3.

[125] Ibid. The Ministry used as an example the driver licensing regime, which uses both a youth age criterion and tests of competency. A young person may not apply for a driver licence until he or she is 15 years old. The current age was originally linked to the school-leaving age when it too was 15. The aim of this baseline limit is to protect young people (and the public) from the dangers of young people driving before they have adequate maturity and skills. Today, under the graduated driver licensing system, a practical competency test is used in addition to the age limit. A system based only on competency, with no lower age limit, would be more complex and costly to administer, and could pose unreasonable risks to road users generally.

[126] Ibid, at 6.

Age-based distinctions should not be relied upon solely where the effect of such reliance would be the automatic exclusion of an examination of the extent to which a young person's capacities had developed. That said, the Ministry's policy does seem to recognise that strict reliance upon age-distinctions could result in inappropriate provision for and protection of children. However, the policy could recognise more explicitly the need to ensure that the age-based distinction serves an important and significant objective given that greater or lesser degrees of autonomy or protection might be necessary. Such an approach could be tied in with the final question regarding whether the youth age policy complies with New Zealand's human rights obligations both nationally and internationally. Having greater regard for the capacity of the individual may be a more reliable tool by which the Ministry may avoid stereotypes that may be demeaning and thus discriminatory. Again, the Ministry's policy seems to recognise this point. In addition to the steps outlined above, the Ministry has outlined a series of questions that policy-makers should take into account when seeking to utilise age-based distinction:

- Does it discriminate against young people?
- Does the youth age withhold, limit access or create age-related barriers to opportunities, benefits or advantages for young people?
- Will the youth age affect certain groups of young people more than others (indirect discrimination)?

Answering yes to any of the above questions then requires policy-makers to justify using a youth age by answering the following questions:

- Do the predicted benefits of the policy override the potential problems of using a youth age?
- Is the result of not using a youth age more serious than the result of not meeting the above criteria?
- Does the use of the youth age fall within one of the exceptions or exemptions to the Human Rights Act 1993 or the New Zealand Bill of Rights Act 1990?

In spite of the fact that the final three questions are a useful means by which to distinguish between legitimate differentiation and discrimination, policy-makers and those vetting such policies would have to ensure that answers to the questions could be verified with regard to empirical evidence so as to avoid paternalistic value judgements that may based on societal consensus, more particularly where such 'consensus' may not be inclusive of young persons' views. In addition, the final question raises some difficulties. Although it is necessary to refer to the relevant legal provisions regarding discrimination, the current language of s 21(1)(i) of the HRA rather negates the requirement to engage in the in-depth examination of policy regarding youth. In fact, the inclusion of the reference suggests that only policies affecting 16- and 17-year-olds need to be vetted as per the Ministry guidelines. The basis for this narrow application lies with the HRA and not the Ministry guidelines but again the outcome would appear to be a two-tiered approach to the determination of children's rights.

Ultimately, potentially arbitrary age-distinctions will remain the trigger. However, the outcome of the trigger effect should be different as age will only be an indicator of autonomy and competency on the part of the child, which may then be rebutted by considerations of what is in the best interests of the child/young person where appropriate. A further problem may arise where a standard of individual competence cannot be determined because, for instance, of likely disagreement on the relevant individual capacities, for example, the relevant competence required to vote. In such instances, arguments in favour of age-based distinctions would appear to be stronger. With regard to the example of the right to vote, both the NZBORA[127] and the Electoral Act 1993[128] set 18 years as the age at which individuals are permitted to vote. Section 86 of the Electoral Act also makes provision for the registration of electors who are mentally incapable, to the effect that a third party appointed under the Protection of Personal and Property Rights Act may register the mentally incapable person,[129] so that mentally incapable persons have the right to vote.

Mentally incapable persons are those persons lacking in capacity for the purposes of the Protection of Personal and Property Rights Act 1988. With regard to the determination of capacity, s 5 of the Act states:

> every person shall be presumed, until the contrary is proved, to have the capacity—
>
> a) To understand the nature, and to foresee the consequences, of decisions in respect of matters relating to his or her personal care and welfare; and
> b) To communicate decisions in respect of those matters.

According to s 8, the primary objectives of a court on an application for the exercise of its jurisdiction under this Part One of this Act are:

> a) To make the *least restrictive intervention possible* in the life of the person in respect of whom the application is made, having regard to the degree of that person's incapacity:
> b) To enable or encourage that person to exercise and develop such capacity as he or she has *to the greatest extent possible*. [emphasis added]

According to s 6(2), the jurisdiction of the court to make orders does not extend to persons under the age of 20 who are not and who have never been

---

[127] Section 12.

[128] Section 268(1)(e).

[129] C.f. s 80 regarding disqualification for registration arising out of an order made under the Mental Health (Compulsory Assessment and Treatment) Act 1992.

married.[130] However, s 6(3) of the Act is most interesting with its provision that:

> The fact that the person in respect of whom the application is made for the exercise of the Court's jurisdiction has made or is intending to make any decision that a person exercising ordinary prudence would not have made or would not make given the same circumstances is not in itself sufficient ground for the exercise of that jurisdiction by the Court.

In other words, the making of an imprudent decision is not to be regarded as a basis for determining lack of capacity.[131] Thus, current law indicates that lack of capacity regarding decision-making as to one's personal care and welfare does not preclude an individual from being regarded having the competence to vote. Applying this analysis, if competency is not a pre-requisite for voting then *all* young persons should be entitled to vote.

Although an age-based limitation may be described as a non-contentious basis on which to limit eligibility to vote because it avoids the need to formulate a competency test and thus avoids divisive tests that may be open to abuse, this needs to be weighed against the restriction on a right to vote where age is an indicator of a lack of competency. As the UK's Electoral Commission Report noted, their consultation activities with young people demonstrated that there were many young people below the minimum voting age who were perfectly capable of taking a responsible attitude to the issue of voting.[132] It may be that whilst the issue of potentially arbitrary age-based distinctions cannot be totally avoided, some of the difficulty with the right to vote may be resolved by lowering the age of majority. Disagreement over required capacities, the capacity to vote for example, should not be replaced with a broad assumption based upon age. As the law currently stands, imprudent decisions are the prerogative of adults.

6.2. Some Legislative and Judicial Responses

Age-based distinctions should be drafted in broad terms where those terms are also linked to specific rights and obligations. A glance through the substantive rights and obligations contained in human rights treaties and legislation reveals that these rights do not make exhaustive reference to these principles. However, the principles of non-discrimination and equality cannot act effectively in a vacuum. They need to be and have been linked to specific rights in

---

[130] The Care of Children Act 2004 applies to those under the age of 20.
[131] See further, *Family Law in New Zealand Vol. 2*, supra note 116, at paras 1538–1540.
[132] Electoral Commission Report, supra note 90, at 25.

order to provide context and also in order to determine whether the right in question is being effectively protected.[133] Equally, rights do not exist in a vacuum and they may be limited where such limits satisfy the requirements of legitimacy, proportionality and necessity – limitations justified by an important and significant objective such as the protection of and provision for a child/young person. Thus, national and international human rights law is underpinned by the principles of non-discrimination and equality, a process that is facilitated by the inclusive language of treaty law and national legislation protecting human rights. Effective implementation of the law, whether at the national or international level, is grounded in the interdependency of general principles and particular rights. With particular reference to children's rights, the interdependent concepts of non-discrimination, best interests of the child, and evolving capacities of the child have been highlighted by the Committee on the Rights of the Child in its General Comment No. 5 with regards to the effective implementation of the Convention.[134]

It is against this background that domestic legislation regarding age-based distinctions can be viewed. In New Zealand, the Minors Contract Act 1969 (MCA) provides a useful basis upon which to model age-based distinctions. It may be noted that, like human rights legislation, the MCA was designed both to protect and delineate individuals' rights. The Act has been described as:

> A uniquely New Zealand response to the age-old problem of preventing persons taking advantage of youthful inexperience without unduly interfering with the ordinary course of commerce and rights of innocent adults.[135]

Broadly speaking, the MCA draws a distinction between minors over the age of 18 years and those under 18 years. With regard to contracts entered into by minors 18 years and older, s 5 states:

> Subject to the provisions of this section, every contract which is—
>
> (a) Entered into by a minor who has attained the age of 18 years; or
> (b) Entered into pursuant to section 66B of the Life Insurance Act 1908 by a minor who has attained the age of 16 years; or
> (c) A contract of service entered into by a minor;
>
> shall have effect as if the minor were of full age.

However, s 5(2) provides the courts with a mechanism to protect the rights of the minor:

---

[133] See, General Comments of the Human Rights Committee, supra note 62.
[134] General Comment No. 5, supra note 39.
[135] *Morrow & Benjamin Ltd v Whittington* [1989] 3 NZLR 122, 124, Thorpe J.

If the Court is satisfied in respect of any contract to which subsection (1) of this section applies that, at the time the contract was entered into,—

(a) The consideration for a minor's promise or act was so inadequate as to be unconscionable; or
(b) Any provision of any such contract imposing an obligation on any party thereto who was a minor was harsh or oppressive,

it may, in the course of any proceedings or on application made for the purpose, cancel the contract, or decline to enforce the contract against the minor, or declare that the contract is unenforceable against the minor, whether in whole or in part, and in any case may make such order as to compensation or restitution of property under section 7 of this Act as it thinks just.

Accordingly, in *National Bank of New Zealand v Ram*,[136] it was unsuccessfully argued that the defendant, who was aged 18 years and 7 months when he guaranteed a loan made by the plaintiff bank to his elder brother, should be entitled to the protection offered by s 5(2)(b). The argument was rejected because there was nothing inherently harsh or oppressive in the loan contract and the guarantee, which were found to be merely standard bank documents.

Section 6(1) provides further protection to minors under the age of 18 years in that it states that contracts entered into by such minors shall be unenforceable against the minor but otherwise shall have effect as if the minor were of full age. In other words, there can be a valid contract between an adult and a minor and the minor can enforce the contract against (i.e. sue) the adult but the adult cannot sue the minor. Section 6(2) permits the court to inquire into the fairness and reasonableness of any contract entered into by a minor under 18 years and in light of such determinations the Court has a discretion to enforce the contract against the minor, cancel the contract in whole or in part and make compensation or restitution orders as it deems necessary.[137] Furthermore, s 6(3) grants the court wide discretion to consider:

(a) The circumstances surrounding the making of the contract:
(b) The subject-matter and nature of the contract:
(c) In the case of a contract relating to property, the nature and the value of the property:
(d) The age and the means (if any) of the minor:
(e) All other relevant circumstances.

Accordingly, greater protection is granted to minors under the age of 18 years as demonstrated in *Morrow & Benjamin Ltd v Whittington*.[138] The plaintiff stockbrokers had started to buy shares for the defendant when he was a 15-year-old

---

[136] (1992) 2 NZBLC 102.
[137] Section 6(2) Minors Contract Act 1969.
[138] Supra note 135.

minor. The defendant had originally paid for the shares in cash but over the course of the following 2-and-a-half years the plaintiffs allowed him to purchase on credit. By 20 October 1987, when the sharemarket collapsed, the defendant's total debt was $35,000 but his shares were only worth $5,000. The plaintiffs sought to sue under s 6 of the MCA. In finding for the defendant, Thorpe J observed that the threshold tests for ss 5 and 6 did not interrelate very easily but was of the opinion that different language had been used as the two formulae were intended to relate to different criteria and to have different results. The threshold of "fairness and reasonableness" in s 6 was not satisfied by merely establishing that there was consideration and that the contract was not harsh or oppressive. Section 6 required more, so that the term "reasonable" would have to take into account the age of the minor and so take account of the purpose of the legislation. Thorpe J was of the opinion that the matters provided for in s 6(3) should be taken into account at the outset of the determination of whether there was a reasonable contract. Using this reasoning, he found that the contracts could not be held to be binding upon the defendant minor. Whilst entry into the contract had been fair, nonetheless, Thorpe J found the contractual terms to be unreasonable given the plaintiff's knowledge of all the circumstances of the case which had resulted from their own failure to implement the proper credit control procedures.

The effect of this legislation is that there is a presumption of capacity to contract on the part of the minor that may be rebutted by the courts with the age-based distinction of 18 years serving a trigger for greater or less degrees of protection. This model provides support for a presumption of capacity to exercise (contractual) rights and strives to provide an equitable balance between the rights of adults and young persons. It could be used more generally in conjunction with age-based distinctions, particularly the considerations that the Court has to consider in s 6(2) and (3).

7. Conclusion

The obligation to protect and provide for young persons can be regarded as an important and significant objective for limiting the rights of young persons but only where such limits are rational and proportionate. There is a difference between adults and young persons, a difference that becomes more difficult to discern as the young person approaches adulthood. The recognised difference between these two societal groups requires differential treatment in order to secure equal treatment and non-discrimination. Inasmuch as one's gender or ethnicity may serve as a trigger for such differential treatment so too should one's age. However, as with all forms of differential treatment, gender, ethnicity or age are not and should not be the sole consideration for such differential treatment. With regard to age-based distinctions, age should be regarded a general indicator of the capacity to exercise rights within a given age group. However, the capacity of the individual member of the group should also be ascertained. As such, the impact of the differential treatment needs to be assessed; a balance between rights has to be struck in addition to the striking of a balance between the rights of individuals. The rebuttable presumption provisions regarding capacity as provided for in New Zealand's Minors' Contracts Act 1969 constitutes one useful model by which this balance may be achieved.

In sum, rather than focusing on age solely as a basis for any legal obligation to protect and provide different treatment for young persons, the justification for such treatment should also incorporate reference to the Guiding Principles of the Convention on the Rights of the Child in order to determine whether the provisions of that legislation do in fact serve to protect and provide for the young person and thereby satisfy the requirement that the limitation contained therein constitutes an important and significant objective. Such an approach underpins the role of equality law, both national and international, which is to ensure that such restrictions are justifiable and amount to a legitimate rights restriction rather than rights violation, where the latter is based upon discrimination rather than difference. The principles of non-discrimination and equality constitute the cornerstone of international human rights treaties which enshrine the notion that dignity and equality is to be accorded to *all* human beings.

Given that children are rights-holders, a framework of equality based on rights should be the most appropriate mechanism for securing the exercise of such rights where equality of choice or autonomy would grant to everyone an "equal set of alternatives [or rights] from which to choose".[139] Perceptions about age, as an indicator of the ability to exercise rights, remain problematic as most analyses of children's rights are, to varying degrees, linked to aged-based limitations to child autonomy. Although children may, theoretically, start off with an equal set of alternatives to choose from, age-based perceptions about children's autonomy may not only constitute an obstacle to a child's choice and pursuit of their own version of the good life but, realistically speaking, their physical and emotional development (or lack thereof) may restrict them in the *actual* pursuit of their version of the good life. Accordingly, we return to a decision-making process based on the best interests of the child that, combined with the right of the child to express his or her views, provides a means by which children 'exercise' their rights. Such an approach resonates with

---

[139] Fredman, supra note 81, at 43.

that of the adoption of dignity as a basis for equality where "[d]ignity is an irreducible minimum"[140] and where "[e]quality based on dignity must enhance rather than diminish the status of individuals".[141] Such an approach to equality legislation could also provide a means for examining any departures from the requirement for equality especially where such a departure constituted an age-based limitation of the rights of the child in order to determine whether the departure was justified or alternatively amounted to discrimination.[142]

The following model suggests an approach that may be followed. First, the inordinate number of legislative distinctions where differing ages are the *sole* determinants of capacity should be abandoned. Second, such legislative distinctions should be replaced by legislation that is formulated with a recognition of age being a useful but *general* indicator of capacity. Third, the adoption of age as a general indicator of capacity should be accompanied by two further rebuttable presumptions: (a) presumption *of* capacity on the part of the child falling *within* a given age group that could be rebutted by a parent/guardian/ court; and (b) a presumption of *a lack of* capacity on the part of a child falling *outside* of that age group which could be rebutted by that child.

The adoption of such a model recognises the acknowledged linkage between one's capacity and the ability to exercise one's rights. However, it should not be regarded as the measure of equality and non-discrimination. As regards any limitations on rights based on the need to achieve a balance between the rights of adults and those of children, the fundamental principles of legitimacy, proportionality and necessity need to be applied with equal stringency as between children and adults as they are between adults themselves.

---

[140] Ibid, at 45.
[141] Ibid.
[142] Ibid, at 56.

CHAPTER TWO

CHILDREN'S RIGHTS AND MEDICAL TREATMENT:
ISSUES OF CAPACITY, CHOICE AND CONSENT

1. Introduction

Much of the (often divergent) discourse surrounding the exercise by children
of their rights is brought sharply into focus by the issue of the child's right to
medical treatment. In New Zealand, the case of Liam Williams-Holloway
brought into sharp focus the conflict between the child's right to medical
treatment, which health practitioners believed to be in the child's best interests, and the rights of the child's parents to choose the course of treatment that
they believed to be in their child's best interests. The polarisation of public
opinion in New Zealand as to whether the child in this case was to be treated
or not, in addition to the extreme measures taken by Liam's parents, illustrates
clearly the issues and questions that have gone to the heart of the rights of the
child and the determination of what is in his or her best interests.[1] In this
chapter, the issue of the child's right to medical treatment is used to demonstrate
the manner in which one of the aims of the Convention on the Rights of the
Child, which recognises the fact that "the child, by reason of his physical and
mental immaturity, needs special safeguards and care, including appropriate
legal protection, before as well as after birth", is achieved, or not, as the case
may be.[2] This chapter focuses on the general degree of success with which the

---

[1] Liam Williams-Holloway was diagnosed with neuroblastoma at the age of three and a half.
When Liam's parents withdrew him from conventional treatment, he was made a ward of court
so that he could continue this type of treatment. Liam's parents brought him to an unknown
location in order to avoid the court orders and to allow him to undertake alternative treatments
which they believed were better suited to Liam. The court orders were ultimately lifted when
it became apparent that Liam's parents would not come out of hiding whilst the orders were in
place. Liam continued to have alternative treatment for his condition until his death at the age of
five. *Healthcare Otago Limited v Brendon Williams Holloway and Trena Williams Holloway* 25/2/99,
Judge Blaikie, FC Dunedin FP012/23/99; *Healthcare Otago Limited v Brendon Williams Holloway
and Trena Williams Holloway* 4/3/99, Judge Blaikie, FC Dunedin FP012/23/99; *Healthcare Otago
Limited v Brendon Williams Holloway and Trena Williams Holloway* 18/3/99, Judge Blaikie, FC
Dunedin FP012/23/99; *Healthcare Otago Limited v Brendon Williams Holloway and Trena Williams
Holloway* 6/5/99, Judge Blaikie, FC Dunedin, FP012/23/99.
[2] Preamble, United Nations Convention on the Rights of the Child, UN Doc. A/44/736,
(1989), UNGA Doc. A/Res/44/25 of 5 December, (1989), 28 I.L.M., 1448, (1989), para 9.

New Zealand legislature and judiciary have succeeded in prioritising the rights of the child over those of his or her parents.[3] This approach has been broadly echoed in the English courts, although more recently, there appears to have been a greater degree of willingness to conflate parental interests with children's rights by the English judiciary.

2. Difference or Discrimination? Paternalism and Autonomy in the Context of Medical Treatment

The issue of the child's right to medical treatment also highlights one of the fundamental problems inherent in the notion of the rights of the child, that is, the often inevitable clash with the rights of parents, most especially in relation to the determination of what is in the child's best interests. Thus, the reality of paternalism and autonomy as a core principles underpinning children's rights is nowhere more immediate than in relation to decision-making where the outcome may mean life or death for the child in question. With regard to children and medical treatment, the first question to be asked is whether the child is sufficiently autonomous or has the requisite capacity to provide consent to the treatment, which lays open to review the extent to which a child may exercise his or her rights. In some cases, this review exercise is simplified by the extreme youth of the child, in which case parents are acknowledged as the appropriate decision-makers and are generally recognised as being best placed to secure the rights of their child. The review process becomes more complex where the exercise of such paternalism is open to challenge by a third party who is of the opinion that the parental decision-making did not secure the rights of the child. It also becomes more complex where the child is older and, accordingly, deemed to possess greater autonomy. In such cases, greater attention should be paid to the views of the child and less to those of the parents, irrespective of whether both views are in accordance or otherwise. In such cases, the State may intervene to adjudicate on how the rights of the child are to be best secured. In the context of the right to medical treatment, State

---

[3] A number of cases have drawn attention to this interrelationship. For example, in *Auckland Healthcare Services v T*, Patterson J referred to Article 6 of the Convention on the Rights of the Child, which places New Zealand, as a State Party to the Convention, under an obligation to recognise that every child has an inherent right to life in stating that parties should ensure to the maximum extent the survival and development of the child: [1996] NZFLR 670, 671. Similarly, in *Auckland Healthcare Services v L*, the Court took into account the provisions of Article 3(1) of the Convention on the Rights of the Child, in conjunction with the provisions pertaining to the right to life in Article 6(1) of the International Covenant on Civil and Political Rights: [1998] NZFLR 998, 1000–1001, 1003.

intervention may prove to be a double-edged sword for children's rights. On the one hand, it may afford greater protection to children's rights by overriding parental wishes, wishes that may eventuate in the death of their child. On the other hand, it may act to limit the autonomy of the, often older, child to exercise his or her right to consent to medical treatment or not, where the wishes of the child may eventuate in his or her own death.

It may be at this point that the question arises as to whether such a limitation is justifiable or whether it is a discriminatory limitation of the child's right to consent or to refuse to consent to medical treatment. Such limitations may be imposed but they should be accompanied by a duty to consult with those young persons who are affected by such limitations.[4] Some young persons may lack the appropriate information and ability to recognise that certain courses of action undertaken in the present may limit their opportunities in later life. In such instances, it is has been suggested that the adult decision-maker should "make some kind of imaginative leap and guess what a child might retrospectively have wanted once it reaches a position of maturity".[5] Examples of theoretical approaches to such difficulties include the concept of 'dynamic self-determination', which has been advanced as a method of decision-making that would have the effect of bringing a child to "the threshold of adulthood with the maximum opportunities to form and pursue life-goals which reflect as closely as possible an autonomous choice".[6] This type of approach allows for the wishes of the young person to constitute a significant factor in the adult's decision. At a more practical level, the issue has been responded to, both legislatively and judicially, in a manner which is sensitive to the ability (or lack thereof) of young persons to take responsibility for their own decision-making in such cases.[7] That said, the determination of capacity (or lack thereof), and consequently the legitimacy of limitation with regard to adolescents remains somewhat difficult to resolve. It is at this point that the

---

[4] Group consultations are equally valuable. See, e.g., ACYA Youth Video Working Group, *Whakarongo Mai / Listen Up* (video), 2003, ACYA, Wellington; H Barwick, A Gray, *Analysis of submissions by children and young people to the Agenda for Children: Children's Discussion Pack*, 2001, Wellington, Ministry of Social Development, http://www.msd.govt.nz/documents/work-areas/sector-policy/agenda-for-children/consultation/consultation-findings-full-children.pdf, as accessed on 20 June 2004; The Electoral Commission, "Minimum Age Limits and Maturity" in *Age of Electoral Majority: Report and Recommendations*, 2004, London, Electoral Commission.

[5] J Eekelaar, "The Emergence of Children's Rights", (1986) 6 Oxford Journal of Legal Studies 161, at 166.

[6] J Eekelaar, "The Interests of the Child and the Child's Wishes: the Role of Dynamic Self-Determinism" (1994) 8 International Journal of Law and the Family, 42, at 53.

[7] Section 8 Family Law Reform Act 1969 marks the first status-based boundary in this area of law. Its effect is to limit the presumption of competence to all patients aged 16 and over.

necessity for the distinction between discrimination and differentiation outlined in the previous chapter becomes more apparent, with the severity of the consequences of the adolescent exercising his or her autonomy being weighed against any benefits to be achieved from limiting that autonomy. Underpinning this balancing act is the internationally and nationally recognised obligation to protect and provide for children, which, in the language of *Oakes*,[8] is regarded as an important and significant objective. Thus, any limitations on the right of the child in the context of medical treatment – whether such limitations arise from the child, parents or the courts – must satisfy not only that objective but they must also satisfy the further requirements of rationality and proportionality.

3. The Child's Right to Medical Treatment

3.1. International Human Rights Law and the Child's Right to Medical Treatment

In international human rights law, the child's right to medical treatment is located mainly in the interrelationship between the rights to life and to health. Article 3 of the Universal Declaration of Human Rights provides that "everyone has the right to life",[9] whilst Article 6(1) of the ICCPR provides that:

> Every human being has the inherent right to life. This right shall be protected by law. No one shall be arbitrarily deprived of his life.[10]

The provision regarding the right to life is reiterated in Article 6(1) of the Convention on the Rights of the Child and is expanded upon in Article 6(2) of the Convention which states that "States Parties shall ensure to the maximum extent possible the survival and development of the child."[11]

In terms of the right to health, Article 12(1) of the ICESCR provides that:

> States Parties to the present Covenant recognise the right of everyone to the enjoyment of the highest attainable standard of physical and mental health.[12]

---

[8] 1986 1 SCR 103 (SCC).

[9] Universal Declaration of Human Rights, G.A. Res. 217A, (III) U.N. Doc. A1810 (1948).

[10] International Covenant on Civil and Political Rights, U.N.G.A. Res. 2200 (XXI), 21 UN GAOR, Supp. (No. 16) 52, U.N. Doc. A16316 (1966).

[11] United Nations Convention on the Rights of the Child, UN Doc. A/44/736, (1989), UNGA Doc. A/Res/44/25 of 5 December, (1989) 28 I.L.M., 1448, (1989).

[12] International Covenant on Economic, Social and Cultural Rights, G.A. Res. (XXI), U.N. GAOR 21st SESS., (Supp. No. 16), at 49, U.N. Doc. A/6316 (1966).

Furthermore, in terms of the right to health and medical treatment, Article 24(1) of the Convention on the Rights of the Child states that:

> States Parties recognise the right of the child to the enjoyment of the highest attainable standard of health and to facilities for the treatment of illness and rehabilitation of health. States Parties shall strive to ensure that no child is deprived of his or her right of access to such health care services.[13]

In terms of the rights of the child, these provisions are to be interpreted in light of Article 19 of the Convention, which places States Parties under an obligation to intervene when the interests of the child are placed at risk. It requires governments to:

> take all appropriate legislative, administrative, social and educational measures to protect the child from all forms of physical and mental violence, injury or abuse, neglect or negligent treatment, maltreatment and exploitation, including sexual abuse, while in the care of parent(s), legal guardian(s) or any other person who takes care of the child.[14]

In terms of the child's right to medical treatment, the above-mentioned provisions should be interpreted in light of Article 3(1), namely that such treatment should be administered in accordance with the standard of the best interests of the child where the child's best interests are weighed between Article 5's recognition of parental rights and responsibilities and Article 12's recognition of the child's right not only to express an opinion but also to have that opinion heard.

3.2. *New Zealand Domestic Legislation and the Child's Right to Medical Treatment*

Although the Convention has provided much of the focus in the debate regarding children's rights and the best interests standard, the Convention, as an instrument of international law, does not bind domestic courts. It merely provides a context in which current social and legal standards may be set, thereby providing a standard according to which ambiguous domestic legislation may be interpreted.[15] Whilst the New Zealand courts may engage in a balancing exercise between the rights and interests of children in domestic law, on the one hand,

---

[13] Ibid.

[14] Convention on the Rights of the Child, supra note 11.

[15] G Austin, "The UN Convention on the Rights of the Child – and Domestic Law" 1(4) Butterworths Family Law Journal (1994) 63–64. In other words, "if a statute touches on the subject-matter of the treaty, its interpretation can be influenced by the principle that the legislature is unlikely to have legislated in a manner contrary to its international obligations": J Burrows, *Statute Law in New Zealand*, Wellington, Butterworths, 1992, at 230.

and New Zealand's international obligations on the other, domestic legislation itself requires the courts to recognise the rights and interests of children.

To that end, extensive recognition has been given to the child's welfare and best interests, as well as recognition of certain rights including the right to consent (or refuse to consent to) medical treatment under the Care of Children Act 2004.[16] According to s 4 of the Act:

> (1) The welfare and best interests of the child must be the first and paramount consideration.
> (2) The welfare and best interests of the particular child in his or her particular circumstances must be considered.
> (3) A parent's conduct may be considered only to the extent (if any) that it is relevant to the child's welfare and best interests.

Section 5 of the Act outlines the Principles relevant to the child's welfare and best interests and recognises that the child's parents and guardians should have the primary responsibility for the child's care, development, and upbringing. However, this section does not prevent the court or other persons from taking into account other matters relevant to the child's welfare and best interests.[17] Section 5 also recognises the importance of broader input from extended family and whanau.

These particular provisions of the Care of Children Act echo s 6 of the Children, Young Persons, and Their Families Act 1989, which states that:

> In all matters relating to the administration or application of this Act . . ., the welfare and interests of the child or young persons shall be *the first and paramount consideration*, having regard to the principles set out in sections 5 and 13 of this Act.[18] [emphasis added]

The requirement that s 6 is to be interpreted in light of ss 5 and 13 would seem to emphasise family responsibility and the child's place within the family. The effect of, and the need for, such an interrelationship has been explained as being based on the consideration that:

> a child's welfare is bound up with his or her family and that if a course of action is likely to cause serious distress and disruption within a family, that too is a factor which must bear on the welfare of the child and therefore weigh with the Court.[19]

The interrelationship between child and family is further recognised by s 5(c) which requires that any decision under the provisions of s 6 must be made so as to take account of the manner in which such a decision would also affect

---

[16] Section 3 Care of Children Act 2004. The 2004 Act reformed and replaced the Guardianship Act 1968.

[17] Ibid, s 4(6).

[18] Children, Young Persons and Their Families Act 1989.

[19] *Director-General of Social Welfare v M* (1991) 8 FLRNZ 498, 504.

the "stability of that child's or young person's family, whanau, hapu, iwi, and family group".[20] This broader interpretation echoes the influence of the Treaty of Waitangi and the suggestion that it also provides a source of protection for children's rights and interests, on the basis that:

> the guarantee of te tino rangatiratanga in article 2 of the Treaty in respect of taonga is considered by some to apply to children. . . . it may be that specific rights for children must be viewed as an aspect of the rights to iwi integrity, well-being and economic viability. Simply put, iwi self-determination may be a way of promoting children's rights.[21]

However, the positioning of the child's best interests within either the family or the broader family has been criticised on the grounds that it:

> presumes that the child's best interests will be advanced by family privacy and responsibility with the state accepting the responsibility of providing no more than a safety net. The New Zealand stance fails to recognise that the focus must be on the best interests of the child, with the child's right to autonomy, identity, a place within their family and community being aspects which must be considered and balanced when determining the best interests of this child in this situation.[22]

In terms of those provisions of domestic law that have particular significance for the child's right to medical treatment, s 8 of the New Zealand Bill of Rights Act, echoing the above provisions of international law, provides that:

> No one shall be deprived of life except on such grounds as are established by law and are consistent with the principles of fundamental justice.

The tone of s 8 is echoed s 4 of the Act, which states that the provisions of the Bill of Rights Act must be interpreted consistently with those of other statutes and that any conflict of meaning must be resolved in favour of the latter. In terms of limitations that give rise to questions of equality and non-discrimination, the justifiable limitations provision (s 5) states that:

> . . . the rights and freedoms contained in this Bill of Rights may be subject only to such reasonable limits prescribed by law as can be fully demonstrably justified in a free and democratic society.

Therefore, any limitations on s 11, the core provision with regard to the child's right to medical treatment, which states that "Everyone has the right to refuse to undergo any medical treatment" must be fully and demonstrably justified.

---

[20] Ibid. C.f. s 5 Care of Children Act 2004.
[21] Austin, supra note 15, at 255.
[22] *Action for Children in Aotearoa 1996: The Non-Governmental Organisation Report to the United Nations Committee on the Rights of the Child*, Youth Law Project/Tino Rangatiratanga Taitamariki, Auckland, 1996, at 36.

In terms of the medical treatment of children, s 36(1) of the Care of Children Act provides that a consent, or refusal to consent to any medical, surgical, or dental treatment or procedure (including a blood transfusion) if given by a child of or over the age of 16 years, has effect as if the child were of full age. Given that the Act does *not* specifically refer to the rights of those children under the age of sixteen to consent to medical treatment, there is a presumption that parental consent is necessary in such a situation, with any dispute arising over parental consent remaining to be resolved by the courts where necessary.

The rights of parents to make decisions that may compromise the best interests of the child may in turn be subject to 'justifiable limitations', as s 27 of the Act permits the court to intervene and deprive a parent of guardianship where consistent with the provisions of s 29 "the Court is satisfied that the parent is for some grave reason unfit to be a guardian of the child or is unwilling to exercise the responsibilities of a guardian" and that "that the order will serve the welfare and best interests of the child".[23] Where parental consent is not forthcoming and the child is in need of medical treatment s 36(3) of the Act allows for consent to be given by a guardian, a person acting in the place of a parent where there is no such guardian, and if no such person can be found, either a District Court Judge or the Chief Executive (of the Department of Child, Youth and Family Services).

Similarly, the Children, Young Persons, and Their Families Act 1989 contains a number of provisions which, in certain circumstances, allow for parental rights to give or refuse consent to medical treatment to be dispensed with and which allow the court to award guardianship of a child to either a particular individual or to the Chief Executive of the Department of Child, Youth and Family Services.[24] These provisions are to be read in conjunction with s 6 of the Act relating to the paramountcy of the welfare of the child.

The Code of Health and Disability Services Consumers' Rights 1996 provides further guidance to decision-makers. The Code gives rights to all health and disability consumers to which children are equally entitled.[25] According to Right 7(1):

> services may be provided to a consumer only if that consumer makes an informed choice and gives informed consent, except where any enactment, or the common law, or any other provisions of the Code provides otherwise.[26]

---

[23] Section 27 of the Act allows for an application to be made to the Family Court or to the High Court for guardianship orders to be made in favour of the Court. This section may come into force when a health practitioner applies for a court-appointed guardian for the purposes of consenting to treatment.

[24] Section 98 Children, Young Persons, and Their Families Act 1989.

[25] Health and Disability Commissioner, *Code of Health and Disability Services Consumer's Rights*, Health and Disability Commissioner, Auckland, 1996.

[26] Ibid.

Under the terms of Right 7(2) every consumer is presumed competent to exercise this right, unless there are reasonable grounds for believing that a person is not competent. Where such competence is lacking services may still be provided under the terms of Right 7(4) where such treatment is:

(a) . . .in the *best interests* of the consumer; and
(b) Reasonable steps have been taken to ascertain the views of the consumer; and
(c) Either, –

    . . .

   (ii) If the consumer's views have not been ascertained, the provider takes into account the views of suitable persons who are interested in the welfare of the consumer and available to advise the provider.[27] [emphasis added]

With regard to a consumer who is a child, a health practitioner must judge whether a particular child is competent to give informed consent. This judgement will be based upon the child's understanding and maturity, and the gravity of the medical procedure in question. Children, as consumers under the Code, must be consulted in a manner relevant to their age.[28] The views of the parents of the child are to be taken into account, however, it remains the responsibility of the practitioner to come to an independent decision on the issue.[29]

The child's right to medical treatment is based upon a combination of international obligations and domestic legislation both of which are informed by the requirement to secure the best interests of the child. The child's right to medical treatment spans his or her right to life, the right to the enjoyment of the highest standard of health, as well as the right to refuse medical treatment. These rights are enforced in the first instance by the child's parents or guardian. However, when parental rights conflict with the best interests of the child, the State may assume guardianship of the child in order to secure what is in his or her best interests. Legislatively, there is an arguably rebuttable presumption that young persons under the age of 16 are lacking the appropriate level of capacity. Failure to rebut this presumption means that their parents or the courts may make such decisions on their behalf.

4. Judicial Interpretation of the Child's Right to Medical Treatment

Limitations have been placed upon a child's right to refuse to undergo medical treatment as parents and/or the State have intervened to limit the rights of children to refuse medical treatment. In cases where such limitations have been found to be in accordance with the law and fully demonstrably justified as

---

[27] Ibid.
[28] Ibid, at 25–26.
[29] See, Ministry of Health, *Consent in Child and Youth Health: Information for Practitioners*, Wellington, Ministry of Health, 1998, at 25.

being in the child's best interests, the child's autonomy is circumscribed by the paternalistic standard of the best interests of the child.[30] The predominant case remains that of *Gillick v West Norfolk and Wisbech AHA*,[31] in which the House of Lords recognised the general principle with regard to a child's right to medical treatment and held that some children are legally competent to consent to some medical treatment. The teenage girl in question, who was seeking contraception without parental consent:

> had the legal capacity to consent to medical examination and treatment if she had sufficient maturity and intelligence to understand the nature and implications of the proposed treatment . . .[32]

Scarman L summed up the matter thus:

> If the law should impose on the process of "growing up" fixed limits where nature knows only a continuous process, the price would be artificiality and a lack of realism in an area where the law must be sensitive to change.[33]

Case law in New Zealand and in England indicates that the judiciary has at the least sought to respond to change in a realistic and sensitive manner, although there may be disagreement over the outcome of some cases.

4.1. *New Zealand Jurisprudence – Medical Treatment of the Young Child*

In New Zealand, the *Gillick* principle as to the legal competency of children with regard to medical issues was considered in *Re X*.[34] The case concerned the right of parents to consent to medical treatment on behalf of their severely mentally handicapped daughter who was 15 years of age but who had the mental age of about 3 to 8 months. The family consulted medical experts and all were in agreement that sterilisation would be in the best interests of the child.[35] In ordering that the operation could proceed under the terms of s 25 of the Guardianship Act, Hillyer J referred to a Canadian decision, which framed the question to be decided as whether it was "in the best interests of Infant K to undergo major surgery in order to avoid the risk of suffering by Infant K which may result if the operation is not performed?"[36] According to

---

[30] Any limitation upon such rights, simply because the right-holder is a child, must be supported by a logical and non-arbitrary reason for so doing that is in proportion to the desired aim of such a restriction: G Austin, "Children's Rights in New Zealand Law and Society" (1995) 25 Victoria University of Wellington Law Review, 249–282, at 254–255.

[31] [1986] AC 112.

[32] Ibid, at 113.

[33] Ibid, at 186.

[34] [1991] NZFLR 49.

[35] Ibid, at 53.

[36] *Re K and Public Trustee* (1985) 19 DLR (4th) 255, at 274–275.

Hillyer J, "Those words from *Re K* were absolutely applicable and apposite in this case."[37] In relation to the question of parental consent, he noted "where a child is under the age of 16 or is intellectually handicapped, such consent is necessary".[38] The difficulty arising from the requirement of parental consent for the under-16-year-old child's right to medical treatment becomes apparent when the consent proviso is turned on its head and parents refuse to allow their children to undergo medical treatment for reasons that pertain more to their rights as parents rather that the rights and interests of the child.

There are no New Zealand cases dealing with teenagers refusing medical treatment. Rather, the courts have been confined to dealing with cases involving quite young children who were deemed to be lacking in capacity and conflict arose between the parents and the courts where the former had sought to refuse medical treatment for their child.[39]

Re J: B and B v Director-General of Social Welfare[40] epitomises the polarisation of parents' rights and children's rights with regard to the child's right to medical treatment. The issue of the child's right to medical treatment, or the exercise of that right by his parents to determine what course of treatment would be in the best interests of their child, was framed in terms of the rights guaranteed to them by the New Zealand Bill of Rights Act and the manner in which their parental rights had been breached.[41] In particular, the parents in *Re J* argued

---

[37] *Re X*, supra note 34, at 54.

[38] Ibid, at 57.

[39] See, e.g., *Re J: B and B v Director-General of Social Welfare* [1995] 3 NZLR 73; [1996] 2 NZLR 134 (CA); *Auckland Healthcare Services v Liu* (1996), Judge Tompkins, HC Auckland, M81/96; *Director-General of Social Welfare v M* (1991) 8 FLRNZ 498, 504.

[40] *Re J*, ibid. The case concerned a three-year-old boy who had suffered a life-threatening nosebleed requiring urgent medical treatment, which included surgery and blood transfusions. His parents, who were Jehovah's Witnesses, did not consent to the blood transfusions. However, both during the surgery and afterwards, blood and blood products were administered to the child in circumstances that were regarded as being essential and urgent to preserve the life of the child. Prior to the surgery, the hospital had sought a court order permitting the use of blood products. The District Court Judge granted this order and also appointed the Director-General of Social Welfare as the child's guardian for the purpose of authorising procedures required to safeguard his welfare. J's parents were subsequently notified of this action. The Director-General of Social Welfare then made a guardianship application to the High Court which made the child a ward of the Court. The High Court subsequently appointed a medical doctor as its agent for the purposes of the consent required for medical treatment involving blood transfusion for the child, and the parents as general agents in respect of all *other* general matters.

[41] In the High Court, Ellis J restricted his judgment to simply concluding that a child's right to health was to override the parents' right to freedom of religion and their general power to decide upon the child's medical treatment. In so doing, he referred to several international conventions as well as to a number of domestic cases which confirmed that the child's welfare is to be the paramount consideration and that parental rights in such cases are to be of secondary importance. He concluded that "the Court will always intervene despite the parents' sincere beliefs where the child's life or well-being is seriously threatened", supra note 39, at 86 (HC).

that ss 13 and 15 of the Bill of Rights Act guaranteed to them the rights to freedom of thought, conscience, religion and belief and to manifest their religion or
belief in worship, observance, practice or teaching and that s 15, in particular,
affirmed that that these rights extended to the right to bring up their children
according to their beliefs and to make decisions as to their medical treatment
according to those beliefs. J's parents further argued that the rights contained in
the Bill of Rights Act could be limited only to the extent justified in a free and
democratic society by virtue of the provisions of s 5, and that such limitations
could only be imposed when the State could prove on the balance of probabil-
ities that the consequent limitation of the rights was justified and was the least
intrusive limitation necessary in the circumstances.

In response to the parent's contentions, the Court of Appeal observed, first,
that the Bill of Rights Act guaranteed J's parents the right "to manifest their
religion or belief in worship, observance, practice or teaching. That is their
personal right, as is the right that they enjoy under s 11 to refuse to undergo any
medical treatment." However, the Court also noted that "the right to manifest
one's religion and belief in practice cannot be absolute . . .".[42] In support of
its interpretation of the Bill of Rights Act, the Court referred to the limitations
imposed by Article 18(3) of the ICCPR, which provides that:

> Freedom to manifest one's religion or beliefs may be subject only to such limita-
> tions as are prescribed by law and are necessary to protect public safety, order,
> health, or morals or the fundamental rights and freedoms of others.[43]

The Court also noted that Article 18(4) of the Covenant provided that the rights
of parents to manifest their religion extended to rearing and educating their
children until such time as their children were able to exercise their freedom
of religion and that this right extended to making decisions for them as to
health and medical treatment.[44] The provisional nature of these rights, guaranteed by both national and international law, became apparent when the
right to medical treatment was balanced against the right to life.

In terms of the right to life, the Court noted that s 8 of the Bill of Rights Act
guaranteed to every child the right not to be deprived of life except on such
grounds as were established by law and consistent with the principles of fundamental justice. Any potential for conflict between the parents' right to manifest their religion, where it would extend to include the right to consent to and
refuse medical treatment for their child, could result in a potential overlap

---

[42] Supra note 39, at 145 (CA).
[43] Ibid.
[44] Ibid.

between that right and the child's fundamental right to life. Such a conflict was not, according to the Court, to be resolved in terms of the provisions of s 5. To do so would be, in the Court's opinion, to frame any action to protect the life or health of a child in terms of a limitation of the parents' right that was prescribed by law and which could be justified in a free and democratic society. The effect of such an approach would be to subsume the right of the child to life within the (limited) right of his parents' to manifest their religion.[45] To that end, the Court stated that:

> It is not an issue of whether the State has established that action to protect the life or health of a child is a limitation of the parents' right that is prescribed by law and can be justified in a free and democratic society.[46]

The Court was of the opinion that any State intrusion to protect the rights of the child was to be indistinguishable from intrusion by the Courts to protect any other rights, it was not a denial (of parental rights) by the State but the securing the rights of the child. To view the conflict as one of a limitation on parents' rights to manifest their religion would be to render the rights of the child as subordinate to those of the parents which, according to the Court, would be in "contradiction to s 23 of the Guardianship Act" which had to be given effect to in this case.

Instead, the Court defined the conflict between the child's right to life and the parents' right to manifest their religion in terms of the scope of s 15. It stated that the parents' right to manifest their religion could not be extended "to imperil the life or health of the child".[47] The Court found itself unable to extend the scope of the right to practice religion to the right to refuse medical treatment for the child on religious grounds even where death would ensue. To do so would be a criminal offence under s 151 of the Crimes Act 1961. Instead, the Court stated that it would be preferable:

> to approach potential conflicts of rights assured under the Bill of Rights on the basis that the rights are to be defined so as to be given effect compatibly. The scope of one right is not to be taken as so broad to impinge upon and limit others.[48]

Accordingly, the Court defined the scope of parental rights to religious freedom as being such as to exclude from the manifestation of religion in practice "doing or omitting anything that is likely to place at risk the life, health, or welfare of their children".[49] It was of the opinion that such an approach was

---

[45] Section 8 New Zealand Bill of Rights Act 1990.
[46] *Re J*, supra note 39, at 146.
[47] Ibid.
[48] Ibid.
[49] Ibid.

consistent, in the present context, with the provisions of the Guardianship Act which recognised that the interests of the child were to be paramount.[50] Finally, the Court noted that this approach would avoid the need to demonstrate that the parents' rights had been infringed before the rights of the child could be secured, an approach which would be inappropriate in the reconciliation of such competing rights.[51] The Court concluded that there was no breach of the parents' rights under the Bill of Rights Act by the exercise of the Court's jurisdiction under the Guardianship Act.

The approach of the Court of Appeal in *Re J* demonstrates the manner in which domestic human rights legislation may be interpreted in a manner that incorporates provisions of international human rights law. Consideration of New Zealand's obligations under Articles 3, 5, 12 and 24 of the Convention on the Rights of the Child would have further strengthened the Court's reasoning.

However, the Convention on the Rights of the Child was referred to in the High Court case of *Auckland Healthcare Services Ltd v T*[52] where the High Court was requested to grant an order to place a twelve-year-old child under the guardianship of the Court so that consent could be given for treatment without which she would die. In following the decision of the Court in *In re J*, Patterson J reiterated that the law was "to have as the first and paramount consideration the welfare of A . . .".[53] Patterson J considered that the parents' position under the Bill of Rights Act had to be compatible with the child's rights and the obligation to ensure the best interests of the child provided for in s 23 of the Guardianship Act.[54] He further noted New Zealand's obligations under Article 6 of the Convention on the Rights of the Child to recognise that every child has the inherent right to life and that, accordingly, the parties were under an obligation to ensure to the maximum extent possible the survival and development of the child.

---

[50] Section 23 Guardianship Act 1969.

[51] Supra note 39, 146. The question of competing rights has not been confined to the right to life. In *Auckland Healthcare Services v Liu*, supra note 39, a 12-year-old boy was made a ward of the court and a medical specialist was appointed as his agent to authorise surgery to re-attach the partially detached retina of the boy's right eye. The child's parents believed that God would heal their son's sight in spite of the medical evidence that indicated that the boy would be rendered totally blind without the surgery, which had a 70% chance of restoring his sight. Judge Tompkins balanced the religious beliefs of the parents with the medical evidence and held that the medical treatment should proceed on the basis of protecting the welfare of the child as provided for under s 23 of the Guardianship Act.

[52] Supra note 3. In this case, the parents of a child who was born with a life-threatening liver defect did not wish their child to undergo transplant surgery and refused to consent to an operation, in spite of the advice of doctors.

[53] Ibid, at 671.

[54] Ibid.

The English Court of Appeal case of *In Re T* stands in stark contrast to the above approach, which prioritises the child's right to life over any parental rights.[55] In her leading judgment, Butler-Sloss LJ concluded, in line with a number of judges in similar cases,[56] that the welfare of the child was the paramount consideration. She also reiterated the fact that although the consent or refusal of parental consent was an important consideration to weigh in the balancing exercise when an application of wardship was made, ultimately the decision was the Court's alone. However, the significance of *In Re T* lies in the fact that the English Court of Appeal did not confine itself solely to a consideration of the medical issues as presented by the case in determining what was in the best interests of the child in question – clinical evidence alone was not regarded as being determinative. Rather, the Court was of the opinion that the best interests of the child would best be determined by balancing his rights with those of his parents, in particular with the rights of his mother who would have been the primary carer of C were the transplant to go ahead. According to Butler Sloss LJ:

> This mother and this child are one for the purpose of this unusual case and the decision of the court to consent to the operation jointly affects the mother and son and it also affects the father. The welfare of this child depends upon his mother.

To that end, Butler Sloss LJ considered the effect on the mother of having to care for a very sick child whose medical treatment she did not condone or consent to. This factor took on added significance in light of expert medical evidence that coercing the mother to care for C after a transplant operation to which she had not consented to "was fraught with danger for the child" on the basis that "the total commitment of the caring parent was essential to the success of

---

[55] *(A Minor) (Wardship: Medical Treatment)* [1997] 1 WLR 242; EWCA Civ 805 (24 October 1996) http://www.bailii.org.ezproxy.waikato.ac.nz:2048/ew/cases/EWCA/Civ/1996/805.html, as accessed on 2 February 2005. C was born with a life-threatening liver defect in the UK. Medical opinion was unanimous that he would not live beyond the age of two and half years if he did not undergo a liver transplant. His parents, who were both health care professionals with experience in the care of sick children, refused to consent to the liver transplant operation. They, along with C, had also moved to another country. The doctors who had treated C while he still lived in England were of the opinion that the parents were not acting in his best interests and referred the matter to their local authority, which applied to the Court to exercise its inherent wardship jurisdiction. At first instance, the Judge held that the mother's refusal to accept the unanimous advice of the doctors and her refusal to consent to the operation was not the conduct of a reasonable parent. He ordered that C be returned to England within 21 days to be assessed for transplant surgery. On appeal this decision was reversed.

[56] *In Re B (A Minor) (Wardship: Medical Treatment)* [1981] 1 WLR 1421; *Re J (A Minor) (Wardship: Medical Treatment)* [1991] Fam. 33; *In Re Z (A Minor) (Identification: Restrictions on Publication)* [1996] 2 WLR 88.

the treatment".[57] She also highlighted the mother's wish to focus on the present peaceful life of the child who had a chance to spend the rest of his short life without the pain, stress and upset of major surgery. In terms of the effect of granting a consent order on C's mother, Butler Sloss LJ considered the fact that C's mother would be required to leave her current country of residence and to return, probably for a long period, to England. This requirement would involve her either leaving C's father behind and losing his support or requiring him to give up his present job and seek one in England. Butler Sloss LJ raised further questions:

> How will the mother cope? Can her professionalism overcome her view that her son should not be subjected to this distressing procedure? Will she break down? How will the child be affected by the conflict with which the mother may have to cope? What happens if the treatment is partially successful and another transplant is needed? The mother may not wish to consent to the further surgery. Is the court to be asked again for consent to the next operation?[58]

Although Butler Sloss LJ acknowledged that the welfare of the child was to be the paramount consideration and recognised the "very strong presumption in favour of a course of action which will prolong life" and the inevitable consequences for C of not giving consent, she also stated that to prolong life was not the sole objective of the court and to require it at the expense of other considerations may not be in a child's best interests. She concluded that, on the "most unusual facts" of the case, it would not be in the best interests of C to require him to return to England for a liver transplant, rather it would be in his best interests to leave his future treatment in the hands of his devoted parents.

The decision of the English Court of Appeal in *In Re T* makes clear that medical profession cannot ignore parental objections to life-saving treatment for a child and that medical evidence alone is not to be regarded as the sole determinant of what is in the best interests of the child.[59] Although the Court's approach can broadly be regarded as being positive, especially with regard to the broader considerations that were taken into account in reaching its decision, other aspects of the reasoning remain very problematic. In particular, there is the difficulty of securing the rights of the child (especially the right to

---

[57] *In re T (A Minor) (Wardship: Medical Treatment)* [1997] 1 WLR 242, http://www.bailii.org.ezproxy.waikato.ac.nz:2048/cgi-bin/markup.cgi?doc=/ew/cases/EWCA/Civ/1996/805.html&query="In+re+T+(A+Minor)+(Wardship:+Medical+Treatment)"&method=all, as viewed 23 May 2005, per Butler-Sloss LJ.
[58] Ibid.
[59] See also, *In Re M.B. (Medical Treatment)* [1997] 2 FLR 426, 439 where Butler-Sloss LJ said, "Best interests are not limited to best medical interests"; and *In Re A (Male Sterilisation)* [2000] 1 FLR 549, 555 where Butler-Sloss, P, said "In my judgment best interest encompasses medical, emotional and all other welfare issues."

life) in the face of Butler-Sloss LJ's stance that, in the case at hand at least, the child's interests were to be treated as being at one with his mother.[60] According to ter Haar,[61] it is difficult to understand on what basis she was able to make such an assertion when the role of the court in this modern age, with regard to its wardship and *parens patriae* jurisdiction, is clearly to protect the vulnerable. If children's interests are to be so intertwined with the parents' that they are seen as one, then this leaves children with very little protection. Previous courts have been at pains to protect children against their parents' views, no matter how sincerely or profoundly those parental convictions are held, but the decision in *In Re T* shows that the court does not always assume this paternalistic role to ensure a child's survival in the face of parental opposition.[62] The Court placed considerable weight upon the likely implications for the mother if the transplant went ahead, namely the possibility of leaving the father behind or forcing him to give up his job and return with them to England. Consequently, the best interests test was no longer to be exclusively focused on the interests of the child but was broadened to take into account the practical difficulties for the parents if the order were made. It was these difficulties that stood in the way of the Court making an order for the liver transplant, with the result that C would be allowed to die in order to accommodate his mother's essentially practical objections. This approach has no regard to the principle that the right to life ought to assume critical importance in determining what is in the best interests of the child. An alternative approach in the case of *In Re T* would have been to recognise that the interests of the mother and the interests of the child were, in fact, conflicting.[63] However, the consequence of the Court of Appeal's reasoning in *In Re T* is that where the child is too young to be reasonably held to be competent in making decisions such as these, where the parent is required to support the treatment in terms of ongoing post-treatment care and where the proposed treatment is invasive, then it ought to be the parent who decides. According to ter Haar:

> The Court of Appeal's decision in *In Re T* suggests that the (English) judicial system is in reality returning to an older ideology, which allowed parents unfettered authority over their children in terms of their proprietorial rights by saying that the child's interests are the same as the mother's, and that his care ought to be left entirely in her hands.[64]

---

[60] Supra note 57, at 252.

[61] C ter Haar, "A Fight to the Death? The Needs, Rights and Welfare of the Child in Need of Life-Saving Medical Treatment" in C Breen (ed), *Children's Needs, Rights and Welfare: Developing Strategies for the 'Whole Child' in the 21st Century*, Victoria, Australia, Thompson-Dunmore Press, 2004, at 32.

[62] Ibid.

[63] Ibid, at 32–33.

[64] Ibid, at 33.

Further concern arises when the practical difficulties referred to above are used as a point of reference in assessing the reasonableness of the views of the parents and thus the extent to which their rights will be taken into account by the Court in the exercise of its wardship jurisdiction. Lord Justice Waite summarised the issue as follows:

> It can only be said safely that there is a scale, at one end of which lies the clear case where parental opposition to medical intervention is prompted by scruple or dogma of a kind which is patently irreconcilable with principles of child health and welfare widely accepted by the generality of mankind; and that at the other end lie highly problematic cases where there is genuine scope for a difference of view between the parent and the judge. In both situations it is the duty of the judge to allow the court's own opinion to prevail in the perceived paramount interest of the child concerned, but in cases at the latter end of the scale, there must be a likelihood (though never of course a certainty) that the greater the scope for genuine debate between one view and another the stronger will be that inclination of the court to be influenced by a reflection that in the last analysis the best interests of every child include an expectation that difficult decisions affecting the length and quality of its life will be taken for it by the parent to whom its care has been entrusted by nature.

> In essence therefore, reliance on the practical difficulties that would be faced by C's mother were she to be obliged to agree to the transplant along with her overall unwillingness to consent to the liver transplant placed the views of C's mother at the opposite end of the spectrum to parental views that were informed by 'scruple or dogma.'[65]

Given that the outcome for C of this approach was death, it conflicts somewhat with the views of Lord Brandon in the House of Lords decision of *In Re F*, where he stated:

> The operation or other treatment will be in their best interests if, but only if, it is carried out in order either to save their lives, or to ensure improvement or prevent deterioration in their physical or mental health.[66]

However, not all cases concerning children's rights are a battle where the right to life is the predominant consideration. In *Auckland Healthcare Services v L*,[67] the High Court endorsed the view that, when presented with medical evidence recommending a particular course of action, to overrule that opinion would be tantamount to an abuse of power that health practitioners owe their patients. That case involved the case of a baby girl who had been born with severe congenital deformities. Her prognosis was hopeless, any treatment would have been unpleasant and her death was inevitable. Nevertheless, her parents felt

---

[65] *In re T*, supra note 57, at 254.
[66] *In re F (Mental Patient: Sterilisation)* [1990] AC 1, 55F.
[67] Supra note 3.

unable to agree to the withdrawal of her life-support systems. Auckland Healthcare requested the Court to relieve the parents of the need to decide when and in what circumstances the baby's life should end. In considering the welfare of the child the Court referred to s 23(1) of the Guardianship Act.[68] It noted the contrast between the case at hand and previous cases where the appropriate legislation was invoked so that the child could receive necessary medical treatment in the absence of parental consent. Nevertheless, despite the lack of authority directly on the point, the Court concluded that the welfare of the child required the discontinuance of life-support.[69] It noted that while the task of the Court is to act to preserve the life of the child, there would still be instances where discontinuing their treatment would be in the child's best interests.[70] The Court also referred to s 8 of the Bill of Rights Act with its provision that no one shall be deprived of the right to life.[71] The Court also drew upon the provisions contained in Article 6(1) of the ICCPR as well as noting the relevance of Article 3(1) of the Convention on the Rights of the Child regarding the best interests of the child. According to the Court, the proposed action would not deprive Baby L of her right to life. In the case at hand, provided that it was in the best interests of the patient to do so, there would be no breach of the Bill of Rights Act in withdrawing treatment, without which natural death would ensue.[72] In terms of the best interests of Baby L, the following "best interests" test was submitted to the Court:

(a) The relevant rights;
(b) The therapeutic or medical benefit of the treatment;
(c) The chance of recovery;
(d) The parents' views;
(e) The impact of the treatment on the child.[73]

The Court held that it was in Baby L's best interests for an order to withdraw treatment to be made. It weighed the child's right to life with her right to be free from pain and discomfort. This trumped her parents' wish for her life to be prolonged as long as possible.[74]

The need to balance the rights of the child with parental rights arose again in the English case of *Re A (Children)*.[75] The children concerned were conjoined twins who for the purposes of the case were identified as Jodie and Mary. The

---

[68] In addition to Article 3(1) of the Convention on the Rights of the Child, supra note 11.

[69] *Auckland Healthcare Services Ltd. v L*, supra note 3, at 1001.

[70] Ibid, at 1003.

[71] Ibid.

[72] Ibid.

[73] Ibid, at 1003–1004.

[74] Ibid, at 1006.

[75] *Re A (Children)* [2000] EWCA Civ 254. http://www.bailii.org.ezproxy.waikato.ac.nz:2048/ew/cases/EWCA/Civ/2000/254.html#sectionIV-1, as accessed on 3 February 2005.

issue before the Court of Appeal was whether it was in the best interests of the children to go against the parents' wishes and order that they be separated, even though such an operation would result in the death of one of the twins and could result in the remaining twin being disabled. In terms of the extent to which the parents' wishes were to be taken into account, Ward LJ reiterated the scale of reasonableness advanced by Waite LJ in *In re T* and noted emphatically that that this too was not a case where opposition was "prompted by scruple or dogma". Nevertheless, Ward LJ remained unconvinced that giving effect to the parents' wishes would be in the children's best interests. In relation to Jodie, the twin who would survive the operation, his Lordship stated that the parents had taken into consideration the worst possible scenario, namely that she would be wheelchair bound and destined for a life of difficulty, and that they had failed to recognise her capacity sufficiently to enjoy the benefits of life that would be available to her were she free and independent. He recognised that Jodie could need special care and attention and that such care could be very difficult to provide fully in the parents' home country. In the face of such difficulties he stated:

> This is a real and practical problem for the family, the burden of which in ordi-
> nary family life should not be underestimated. It may seem unduly harsh on
> these desperate parents to point out that it is the *child's* best interests which are
> paramount, not the *parents'*. Coping with a disabled child sadly inevitably casts a
> great burden on parents who have to struggle through those difficulties. . . . They
> surely cannot so minimise Jodie's rights on the basis that the burden of possible
> disadvantage for her and the burdens of caring for such a child for them can
> morally be said to outweigh her claim to the human dignity of independence
> which only cruel fate has denied her. . . . In their natural repugnance at the idea
> of killing Mary they fail to recognise their conflicting duty to save Jodie and they
> seem to exculpate themselves from, or at least fail fully to face up to the conse-
> quence of the failure to separate the twins, namely death for Jodie. In my judg-
> ment, parents who are placed on the horns of such a terrible dilemma simply
> have to choose the lesser of their inevitable loss.[76]

The extreme youth of many of the children at the centre of the above cases means that issues of child competency and autonomy and their impact on limitations on imposed on the ability of the child *itself* were simply by-passed. Rather, the cases involving conflicts of rights between parents and young children over the latter's right to medical treatment are aimed at resolving that conflict by achieving the appropriate balance of rights between the individuals involved. In particular, the ability of parents to limit the right to life of their children has itself been limited by legislation and judicial interpretation thereof in a manner not dissimilar to the manner in which national and international human rights law has sought to circumscribe, where necessary, the vertical

---

[76] Ibid.

effects of such rights. However, the limitation on the rights, whether those of the parent or the child, are, nevertheless, to be examined in order to ensure that the differential treatment is legitimate, proportionate and necessary and, thus, non-discriminatory.

4.2. The Medical Treatment of Adolescents

There is a dearth of cases involving the rights of adolescents to refuse medical treatment. The English Courts have been forced to deal with this issue on numerous occasions, cases where, contrary to the facts of *Gillick*, young persons have *refused* life-saving medical treatment. The cases revolved around the meaning of s 8 of the Family Law Reform Act 1969, which provides:

> The consent of a minor who has attained the age of sixteen years to any surgical, medical or dental treatment which in the absence of consent would constitute a trespass to his person, shall be effective as it would be if he was of full age.

In *Re W (a minor) (medical treatment)*,[77] W was 16 years old and dangerously ill with anorexia nervosa. She refused to undergo medical treatment for her condition without which she was likely to die. The Court of Appeal acknowledged that the question of whether W had sufficient competence had to take into account one of the features of anorexia nervosa, which was to destroy the ability to give informed consent.[78] The jurisdiction of the Court to order medical treatment in the face of a minor's refusal to consent to such treatment was outlined by Lord Donaldson MR, who in ordering that W be treated, stated:

> There is ample authority for the proposition that the inherent powers of the court under its *parens patriae* jurisdiction are theoretically limitless and that they certainly extend beyond the powers of a natural parent . . . There can therefore be no doubt that it has the power to override the refusal of a minor, whether over the age of 16 or under that age but 'Gillick competent'.[79]

Lord Justice Balcombe provided the most explicit encapsulation of the nature and extent of the powers of the Court in instances where a child was refusing medical treatment:

> If the court's powers are to be meaningful, there must come a point at which the court, while not disregarding the child's wishes, can override them in the child's own best interests, objectively considered. Clearly such a point will have come if the child is seeking to refuse treatment in circumstances which will in all probability lead to the death of the child or to severe permanent injury.[80]

---

[77] [1992] 4 All ER 627.
[78] Ibid, at 637, 641.
[79] Ibid, at 637.
[80] Ibid, at 643 (emphasis added).

The relevance of *Gillick* competence to cases where perhaps otherwise *Gillick* competent minors refuse life-saving treatment was described as follows by Nolan J:

> It is of the essence of that jurisdiction that the court has the power and the responsibility in appropriate cases to override the views of both the child and the parent in determining what is in the child's best interests. Authoritative and instructive as they are, the speeches in Gillick do not deal with the principles which should govern the exercise of this court's jurisdiction in the present case. In my judgment, those principles are to be found in s 1 of the Children Act 1989. *The child's welfare is to be the paramount consideration: see s 1(1).*[81]

In *Re E (a minor) (wardship: medical treatment)*,[82] the adolescent in question, A, was a 16-year-old teenage boy who, because of the strength of his Jehovah's Witness beliefs, refused to undergo blood transfusions as part of his treatment for leukaemia. Justice Ward framed the issue as one of whether or not A's refusal was a refusal of such a nature that it could enable him to override parental choice or even the *parens patriae* jurisdiction of the Court. In other words, was A *Gillick* competent? According to Ward J, E lacked *Gillick* competence on the grounds that E had:

> No realisation of the full implications which lie before him as to the process of dying. He may have some concept of the fact that he will die, but as to the manner of his death and to the extent of his and his family's suffering I find that he has not the ability to turn his mind to it nor the will to do so. Who can blame him for that.[83]

In so deciding, Ward J returned to the inherent wardship jurisdiction of the Court, which has the welfare of the child as its core. In determining whether A's choice to die was a choice that a judge in exercising a wardship jurisdiction could find to be consistent with the welfare of the child, Ward J held such a choice to be "inimical to his well-being".[84]

In *Re S (A Minor) (Consent To Medical Treatment)* was a further case involving a 15-and-a-half-year-old girl whose strong Jehovah's Witnesses beliefs prevented the life-saving blood transfusions required by the congenital disease from which she was suffering.[85] According to Johnson J, "S's case is simply that she is now of an age when she has the right to decide whether she should

---

[81] Ibid, at 647.

[82] [1993] 1 FLR 386.

[83] Ibid, at 391.

[84] Ibid, at 393. However, as soon as E turned 18, he exercised his right as an adult to refuse medical treatment and subsequently died.

[85] [1995] 1 FCR 604; [1994] 2 FLR 1065; [1995] Fam Law 20; http://www.lexisnexis.com.au.ezproxy.waikato.ac.nz:2048/cui/uni-login/default.htm?login.asp?uni=waikato, as accessed on 28 February 2005.

have this treatment or not . . .".[86] After canvassing the law regarding the balance to be struck between the autonomy and the welfare of the child as set out in *Re W*[87] and *Re E*,[88] Johnson J unhesitatingly started from the position that S's wish should be given effect unless there were strong countervailing factors to the contrary. While he recognised that S's right to determine what happened to her body was not to be overridden lightly, he also noted that, on the other hand, there were other considerations to be weighed in the balance. He was of the opinion that S did not understand the full implications of what would happen to her. According to Johnson J:

> It does not seem to me that her capacity is commensurate with the gravity of the decision which she has made. It seems to me that an understanding that she will die is not enough. For her decision to carry weight she should have a greater understanding of the manner of the death and pain and the distress.[89]

This was the standard set by Johnson J in determining whether S was '*Gillick* competent'. In spite of the fact that his initial approach was that the case at hand was a case of a child who was *Gillick* competent, given that she was 15-and-a-half years old, having later seen her and heard about her, Johnson J was in no doubt at all that she was not *Gillick*-competent:

> 'When I was a child, I spoke as a child.' That seemed to me to be how S feels and speaks. There are those who are children and those who are adults and those who are in-between. I do not believe that S is in-between. She is still very much, in my view, a child. Whilst as she gave evidence I was so very strongly impressed by her integrity and her commitment, I believe they were the integrity and commitment of a child and not of somebody who was competent to make the decision that she tells me she has made. She hopes still for a miracle. My conclusion is, therefore, that she is not 'Gillick-competent'.[90]

The centrality of the welfare of the child was returned to, and expanded upon, by Wall J in *Re C (Detention: Medical Treatment)*.[91] In determining that the powers of the Courts could be extended to include the detention of C in order for her to receive medical treatment, Wall J stated:

> the test which I have to apply if I exercise the inherent jurisdiction is whether or not an order such as that being sought is in C's best interests. It is also common ground that in deciding what is in C's best interests I must have regard to her

---

[86] Ibid.
[87] Supra note 77.
[88] Supra note 82.
[89] *Re S*, supra note 85.
[90] Supra note 84.
[91] [1997] 2 FLR 180, http://www.lexisnexis.com.au.ezproxy.waikato.ac.nz:2048/cui/uni-login/default.htm?login.asp?uni=waikato, as accessed on 25 February 2005.

wishes and feelings, although, plainly, I can override her wishes if what she wants is not in her best interests.

C's capacity to give or refuse consent to treatment is relevant to my decision, but is not determinative of it. Clearly, however, if the evidence is that C has the capacity to give or refuse consent then the weight which should be given to her wishes is increased.[92]

The balance between competency and welfare was more struck more clearly by Stephen Brown P in *Re L (Medical Treatment: Gillick Competency)* which concerned a 14-year-old girl who refused life-saving medical treatment because of her strongly held Jehovah's Witness belief.[93] In determining that L was not '*Gillick* competent', Stephen Brown P made reference to her 'sheltered life', her sincere beliefs and also to the fact that she was unaware of the full consequences that would flow from her refusal of medical treatment. This determination led him to consider that the recommended treatment was not only in her best interests but was vital for her survival given the grave nature of her situation. He accordingly made an order for medical treatment to be given adding that "without any doubt at all, that it would be the appropriate order to make even if I were not justified in coming to the conclusion that she was not so-called '*Gillick* competent'".

The cases regarding the medical treatment of adolescents, in particular, demonstrate that the age of 16 is only useful as a trigger to determine and then often to disregard the level of competency of a young person – a clear example of the tension between the paternalistic notion of welfare and autonomous notion of rights. Although, in some instances, there may not be much difference between the ability of a minor and an adult in terms of their ability to comprehend the full extent of the consequences of their decision to refuse medical treatment and thus the drawing of a distinction between levels of competency may appear discriminatory. Nevertheless, the balance to be struck by the courts lies very much in favour of the welfare of the child and, on first appearances, seems to be at odds with greater recognition for the rights of the child and increased levels of autonomy. The issue of whether the Courts' apparent disregard for the levels of competency demonstrated by the minors in question is discriminatory, may be answered by examining the justifiability of

---

[92] Ibid.

[93] [1998] 2 FLR 810; [1999] 2 FCR 524; [1998] Fam Law 591, http://www.lexisnexis.com.au. ezproxy.waikato.ac.nz:2048/cui/uni-login/default.htm?login.asp?uni=waikato, as accessed on 25 February 2005. This approach was followed the following year in *Re M (child: refusal of medical treatment)* [1999] 2 FCR 577; 52 BMLR 124; 29 [1999] Fam Law 753. Johnson J overrode M's refusal to a life-saving transplant given that the consequence of such a refusal was death.

the apparent discrimination and whether the differential treatment is legitimate, proportionate and necessary (in a democratic society).

4.3. Limiting the Child's Right to Medical Treatment and the Child's Right to Refuse Medical Treatment: Differential or Discriminatory Treatment?

The jurisprudence of the New Zealand and English Courts demonstrates that the right to consent to medical treatment, whether it derives from the Care of Children Act (NZ) or the Family Law Reform Act (UK), carries with it a right to refuse medical treatment. Thus, the law allows for either the child's right to be limited by his or her parents or for the child himself or herself to act autonomously and to refuse medical treatment. This right, irrespective of who exercises it, must be balanced with, or limited by, the inherent *parens patriae* jurisdiction of the courts and/or national legislation,[94] both of which serve as echoes of the internationally recognised principle of providing for and protecting children. Such judicial and legislative measures also echo the initial requirement of determining whether differential treatment is in fact discriminatory treatment. In terms of the first part of the *Oakes* test,[95] the question to be determined is whether the limitation on the child's right to medical treatment, or the right to refuse medical treatment, serves an important and significant objective. In the cases considered above, the objective was to preserve the life of the child where painful and distressing deaths were regarded as being 'inimical to the child's well-being'. Thus, the Courts, exercising their inherent jurisdiction of *parens patriae*, could legitimately limit the rights of the child – or their parents – and tip the balance of rights in favour of life rather than death.

Once the requirement of legitimacy or the serving of an important and significant objective has been satisfied, the requirements of rationality and proportionality still remain to be considered. Arguably, the rationality of limitation measures predates the adoption of the language of the human rights of children (and any restrictions thereof). The notion of *parens patriae* has been described as:

> an ancient jurisdiction . . . which extends as far as necessary for the protection of those who are subject to it. . . wherein the court has power to protect the ward from any interference direct or indirect.[96]

This 'ancient jurisdiction' has also found expression in English and New Zealand legislation. This combination of the ancient and the modern recognition of

---

[94] For example, s 1 Children Act 1989, with its emphasis on the welfare of the child.
[95] *R v Oakes* [1986] 1 SCR 103; 1986 CanLII 46 (SCC), http://www.canlii.org.ezproxy.waikato.ac.nz:2048/ca/cas/scc/1986/1986scc7.html as viewed on 7 February 2005.
[96] *Re E*, supra note 82, at 391, Ward J.

the need to protect the vulnerable child, not only from others but also from himself or herself, in addition to promoting the welfare of the child, may thus be regarded as providing a rational limitation to the rights of the child to refuse medical treatment. The rationale behind the need to protect the child is further strengthened by the fact that, in the instant cases, failure to do so would have resulted in death. Although orders in favour of medical treatment would, on the whole, have extended the child's suffering, they would also have provided the child with further opportunity to exercise rights such as the right to life or the right to health. Such opportunity could equally translate into a right to reconsider their decision, as an adult, and the consequences thereof. In the words of Article 5 of the Convention on the Rights of the Child. The Courts could be described as securing the right of the child to evolve further, even where evolution may not ultimately make a difference to the wish of the child to die, as in the case of *Re E*. Legislation and the judiciary recognise that death provides no such opportunity for the child to exercise autonomy. Equally, this basis for rationality also provides the basis for satisfying the requirement that the limitation in question be proportionate to any limitation on the right of the child to either medical treatment or to refuse medical treatment being weighed against the consequences of the actual exercise of that right. Bluntly speaking, the pain and suffering (both physical and mental) to be endured by the child as a consequence of the medical treatment required would have to be balanced against the decision to forgo such treatment which, in the instant cases, could include death or severe permanent injury. The proportionality may be determined by the prospects for survival and a reasonable quality of life arising from the medical treatment in question, as judges both in the New Zealand and English Courts have recognised that such treatment would only serve the welfare of the child, if and only if, it was carried out in order either to save their lives, or to ensure improvement or prevent deterioration in their physical or mental health.[97]

5. Conclusion

The Courts have been governed by the rule that some children are legally competent to consent to medical treatment. Where such competency is lacking, the Courts have acknowledged the rights of parents to make decisions regarding medical treatment that is in the best interests of their child. Equally, however, the Courts have sought to constrain the rights of parents where they

---

[97] See, *In re F*, supra note 66, 55, *Auckland Healthcare Services v L*, supra note 3, and *Re A (Children)* supra note 76.

conflict with the best interests of the child. Not only that, the courts themselves have clearly expressed their willingness to disregard the wishes of the '*Gillick* competent' child in the face of life-threatening choices. However, children, parents and the Courts need to ensure that the exercise of the right to medical treatment, including the right to refuse such treatment is as a result of differential treatment which is legitimate and perhaps reflective of a course of action that is necessary to avoid discrimination.

CHAPTER THREE

HUMAN-ASSISTED REPRODUCTION AND
THE CHILD'S RIGHT TO IDENTITY

1. Introduction

Human-assisted reproduction is one of a number of issues that is illustrative of the, often difficult, relationship between law and technology. Such difficulties arise out of the struggle of law to keep pace with rapid technological advances, which has resulted in a number of legal lacunae. This chapter focuses on one particular issue affecting the human rights of children born through assisted human reproduction (AHR),[1] namely the right to identity. More specifically, the right to access information regarding the genetic identity of such children is often compromised by a number of limitations governing if, when, and what type of information may be accessed. Such limitations may result in a number of different potentially discriminatory practices. First, such limitations allow for differential treatment as between various groups of children within society as the current law in New Zealand, which is reflective of overseas legislative trends, provides no means of signalling to donor-conceived children that they are not genetically related to either one or both of their birth parents. Second, even if such children become aware that their genetic parentage may be different to their birth parentage, access to information regarding their genetic parents is restricted. These restrictions are age-based, with greater degrees of information becoming available when the donor-conceived child turns 18 years of age. Following the theme of this book, the issue to be determined is whether such limitations are discriminatory or are simply legitimate differential treatment.

Children's rights issues arising out of AHR, such as the right to identity, are gaining greater significance. It has been observed that the numbers of children created by reproductive technology is increasing and that families are being formed in ways that once were previously unimaginable.[2] The child born with the assistance of reproductive technology may have up to five individuals who

---

[1] Such children are also referred to as donor-conceived children or donor-conceived offspring. All three terms are used interchangeably in this chapter.

[2] M Roberts, "A Right to Know for Children by Donation – Any Assistance from Down Under" (2000) 12(4) Child and Family Law Quarterly, 371–382, at 371.

could be considered to be parents.[3] In New Zealand, as elsewhere, debates about the ethics of AHR have been the subject of a great deal of analysis by various interested bodies, including experts in law, sociology, and medicine.[4] This debate reflects the concern with the impact of AHR upon the family and society, a concern echoed in legislation such as the Care of Children Act 2004. Traditionally, much of the current discourse regarding AHR, both in New Zealand and overseas, tends to focus on the needs and rights of parents, whether they are social parents or those donating gametes, at the expense of careful consideration of the rights of the child.[5] The focus of this tension between rights used to be the perceived need for secrecy to protect the rights of adults, resulting in restrictions on the rights of the child to access information on their genetic origins. However, a number of jurisdictions have become increasing aware of the need to give greater recognition to the rights of individuals born of AHR, in particular the right to be free from discrimination regarding access to identifying information which underpins the child's right to identity. Nevertheless, legislation governing AHR continues to be reflective of parental bias.

Before considering the New Zealand approach to the rights of children born of AHR, it is worth considering some of the international legal backdrop. To that end, Part 2 of this chapter considers the AHR debate from a general human rights perspective. It then turns to the rights of the child with particular emphasis

---

[3] For example, an embryo may be conceived with the assistance of donated sperm and a donated egg, and the resulting embryo could be implanted in the womb of a surrogate mother who may ultimately give birth to a child who may be cared for by two other individuals, the social parents.

[4] See, e.g., Ministerial Committee on Assisted Reproductive Technologies (MCAHR), *Assisted Human Reproduction: Navigating Our Future: Report of the Ministerial Committee on Assisted Reproductive Technologies*, Wellington, Department of Justice, 1994; Interim National Ethics Committee on Assisted Reproductive Technologies (INECAHR), *Non-Commercial Surrogacy by Means of In-Vitro Fertilisation: Report of the Interim National Ethics Committee on Assisted Reproductive Technologies*, Wellington, Ministry of Health, 1995; B Atkin, "Medico-Legal Implications of AHR" (1994) 1(5) Butterworths Family Law Journal, 90–96; Human Rights Commission, *Submission of the Human Rights Commission to the Ministerial Committee on Assisted Reproductive Technologies*, Auckland, Human Rights Commission, 1994; Department of Justice, *Assisted Human Reproduction: A Commentary on the Report of the Ministerial Committee on Assisted Reproductive Technologies*, Wellington, Department of Justice, 1995; and J Caldwell and K Daniels, "Assisted Reproduction and the Law" in M Henaghan and B Atkin (eds), *Family Law Policy in New Zealand*, Auckland, Oxford University Press, 1992, at 256–303.

[5] See, e.g., Freeman's observation that there is a sharp contrast between recognition of children's rights and the responsibilities incumbent on parents and society in general and upon science in particular, on the one hand, and the "cacophony of sound and fury produced by feminists on the woman question and reproductive technology": M Freeman, "The New Birth Right? Identity and the Child of the Reproduction Revolution" (1996) 4 International Journal of Children's Rights, 273–297, at 273.

on the child's right to access information relating to genetic parentage and the related right to identity. Part 3 considers some relevant overseas legislation from Britain and Australia, which is used to illustrate the evolution of such legislation away from the secretive approach that underpinned the protection of donor parents' rights and towards attempts at increased openness that is based ultimately upon the recognition of the child's right to identity. Part 4 outlines current law in New Zealand regarding children born through AHR. It measures New Zealand's compliance with its international obligations to put the rights of donor-conceived children at least on an equal footing with those of parents and other children, and considers whether the legislative measures in place are discriminatory.

2. *International Human Rights Law and Human-Assisted Reproduction*

The approach adopted in this part is that of providing an overview of the principles and provisions contained in a number of international human rights treaties which have particular significance for a rights-centred analysis of AHR. This analysis reveals that although some of the older human rights instruments, such as the International Bill of Rights[6] and the European Convention,[7] and even the comparatively recent Convention on the Rights of the Child,[8] do not contain rights provisions that readily extend to rights issues raised by AHR, certain provisions contained therein form a backdrop for any analysis of the human rights of individuals born of AHR. For example, the broad language of such treaties, particularly with regard to the fundamental principles of non-discrimination and dignity, may usefully inform more general discussion on human rights and AHR. In terms of the rights of the child, the Guiding Principles of non-discrimination,[9] best interests,[10] evolving capacities,[11] and expression of views[12]

---

[6] Universal Declaration of Human Rights, G.A. Res. 217A, (III) U.N. Doc. A1810 (1948); International Covenant on Civil and Political Rights, U.N. G.A. Res. 2200 (XXI), 21 UN GAOR, Supp. (No. 16) 52, U.N. Doc. A16316 (1966); International Covenant on Economic, Social and Cultural Rights, G.A. Res. (XXI), U.N. GAOR 21st SESS., (Supp. No. 16), at 49, U.N. Doc. A/6316 (1966).

[7] European Convention for the Protection of Human Rights and Fundamental Freedoms, 213 U.N.T.S., p. 221, no. 2889; Council of Europe, European Treaty Series, 4 November 1950, no. 5; Council of Europe, Collected Texts, Strasbourg (1987).

[8] United Nations Convention on the Rights of the Child, UN Doc. A/44/736, (1989), UNGA Doc. A/Res/44/25 of 5 December, (1989) 28 I.L.M., 1448, (1989).

[9] Article 2.

[10] Article 3.

[11] Article 5.

[12] Article 12.

underpin any interpretation of the substantive rights contained in the Convention on the Rights of the Child as well as the spirit and purpose of the Convention. Thus with regard to the determination of rights of children born of AHR, for example, the ambiguous language of the Convention may be of benefit when read alongside the provisions of Article 3, which sets the child's interests as paramount. That is to say, given that the Convention is clear as to the child's interests prevailing in the balancing of rights and interests between child and parent (whether social or genetic), it is the interests of the child that should prevail, irrespective of the provisions regarding parental responsibilities contained in Article 5.[13]

In contrast to earlier human rights treaties, the Charter of Fundamental Rights of the European Union (the European Charter)[14] and the European Convention for the Protection of Human Rights and Dignity of the Human Being with Regard to the Application of Biology and Medicine (the Oviedo Convention)[15] are two more recent European treaties which have had the benefit of being able to reflect the legal dimension arising from advances in biotechnology that are fuelling the exponential growth in the bioethics discourse. These treaties combine the same foundational principles as their predecessors with recognition of the increasing impact of science and technology on the protection of human rights. For example, in relation to AHR, the European Charter contains numerous rights relating to data protection and bioethics.[16] The Preamble not only states that the European Union "is founded on the indivisible, universal of human dignity, freedom, [and] equality . . ."[17] but goes further, recognising the necessity of strengthening "the protection of fundamental rights in the light of changes in society, social progress and *scientific and technological developments*. . .".[18] [emphasis added]. Moreover, it notes that "Enjoyment

---

[13] A similar conflict between parental rights and children's rights has also arisen in the context of the corporal punishment of children by their parents. Proponents of corporal punishment have contended that Article 5 justifies reasonable physical chastisement. In response, the Committee on the Rights of the Child has observed that "A way should thus be found of striking the balance between the responsibilities of the parents and the rights and evolving capacities of the child that was implied in Article 5 of the Convention. There was no place for corporal punishment within the margin of discretion accorded in Article 5 to parents in the exercise of their responsibilities." See, Summary Record of the 205th Meeting, U.N. GAOR, Comm. on the Rts. of the Child, 8th Sess., 205th mtg., U.N. Doc. CRC/C/SR.205 (1995), at p 17.

[14] Charter of Fundamental Rights of the European Union, 2000/c 364/01.

[15] The Convention for the Protection of Human Rights and Dignity of the Human Being with regard to the Application of Biology and Medicine: Convention on Human Rights and Biomedicine (the Oviedo Convention), ETS No. 164, 1996.

[16] http://europa.eu.int/comm/justice_home/unit/charte/en/faq.html.

[17] Preamble, European Charter, supra note 14, at para 2.

[18] Ibid, at para 4 (emphasis added).

of these rights entails responsibilities and duties with regard to other persons, to the human community and to *future generations*."[19] [emphasis added]. Therefore, not only are fundamental human rights principles given an update, they are also given a rights basis. As such, the significance of human dignity is highlighted in Article 1, which states that "Human dignity is inviolable. It must be respected and protected." Much more significantly, however, is Article 21 which states that "[A]ny discrimination based on any ground such as . . . *genetic feature*, [and] birth . . . shall be prohibited."[emphasis added]

Similarly, the Preamble to the Oviedo Convention notes the impact of technological advances upon human rights. It provides that the Member States of the Council of Europe, other States and the signatories to the European Community being "Conscious of the accelerating developments in *biology and medicine*" [emphasis added] and being "Convinced of the need to respect the human being both as an individual and as a member of the human species and recognising the importance of ensuring the dignity of the human being" have resolved "to take such measures as are necessary to safeguard human dignity and the fundamental rights and freedoms of the individual with regard to the application of biology and medicine." Like the European Charter, these principles are elevated to rights status, as Article 1 states that the purpose and object of the Convention is to "protect the dignity and identity of all human beings and guarantee everyone, without discrimination, respect for their integrity and other rights and fundamental freedoms with regard to the application of biology and medicine" and requires that "Each Party shall take in its internal law the necessary measures to give effect to the provisions of this Convention." Of greater significance to the AHR and human rights discourse is Article 2, which gives effect to the primacy of the human being, stating that "The interests and welfare of the human being shall prevail over the sole interest of society or science." Moreover, Article 11 of the Oviedo Convention states that "Any form of discrimination against a person on grounds of his or her genetic heritage is prohibited."

2.1. *Substantive Human Rights and AHR*

Whilst the principles of non-discrimination and dignity underpin the substantive provisions of all human rights treaties, the substantive provisions of only some treaties are relevant to a discussion of the rights of the individual born of AHR. These provisions range from those that do not specifically refer to human rights and AHR, and which necessitate a broad reading to include the rights of individuals born of AHR, to those treaty provisions that deal specifically

---

[19] Ibid, at para 6.

with the rights of those born of AHR. Particular human rights which may
extend to cover the rights issues raised by AHR include the right to respect for
family and private life, the right to respect for identity, the right to know one's
parents and the right to access to information.

2.1.1. *The Right to Respect for Family and Private Life*

Recognition of the right to respect for family and private life can be traced
back to Article 12 of the Universal Declaration, which provides:

> No one shall be subjected to arbitrary interference with his privacy, family, home
> or correspondence, nor to attacks upon his honour and reputation. Everyone has
> the right to the protection of the law against such interference or attacks.

In addition, Article 16(3) of the Declaration provides that the "family is the
natural and fundamental group unit of society and is entitled to protection by
society and the State".[20] Recognition of this right is reiterated by Article 23(1)
of the ICCPR,[21] whilst Article 17 of the ICCPR states:

> 1. No one shall be subjected to arbitrary or unlawful interference with his pri-
>   vacy, family, home or correspondence, nor to unlawful attacks on his honour
>   and reputation.
> 2. Everyone has the right to the protection of the law against such interference
>   or attacks.[22]

The special protection to be accorded to the family is framed more broadly in
Article 10(1) of the ICESCR, which states that:

> [T]he States Parties to the present Covenant recognize that:
> The widest possible protection and assistance should be accorded to the family,
> which is the natural and fundamental group unit of society, particularly for its
> establishment and while it is responsible for the care and education of depend-
> ent children.[23]

Further protection is provided to the family by Article 23(1), which states that
"the family is the natural and fundamental group unit of society and is entitled
to protection by society and the State." As indicated in Chapter 1, Article 24
of the Covenant makes particular reference to the rights of the child to be free
from discrimination.[24]

---

[20] Universal Declaration, supra note 6.
[21] ICCPR, supra note 6. Article 23(1) also states, "The family is the natural and fundamental group unit of society and is entitled to protection by society and the State." See also, CCPR,
GENERAL COMMENT 19: *Protection of the family, the right to marriage and equality of the spouses
(Art. 23) 27/07/90.*
[22] Ibid.
[23] ICESCR, supra note 6.
[24] See, Chapter 1, note 59 and accompanying text.

In regional terms, Article 8 of the European Convention expresses the right to respect for family and private life in terms similar to that of the Covenant, with its provision that:

1. Everyone has the right to respect for his private and family life. . . .
2. There shall be no interference by a public authority with the exercise of this right except such as is in accordance with the law and is necessary in a democratic society in the interests of national security, public safety or the economic well-being of the country, for the prevention of disorder or crime, for the protection of health or morals, or for the protection of the rights and freedoms of others.[25]

With regards to the spectrum of substantive rights which may cover AHR, Article 8 lies at that end where a broad interpretation is required, an interpretation which it has been given by the European Court of Human Rights. Thus, in *Gaskin v United Kingdom*[26] the Court interpreted this right as extending to the provision of information to those who "have a vital interest, protected by the Convention, in receiving the information necessary to know and to understand their childhood and early development".[27] However, according to the Court in *Gaskin*, this right would be sufficiently protected by the establishment of an independent authority which could finally decide that access has to be granted when a contributor to the records either is not available or improperly refuses consent.[28] In terms of its application to AHR, the requirement for a dedicated authority would be satisfied by the establishment of a body such as that of the UK's Human Fertilisation and Embryology Authority set up

---

[25] European Convention, supra note 7. Similarly, the European Charter states, "Everyone has the right to respect for his or her private and family life, home and communications." European Charter, supra note 14.

[26] *Gaskin v United Kingdom*, Judgment of 7 July 1989, Series A, no. 160, (1989).

[27] Ibid, at para 49. Gaskin had been put in care as a child and had sought access for records kept during that period. In relation to the issue of provision of information, the Court also noted that "confidentiality of public records is of importance for receiving objective and reliable information, and that such confidentiality can also be necessary for the protection of third persons." Ibid. Gaskin also claimed that his right to receive information provided for by Article 10 had been violated. However, the Court, following its decision in *Leander v Sweden* (Series A no. 116, p. 29, para. 74), held that, "the right to freedom to receive information basically prohibits a Government from restricting a person from receiving information that others wish or may be willing to impart to him". It found that in the circumstances of the present case, Article 10 did not embody an obligation on the State concerned to impart the information in question to the individual. Ibid, at para 52. It has been asserted, however, that, "*Gaskin* is no authority for a child's right to know the identity of her father" on the basis that the European Commission on Human Rights distinguished between Gaskin applying as an adult and Gaskin applying as a child. Had Gaskin applied as a child, access to his records would have been refused. See, also G Van Bueren, "Children's Access to Adoption Records – State Discretion or an Enforceable Right" (1995) 58(1) Modern Law Review, 37–53, at 45.

[28] *Gaskin*, supra note 26, at para 49.

under the provisions of the Human Fertilisation and Embryology Act 1990.[29] Only those who have reached the age of 18[30] may ask the Authority for information, and then may only be provided with information which the Authority is required by regulations to give.

This continued focus on the rights of the donor, whether it is at the level of the European Court of Human Rights or at the domestic level, is reflective of an approach which is more orientated towards protecting the rights and interests of the genetic and/or social parents. The skewing of the balance away from the rights of the child born of AHR is evident in the decision of the Court in *X, Y and Z v United Kingdom*.[31] The Court's finding that X's right to respect for his family life had not been violated was based, in part, on its recognition of the difficulties associated with attempting to protect the best interests of children in Z's position. According to the Court, such difficulties stemmed from the lack of consensus amongst States Parties on the issue of filiation in cases of medically-assisted procreation. Most significantly, the Court also noted the lack of consensus on whether the interests of the child were best served by preserving the anonymity of the donor of the sperm or whether the child should have the right to know the donor's identity.[32] It remains to be seen whether the advances made by the European Court in securing the rights and interests of the child in other areas of its jurisprudence will be extended to securing more fully the rights and interests of the child born of AHR.[33]

---

[29] Section 31(3)(a) of the Act provides for the establishment of an authority to keep a register of information relating to the provision of treatment services. The keeping or use of gametes of any identifiable individual or of an embryo taken from any identifiable woman "or if it shows that any identifiable individual was, or may have been, born in consequence of such treatment services."

[30] Section 31(3) Human Fertilisation and Embryology Act 1990.

[31] *X, Y and Z v United Kingdom*, Judgment of 22 April, Reports II, (1997). The first applicant, X, a female-to-male transsexual had been living in a permanent and stable relationship with Y, a woman, since 1979. In 1992, Y gave birth to Z who had been conceived through artificial insemination by donated sperm (AID) with the agreement of the hospital ethics committee. Prior to the birth of Z, X had enquired of the Registrar General whether there would be any objection to his being registered as the father of Z. He was informed by the Minister of Health that, after taking legal advice, the Registrar General believed that only a biological man could be regarded as a father for the purposes of registration. However, Z could lawfully bear X's surname. The applicants claimed that the lack of legal recognition of the relationship between X and Z amounted to a violation of Article 8 of the Convention, as they had shared a 'family life' within the meaning of Article 8 since Z's birth, emphasising that, according to the jurisprudence of the Court, social reality, rather than formal legal status, was decisive.

[32] Ibid, at para 44.

[33] See, e.g., *A v United Kingdom*, Judgment of 23 September 1998, Reports VI (1998) which found that the corporal punishment of a child by his step-father was a violation of Article 3. The Court's concern with securing the best interests of the child may also be seen in relation to custody and access proceedings and the right to respect for family life under the provisions of Article 8 as in *Olsson v Sweden*, Judgment of 24 March 1988, Series A, no. 130, (1988).

In *Mikulić v Croatia*,[34] the Court noted that it had previously held, in *Gaskin*,[35] that respect for private life required that everyone should be able to establish details of their identity as individual human beings and that an individual's entitlement to such information is of importance because of its formative implications for his or her personality. In the instant case, the applicant was a child born out of wedlock who was seeking, by means of judicial proceedings, to establish the identity of her natural father. She had instituted paternity proceedings which were intended to determine her legal relationship with her putative father through the establishment of the biological truth. Consequently, according to the Court, there was a direct link between the establishment of paternity and the applicant's private life.[36] With regard to the question of compliance with the provisions of Article 8, the Court reiterated that while the essential object of Article 8 was to protect the individual against arbitrary interference by the public authorities, it did not merely compel the State to abstain from such interference but it allowed for the imposition of positive obligations in order to provide effective respect for private or family life. Private life, according to the Court, "includes a person's physical and psychological integrity and can sometimes embrace aspects of an individual's physical and social identity".[37] Positive obligations in this context could involve the adoption of measures designed to secure respect for private life even in the sphere of the relations of individuals between themselves.

In determining whether or not such an obligation existed, the Court said that regard must be had to the fair balance which has to be struck between the general or public interest and the interests of the individual and that, in both contexts, the State enjoyed a certain margin of appreciation. Furthermore, in the Court's opinion, persons in the applicant's situation have a vital interest, protected by the Convention, in receiving the information necessary to uncover the truth about an important aspect of their personal identity. Furthermore, in determining an application to have paternity established, the Courts were required to have regard to the basic principle of the child's interests. In *Mikulić*, the Court found that the procedure available to the applicant did not strike a fair balance between the right of the applicant to have her uncertainty as to her personal identity eliminated without unnecessary delay and that of her supposed father not to undergo DNA tests. It considered that the protection

---

[34] *Mikulić v Croatia*, Judgment of 04/09/2002, http://cmiskp.echr.coe.int/tkp197/view.asp?item=1&portal=hbkm&action=html&highlight=Mikuli%u0107%20%7C%20v.%20%7C%20Croatia&sessionid=1298569&skin=hudoc-en, as accessed on 3 March 2005.

[35] *Gaskin*, supra note 26, at 16, §39.

[36] *Mikulić*, supra note 34, at para 53.

[37] Ibid, at paras 54–55.

of the interests involved was not proportionate[38] and was in violation of
Article 8.

However, the broad issue that the Court found itself faced with in *X, Y, and
Z*, in terms of the lack of consensus on whether the interests of the child were
best served by preserving the anonymity of the sperm donor or whether the
child should have the right to know the donor's identity, was revisited in
Odièvre v France.[39] Although the case did not deal with assisted conception, it did
concern the principle of confidentiality in respect of the identity of the applicant's birth parents and the resulting impossibility for the applicant to obtain
information about her origins. The applicant (who was adopted) complained
that her inability to secure the disclosure of identifying details about her birth
family and possible siblings amounted to a violation of her rights under Article 8.
She also submitted that the principle of confidentiality, as established in France,
amounted to discrimination based on birth, and relied on Article 14 (prohibition of discrimination) of the Convention.

The Court considered the matter to be one regarding the right to private
life as the applicant's claim to be entitled, in the name of biological truth, to
know her personal history was based on her inability to gain access to information about her origin and related identifying data.[40] The Court's comments
in the context of issues related to AHR are illuminating, as it noted that:

> Article 8 protects a right to identity and personal development, and the right to estab-
> lish and develop relationships with other human beings and the outside world. . . .
> The preservation of mental stability is in that context an indispensable precondition
> to effective enjoyment of the right to respect for private life." (*Bensaid v. United Kingdom*,
> no. 44599/98, 06.02.2001, § 47). Matters of relevance to personal development
> include details of a person's identity as a human being and the vital interest protected
> by the Convention in obtaining information necessary to discover the truth concern-
> ing important aspects of one's personal identity, such as the identity of one's parents
> (*Mikulic v. Croatia, no. 53176/99*, 07.02.2002, §§ 54 and 64). Birth, and in particular
> the circumstances in which a child is born, forms part of a child's, and subsequently
> the adult's, private life guaranteed by Article 8 of the Convention.[41]

---

[38] Ibid, at para 65.
[39] *Odièvre v France*, Judgment of 13 February 2003, http://hudoc.echr.coe.int/hudoc/
ViewRoot.asp?Item=0&Action=Html&X=510020552&Notice=0&Noticemode=&Related
Mode=0, as accessed on 10 May 2004. Somewhat uniquely, Articles 341 and 341-1 of the Civil
Code, in essence, allow for mothers to give birth anonymously as they may request that their
admission to hospital and identity shall remain secret. This has the effect of rendering confiden-
tial any information about a child's origins. The applicant alleged that the fact that her birth
had been kept secret with the result that it was impossible for her to find out her origins
amounted to a violation of her rights guaranteed by Article 8 of the Convention and discrimination contrary to Article 14 of the Convention.
[40] Ibid, at para 28.
[41] Ibid, at para 29.

Nevertheless, the Court observed that there were two competing interests in the case before it: on the one hand, the right to know one's origins and the child's vital interest in its personal development and, on the other, a woman's interest in remaining anonymous in order to protect her health by giving birth in appropriate medical conditions. In the Court's opinion, those interests were not easily reconciled, as they concerned two adults, each endowed with free will.

The Court noted that the applicant had already been given access to non-identifying information about her mother and natural family that had enabled her to trace some of her roots, while ensuring the protection of third-party interests. In addition, while preserving the principle that mothers were entitled to give birth anonymously, legislation passed in January 2002 facilitated searches for information about a person's biological origins by setting up a National Council on Access to Information about Personal Origins. According to the Court, the applicant could use it to request disclosure of her mother's identity, subject to the latter's consent being obtained.[42] The legislation in question had thus sought to strike a balance and to ensure sufficient proportion between the competing interests. In recognising the complex and sensitive nature of the issue of access to information about one's origins, an issue that concerned the right to know one's personal history, as well as the choice of the natural parents, the existing family ties and the adoptive parents, the Court found that there had been no violation of Article 8 of the Convention.[43] In spite of the fact that the applicant was unsuccessful, the comments by the Court with respect to the importance to be attached to personal identity crystallise the issue from a human as well as a human rights perspective and may extrapolated to include the rights of children born of AHR.[44]

In addition to the provisions of the European Convention, Article 7 of the European Charter states that "Everyone has the right to respect for his or her private and family life. . . ." Given that this provision is based upon Article 8 of the European Convention, it can be imagined that Article 7 of the Charter could be given a similar interpretation, although the question of the Charter's force is an issue to be considered within the European Union at a later date.[45] It is to be imagined that the Charter will become binding "through its being

---

[42] Ibid, at paras 44–49.

[43] In so doing, the Court reiterated its approach in *X, Y and Z v United Kingdom*, supra note 31, that X's right to respect for his family life had not been violated was based, in part, on its recognition of the difficulties associated with attempting to protect the best interests of children in Z's position.

[44] For a consideration of the correlation between the rights and interests of children born of AHR and adopted children see Freeman, supra note 5, at 279–282.

[45] http://europa.eu.int/geninfo/key_en.htm.

interpreted by the Court of Justice as enshrining the general principles of Community law".[46] Significantly, Article 8 of the Charter states that "[E]very-one has the right of access to data which has been collected concerning him or her."[47]

2.1.2. The Child's Right to Identity and the Right to Information Necessary to Establishing that Identity

The Convention on the Rights of the Child draws together many of the issues raised by the right to respect for family and private life as "the preservation of family relations is one component of a child's right to identity".[48] Article 7 of the Convention states that the child shall "as far as possible have the right to know . . . his or her parents" whilst Article 8 provides that "States Parties shall undertake to respect the right of the child to preserve his or her identity, including family relations as recognised by law without unlawful interfer-ence."[49] In terms of Article 7, the difficulty arises with the phrase "as far as possible" which, it has been commented, renders the right of knowledge of one's parents meaningless.[50] Part of the reason for the insertion of this phrase was based on the domestic legislation of a number of delegations regarding the right of secret adoption, whereby the adopted child did not possess the right to know his or her parents.[51] According to these delegations, the "right to know one's parents" could not be absolute.[52] Similar difficulties can be identified in terms of the right to identity and the vague obligations imposed on States Parties by Article 8 to undertake to respect without lawful interfer-ence the right of the child to preserve his or her 'family relations' where the route to such preservation may be through access to information regarding such family relations. The vague language of the provision was the ultimate result not only of a number of delegations' concern over the necessity of the

---

[46] http://europa.eu.int/comm/justice_home/unit/charte/en/faq.html.

[47] It would seem that the drafters of this Article were primarily concerned with the issue of data protection, echoing the European Court of Human Rights' decision in *Leander*, supra note 27, and *Gaskin*, supra note 26. Nevertheless, given that the Charter recognises changes in tech-nology and their potential impact for human rights, an interpretation of this right to access data in order to incorporate the rights of those born of AHR may still be forthcoming.

[48] Van Bueren, supra note 27, at 47.

[49] The inclusion of Article 8 was as a result of Argentina's wish to create an international mechanism to prevent a repetition of the abductions of children born in secret detention cen-tres, who were then illegally given to childless military and police couples to raise as their own. See, S Detrick, *A Commentary on the United Nations Convention of the Child*, Dordrecht, Martinus Nijhoff, 1999, at 59–162.

[50] Ibid, at 153.

[51] Ibid.

[52] Ibid.

inclusion of such an article but also of their concern about the application of Article 8 to situations arising from AHR.[53]

The provisions of the Convention relating to the right to identity of the child born of AHR face the twin problem of vague language and the imposition of ambiguous obligations upon States Parties, in addition to the non-absolute right to know one's parents and the expression of concern during the drafting process regarding the extension of Article 8(1)'s right to identity to cover the rights of the child of born of AHR. Within the right to freedom of expression accorded to the child by Article 13, is the freedom "to seek, receive and impart information . . . of all kinds" with "The exercise of this right [being] subject to certain restrictions, but these shall only be such as are provided by law and are necessary . . . for respect of the rights of others."[54] The provisions of Article 13 echo those of Article 19(2) of the ICCPR and the issue arising from both provisions is the restrictions they impose on the right to seek and receive information. Once again, the restrictions imposed upon the rights of the child is a consequence of the perpetual balancing act between children's rights and parents' rights, which pervades any discussion of the rights of children born of AHR. Doubtless, a similar difficulty could be identified in Article 16's recognition of the right of the child to be free from arbitrary or unlawful interference with his or her private life or family.

In any discussion regarding the best interests of the child born of AHR, a comparison will inevitably be drawn between the child born of donation and the adopted child as the issue of the right to identity is common to both. Studies of adopted children have led to a wider recognition that a child's knowledge of his or her biological heritage is crucial to the formation of positive self-identity. It has also been generally recognised that being open about the child's status is in the best interests of that child and that donation, like adoption, may result in the severance of all legal ties with one's biological parentage.[55] The observation has also been made that the adopted child's need to know his or her biological ancestry is merely a social construct and is not supported by empirical evidence.[56]

---

[53] Ibid, at 165.

[54] Article 13(2) Convention on the Rights of the Child, supra note 8.

[55] S Maclean and M Maclean, "Keeping Secrets in Assisted Reproduction – the Tension between Donor Anonymity and the Need of the Child for Information" (1996) 8(3) Child and Family Law Quarterly, 243–251, at 250. This parallel was further explored in a 1992 British Government Working Group report which, in the process of reviewing adoption practices, stressed the importance of openness in adoption and stated that there was no inherent reason why adoption "should preclude the possibility of some contact being maintained, nor should it preclude the possibility that there is no contact at all": Review of Adoption Law, at para 5.1, quoted in Maclean, ibid.

[56] K O'Donovan, "What Shall We Tell the Children?" in R Lee and D Morgan, *Birthrights, Law and Ethics at the Beginnings of Life,* New York, Routledge, 1989, 96.

Conversely, it has been noted that some children do in fact care very much about their biological origins and go to great lengths to trace their birth parents.[57] The notion of genealogical bewilderment, as it has applied to adopted children, contends that the restriction or prohibition of access to information upon adopted children results in confusion and uncertainty, which fundamentally undermines the child's sense of security, thereby affecting their mental health.[58] More recently, the debate has been added to by comments that the traditional biological concept of family has been added to by a new biologism whereby the true essence of a person is rooted in the primordial difference of gender, race, ethnicity and genes. The implications for this new biologism encompass the search for genetic roots and adopted persons seeking out their birth parents, and should also encompass access to genetic origins in donor-assisted conceptions.[59]

Irrespective of the merits of any of the above arguments, it has been observed that the impact of the development and adoption of children's rights issues (and the ensuing development of children's rights jurisprudence) has reached too great an international consensus that children can no longer be regarded as chattels. Secrecy over access to information over one's genetic origins may be the last vestige of the outdated concept that children can be regarded as parental property or, at the very least, that parents have rights over their children. Any other alternative serves to condone the notion that parents have rights over their children and it is this claim "that has through the centuries sought to deny that children can be rights holders".[60]

The issue of the right of the child to know his or her origins has also been considered within the Council of Europe by the Committee of Experts on Family Law (CJ-FA). In 2002, the CJ-FA published a *"White Paper" on Principles Concerning the Establishment and Legal Consequences of Parentage*.[61] The White Paper flowed on from an analysis of the issue undertaken by a Working Party on the legal status of children within the Committee of Experts on Family Law.[62]

---

[57] The Glover Report on Reproductive Technologies to the European Commission, *Fertility and the Family*, London, Fourth Estate, 1989, at 37, quoted in Maclean, supra note 56, at 251.

[58] See, K Tefft Stanton, "Secrecy as a Social and Political Process" in K Tefft Stanton (ed), *Secrecy: A Cross-Cultural Perspective*, New York, Human Sciences Press, 1980, at 339, H Sants, "Genealogical Bewilderment in Children with Substitute Parents" in P Bean (ed), *Adoption: Essays in Social Policy, Law, and Psychology*, London, Tavistock, 1994, at 67.

[59] See, generally, A Skolnick, "Soloman's Children: The New Biologism, Psychological Parenthood, Attachment Theory and the Best Interests Standard", in A Mason, A Skolnick, and A Sugarman (eds), *All Our Families: New Policies for a New Century*, New York, University Press Oxford, 1998, at 240.

[60] See Van Bueren, supra note 27, at 42–43.

[61] "White Paper" on Principles Concerning the Establishment and Legal Consequences of Parentage 2002, CJ-FA (2001) 16 rev.

[62] The Draft Report on Principles Concerning the Establishment and Legal Consequences of Parentage (the Legal Status of Children) 2001, Draft No.1 Council of Europe (02/08/01).

Part A of the White Paper is concerned with principles relating to the establishment of legal parentage including the cases of medically-assisted procreation in the establishment of paternal affiliation; contestation of parentage and the change of parentage. Part A also outlines the main principles governing the establishment and legal consequences of parentage in order to provide guidelines to States when introducing or considering legislative reforms in this field and, to that end, refers to the main principles established by the former European Commission of Human Rights and the European Court of Human Rights arising from Articles 8 and 14 respectively.[63]

Part A of the White Paper also confines the principles considered therein to issues relating to legal parentage, "since the establishment of biological parentage is a medical matter", where 'legal parent' is defined as a person whose parentage has been established in a manner prescribed by law.[64] The White Paper also notes that although the best interests of the child should be the paramount consideration:[65]

> Other interests, such as the interest of the family as well as the public interest may also be taken into account in addition to the best interests of the child. Therefore the law may opt not to allow the parentage to be established on the basis of biological affiliation, for instance in cases of medically assisted procreation with an anonymous donor of sperm.[66]

According to the CJ-FA, the application and interpretation of the principles of the White Paper sought to balance "the biological truth", reflecting primarily biological and genetic parentage, and "social parenthood", reflecting the child's living situation and who is taking care of him of her, favouring the latter.[67] Against the background of such General Principles, Part B of the White Paper deals with principles relating to legal consequences of parentage, including the right of the child to know his or her origins. The CJ-FA referred to the earlier discussions of the Working Party and, in this regard, noted the controversial nature of this right. According to the Committee, Principle 28 of the White Paper, in stating that "The interest of a child as regards information on his or her *biological* origin should be duly taken into account in law",[68] went further than Article 7 of the Convention on the Rights of the Child, which referred simply to the right of the child to know his or her parents and which had not been uniformly interpreted [emphasis added]. The CJ-FA noted that although

---

[63] "White Paper", supra note 61, at paras 6–7.
[64] Ibid, at para 8.
[65] Ibid, at para 9.
[66] Ibid, at para 10.
[67] Ibid, at para 11.
[68] Ibid, at para 87.

the Working Party did not draft a principle which would establish the absolute right of the child to know his or her origins, it did recognise that all children have a legitimate interest with respect to their origins. The Working Party had also recognised that in certain situations, the best interests of the child or of other persons involved could justify withholding from the child such information or certain parts of it, and referred to the *Gaskin* case as a case on point.[69]

3. *Children's Rights and the Law Regarding AHR in the United Kingdom and Australia: A Comparison of Approaches*

The initial point of departure for much of the legislation regarding technological advances in human reproduction has been to focus on clarifying the status of a child born of donated gametes. For example, in the United Kingdom, s 27 of the Human Fertilisation and Embryology Act 1990 (the HFE Act) provides that the gestational mother is the legal mother, whilst s 28 provides that, if treatment takes place at a licensed centre in accordance with the HFE Act, the husband of the woman receiving treatment will be the legal father of the child, provided that he consented to the treatment. Section 28(2) provides that this presumption can be rebutted if the husband can show that he did not consent to the treatment and, legally speaking, the child will be fatherless. Similarly, in Australia, the Family Law Act 1975 contains amendments to federal legislation regarding the status of children born using donated gametes or embryos. The legislation is very similar to that of the HFE Act and s 60H provides that where a child is born using donated gametes, the birth mother is the legal mother and if her husband or partner consented to the treatment, he is the legal father. Similar legislation regarding the status of children is to be found in state legislation.[70] Both federal and state law provide that the donor bears no legal rights or responsibilities towards the child.[71]

3.1. *The Right to Identity of Donor-Conceived Children in the United Kingdom*

Although clarification of the legal status of the child born of medically-assisted reproductive techniques goes some way to securing the best interests of the child in terms of determining his or her legal parentage, nevertheless, such

---

[69] Ibid, at para 87–89.

[70] Victoria: Status of Children Act 1974; South Australia: Family Relations Amendment Act 1984; New South Wales: Artificial Conception Act 1984; Tasmania: Status of Children Amendment Act 1994; Queensland: Artificial Conception Act 1985; West Australia: Artificial Conception Act 1986.

[71] See, e.g., s 5A Family Law Act (Cth).

legislation traditionally tends to reinforce the secrecy that surrounds AHR. The practical outcome of such legislation was that birth certificates recorded the names of the legal parents and did not indicate that the child may have not have had a genetic or biological link with either one or both of his or her parents. Much of this secrecy stemmed from the according of greater concern to the needs of the social parents and the delineation of the rights of both donor and social parents. Very little focus was placed on the interests and rights of the child in spite of the fact that a number of committees of inquiry were set up to consider the social, legal and ethical issues arising from AHR in relation to the right of children to know the identity of their genetic parents. In the United Kingdom, this right was confined to the need for such knowledge in terms of medical history,[72] and whilst it was recommended to parents to be open about the means of conception[73] the British committee of enquiry did not recognise that children born of AHR had a right to know the identity of their genetic parents. A similar approach was adopted in Australia.[74] In both jurisdictions, legislation did not impose any requirement upon parents to tell their children that they were conceived by donation. Rather, the onus was put back on children to determine whether they were conceived through donated gametes or embryos, a situation complicated by the fact that such children may have no formal indication from their birth certificate.

Putting the onus back on the child places the child born of AHR at a legislatively mandated disadvantage, which violates the principles of equality and non-discrimination that underpin international human rights law and domestic law. For example, s 31 of the UK HFE Act provides that children, who have reached the age of 18, may find out if they were conceived in such a manner. The Human Fertilisation and Embryology Authority (HFEA) is under a statutory duty to keep a register of information acquired from licensed centres, including identifying information on donors, recipients, and resulting children.

Until recently, the requirement of absolute anonymity meant that the donor could not be identified and neither could the recipients or the child.[75]

---

[72] M Warnock, *A Question of Life: the Warnock Report on Human Fertilisation and Embryology*, Oxford, Oxford University Press, 1985, at para 4.21. See also, the Royal Commission on New Reproductive Technologies, *Proceed with Care: Final Report on New Reproductive Technologies*, Ottawa, Canada Communications Group, 1993, at 465.

[73] Warnock, ibid, at para 4.25.

[74] See, e.g., the Committee to Consider the Social, Ethical and Legal Issues Arising from In Vitro Fertilisation, *Report on Donor Gametes In IVF*, Victoria, CCSELIAIVF, 1983, at paras 3.30, 3.35 and 3.37, and South Australian Council on Reproductive Technology (SACRT), Discussion Paper of the South Australian Council on Reproductive Technology, *Conception by Donation, Access to Identifying Information in the Use of Donated Sperm, Eggs and Embryos in South Australia*, South Australia, SCAHR, 2000.

[75] Section 31(3) and (4) Human Fertilisation and Embryology Act 1990.

In July 2004, however, the Human Fertilisation and Embryology Authority (Disclosure of Donor Information) Regulations 2004[76] came into force. These Regulations were made under ss 31(4)(a) and 45(1) to (3) of the HFE Act. They prescribe the information which the HFEA will provide in response to a request from a person who has attained the age of 18 and who was, or may have been, born in consequence of treatment services provided under the Act. The Authority will provide information entered on its register in response to applications from adult donor-conceived persons at any time since the register was started in 1991. However, it will not provide information as to the identity of donors of sperm, eggs, or embryos. Regulation 2(3) allows for the provision of identifying information about donors to adult donor-conceived person from 1 April 2005.

In spite of the greater openness signalled by the coming into effect of the Regulations, the structure of the Act in terms of identifying information is very much reflective of the emphasis placed upon the welfare of the child, with s 13(5) simply stating that those providing the treatment are to take account of the welfare of any child born of such treatment. However, the HFE Act does not explicitly define what needs to be taken into account when determining the welfare of the child (other than perhaps the need of a child for a father). The task of determining what steps are to be taken to secure the (undefined) welfare of the child fell to the HFEA, which has published a Code of Practice.[77] Unfortunately, the Code itself is unclear regarding the prioritisation of the welfare of the child. On the one hand, its states that centres, in deciding whether to offer treatment or not, "should take account of the wishes and needs of the people and of the needs of any children who may be involved. Neither consideration is paramount over the other".[78] On the other hand, it states that if the treatment involved is required to be licensed under the Act and "particularly if it involves the use of donated gametes" then the degree of consideration necessary to determine the welfare of the child will be greater.[79] But the Code also goes further and states that "treatment should be refused if the centre believes that it is not in the interests of any resulting child, or any child already existing".[80] In terms of the child's right to identity, the Code does identify a

---

[76] Human Fertilisation and Embryology Authority (Disclosure of Donor Information) Regulations 2004 (SI 2004/1511).
http://www.bailii.org.ezproxy.waikato.ac.nz:2048/uk/legis/ num_reg/2004/20041511.html, as accessed on 13 October 2004.
[77] Human Fertilisation and Embryology Authority, *Code of Practice: Explanation*, London, HFEA, 1993.
[78] Ibid, at 10.
[79] Ibid, at 13.
[80] Ibid, at 16.

number of factors which centres should consider, one of which is the child's potential need to know about his or her genetic origins.[81]

This greater recognition of the rights of donor-conceived children reflected other developments in the area of the child's right to identity. This right was considered by the English High Court in 2002, in the case of *Rose & Another v Secretary of State for Health*.[82] Both claimants were children born of artificial insemination by donor (AID). The first claimant was born in 1972 and sought access to non-identifying information, and, where possible, identifying information about the anonymous donor, in addition to requesting that regulations be passed to alleviate the types of difficulties that she, as a donor-conceived child, had experienced. The second claimant was born in 1996 and her parents, on her behalf, sought non-identifying information about their donor and the steps undertaken by the British Government to establish a contact register. Both claimants argued, in essence, that their requests fell within the ambit of Articles 8 and 14 of the European Convention which been brought into UK law by the Human Rights Act 1998. In discharging its obligations under these two articles, the claimants argued that the State was under a positive obligation to ensure the collection of certain vital non-identifying information about donors and that such information should be made available to the parents and their children born of AID who sought such information. According to the claimants, Article 14 was also engaged as the current regime discriminated between those born of AID and adoptees and as between those AID offspring born before and after the HFE Act. The claimants also argued that the State had to establish a voluntary register to facilitate the exchange of information and contact between willing donors and children and that a failure to take all of these steps amounted to an unjustifiable breach of the claimants' rights under Articles 8 and 14. In light of the fact that the Government was engaged in a review of how to deal with these types of issues at the time of the case, Scott Baker J confined his reasoning, inter alia, to whether the claimant's arguments engaged Article 8.

After considering the relevant jurisprudence of the European Court, Scott Baker J stated that he did not consider the issue in the present case to be essentially a question of whether the relationships of the claimants and the donors fell within the ordinary concept of family life. Rather, it was really an identity case and involved the claimants' rights to know about their origins. The emphasis therefore was much more on 'private life' than 'family life'.[83] After

---

[81] Ibid, at para 3.12.
[82] [2002] EWHC 1593 (Admin).
[83] Ibid, at para 28.

consideration of relevant English case law, Scott Baker J stated that, in his opinion, "the bottom line . . . is that the donor provided half of each Claimant's genetic identity and it is this that creates the interest of the Claimant to seek information about him".[84] He was satisfied that the requests for information made by the claimants fell within the provisions of Article 8 although he refrained from determining whether there had been a breach of that provision.[85] However, he did state that it was:

> entirely understandable that A.I.D. children should wish to know about their origins and in particular to learn what they can about their biological father or, in the case of egg donation, their biological mother. The extent to which this matters will vary from individual to individual . . . I do not find this at all surprising bearing in mind the lessons that have been learnt from adoption. A human being is a human being whatever the circumstances of his conception and an A.I.D. child is entitled to establish a picture of his identity as much as anyone else. We live in a much more open society than even 20 years ago. Secrecy nowadays has to be justified where previously it did not . . . Respect for private and family life has been interpreted by the European Court to incorporate the concept of personal identity [which also held that] everyone should be able to establish details of his identity as a human being . . . That, to my mind, plainly includes the right to obtain information about a biological parent who will inevitably have contributed to the identity of his child. There is in my judgment no great leap in construing Article 8 in this way. It seems to me to fall naturally into line with the existing jurisprudence of the European Court.[86]

3.2. The Right to Identity of Donor-Conceived Children in Australia

In Australia, both federal and state law generally follow the same process as British legislation. The National Health and Medical Research Council (NHMRC) 1996 guidelines (currently under review)[87] require donor records to be maintained indefinitely[88] and support the right of children conceived by donation "to knowledge of their biological parents."[89] However, these are only guidelines and are subordinate to any legislation. Victoria, Western Australia and South Australia are the only three Australian states with legislation regulating assisted reproduction. The Victorian Infertility Treatment Act 1995, which

---

[84] Ibid, at para 38.
[85] Ibid, at para 46.
[86] Ibid, at paras 47–48.
[87] National Health and Medical Research Council (NHMRC), *Ethical Guidelines on Assisted Reproductive Technology*, Australian Government Publishing Services, 1996.
[88] Ibid, at para 8.5.
[89] Ibid, at para 3.1.5.

regulates the practice of assisted reproduction, is the most advanced in terms of the right to identity.[90] In terms of the rights and interests of the child, this piece of legislation is very significant. Section 5(1)(a) of the Act contains the most important of its guiding principles which is that "the *welfare* and interest of any person born or to be born as a result of a treatment procedure are *paramount*" [emphasis added]. The paramountcy of the welfare of the child is also reflected in the statutory provisions requiring the maintenance of a central register of all births from medically-assisted reproduction. Moreover, s 79(1)(b) of the Act provides children conceived by donation with access to identifying information when they reach the age of 18 years. Although this right to information is not given retrospectively (it only applies to those born following donations given after 1 January 1998) it does mean that donors cannot veto the giving of identifying information; they donate knowing that such information may be provided upon request. However, the significance or potential impact of this provision upon the rights of the child is limited by the fact that the Act does not require that any indication be given on the child's birth certificate which allows parents to conceal the fact that the child's birth was a result of donated gametes or a donated embryo. The outcome is that a child may never suspect or know his or her true genetic parentage. The failure to impose a duty upon parents to disclose such information constitutes a prioritising of parental rights over those of the child, especially during the latter's childhood, and flies in the face not only of the child's right to an identity as provided for under the Convention on the Rights of the Child, but also the notion of the developing autonomy of the child as provided for under the Convention.[91]

---

[90] C.f. the Western Australian Act, the Human Reproductive Technology Act 1991, s 4(1)(iv) of which states simply "that the prospective welfare of any child to be born consequent upon a procedure to which this Act relates is properly taken into consideration . . .". The South Australian legislation, Reproductive Technology (Clinical Practices) Act 1988, makes no such reference. In December 2003, a Consultation Draft bill, the Assisted Reproductive Technology Bill 2003, was issued by the New South Wales Parliament. The Bill includes provision for the establishment of a central register of identifying and non-identifying information which is to be made available to children born of ART, cl. 38.

[91] This prioritising of parental rights over those of the child is echoed in the legislative provisions of South Australia (Reproductive Technology Act 1988 (SA)) and West Australia (Human Reproductive Technology Act 1991 (WA). In fact, the South Australian legislation makes it a criminal offence to reveal the identity of a donor without consent. Non-identifying information may be revealed to prospective parents at the time of conception with the child having to wait until the age of 16 years. In Western Australia, the right of access to information is limited to non-identifying information. A central register established in the Health Department contains information about donors, recipients and children born by donation and a 1999 Select Committee Report on the Act has recommended that identifying information should be made known to children born by donation.

4. International Obligations and Overseas Jurisdictions: the Impact for New Zealand Legislation

As stated earlier, the aim of this chapter is to consider whether New Zealand's legislative provisions relating to AHR are discriminatory with regard to the child's right to identity. In many respects, the right to identity, or more specifically, the right to access information regarding one's genetic identity, is indicative of the balance between the two sets of rights involved in any discussion of AHR – those of the adult donor and those of the donor offspring. Despite recent legislative moves towards openness in AHR, the balance still lies in favour of the adult and the following early observation on the matter still holds currency:

> While the law asserts that the rights of a child are paramount, surrogacy is inherently adult centred and the current law does not respect a child's wish to know his or her identity and whakapapa.[92]

Although this observation makes specific reference to surrogacy arrangements, the underlying observation is equally applicable to other forms of AHR. Moreover, the right to access to information regarding one's identity has a greater and different importance for Maori than Pakeha given the greater emphasis placed by Maori on genealogical identity so that "[T]his concern with identity will be of significance from the child's welfare perspective."[93] It has also been asserted that New Zealand's legislative statements on parenthood in relation to AHR and surrogacy "are really statements of deception".[94] This is because typically the issues raised by the question of the child's right to identity have focused largely on parent and/or donor concerns. Such concerns typically relate to avoiding the prospect of an unwanted relationship as between donor and donor-conceived offspring and/or avoiding the perceived social stigma surrounding infertility. Similarly, parental concerns may also have arisen with regard to the prospect of an unwanted relationship between the donor-conceived offspring, their child legally speaking, and the donor(s) involved. New Zealand legislation is aimed at defusing some of these parental and donor concerns but it does not go far enough to remove the potential for secrecy as it may not be readily apparent to the child that he or she is not genetically related to one or either parent.

---

[92] INECAHR Report, supra note 4.

[93] *Submission of the Human Rights Commission to the Ministerial Committee on Assisted Reproductive Technologies*, supra note 4, at p 6.

[94] Caldwell and Daniels, supra note 4, at 262, quoting H Gamble, "Fathers and the New Reproductive Technologies: Recognition of Donor as Parent" (1990) 4 Australian Journal of Family Law, 131.

4.1. The Rights of New Zealand Children born of Assisted Human Reproduction

There are two pieces of legislation that govern the rights of donor-conceived children and the rights of donors. Broadly speaking, the Status of Children Amendment Act 2004 (SCAA) governs the legal relationship as between parents, donors and, to a more limited extent, donor offspring whilst the Human Assisted Reproductive Technology Act 2004 (HART Act) governs the issues regarding the rights of donors of gametes and delineates surrogacy arrangements. The SCAA is useful insofar as it delineates, and therefore provides a degree of (legal) certainty with regards to the relationship between parents and their donor-conceived children and the lack of legal relationship, with some exceptions, between donors and their offspring. However, it makes no reference to the HART Act's provisions relating to access to information about either donor. This omission does not strengthen the, somewhat limited, rights accorded to donor-conceived children under the latter Act. Any relationship between the two pieces of legislation has to be inferred. Perhaps the significance of the relationship between the two Acts lies in the fact that it is the legal parent for the purposes of the SCAA who is the guardian and who may access identifying information regarding donors for the purposes of the AHR. This situation tends to reinforce the emphasis on parental rights, continued secrecy and the consequent limitations on the children's rights in question, especially since neither piece of legislation includes an effective mechanism by which donor-conceived children may access much, if any, of the information that should be available to them under either piece of legislation, but particularly with reference to the AHR.

4.1.1. The Human Assisted Reproductive Technology Act 2004
The HART Act governs the right to identity of the child born of AHR. The purposes of the Act include securing:

> the benefits of assisted reproductive procedures, established procedures, and human reproductive research for individuals and for society in general by taking appropriate measures for the protection and promotion of the health, safety, dignity, and rights of all individuals, but particularly those of women and children, in the use of these procedures and research.[95]

A further purpose, that gives to general recognition to the child's right to identity, is the provision for the establishment of a comprehensive information-keeping regime to ensure that people born from donated embryos or donated cells can find out about their genetic origins.[96]

---

[95] Section 3(a).
[96] Section 3(f).

Section 4 of the Act identifies a number of principles that are to guide all persons exercising powers or performing functions under the Act. In terms of children's rights, the Act states that:

(a) the health and well-being of children born as a result of the performance of an assisted reproductive procedure or an established procedure should be *an important consideration* in all decisions about that procedure . . . [emphasis added]

(e) donor offspring should be made aware of their genetic origins and be able to access information about those origins.

In terms of the emphasis placed by Maori on genealogical identity or whaka-papa, s 4(f) provides that "the needs, values, and beliefs of Maori should be considered and treated with respect".

With regard to the issue of the right to identity, the Act provides the means by which donor offspring, as well as donors themselves, may access information about each other. To that end, the Act places providers[97] of AHR procedures and services under an obligation to obtain information, both identifying and non-identifying, about the donor.[98] Moreover, providers are under a further obligation to keep all such donor information in relation to any donated embryo or a donated cell and they may pass such information on to the Registrar-General (currently, the Registrar of Births, Deaths and Marriages).[99] Thus, the Act does not provide for the establishment of a central AHR specific register. The loose nature of the legal provisions regarding the recording of information is emphasised by the fact that it is up to the provider to ensure that, at all times, there is in place an effective system for being notified of, or otherwise becoming aware of, the births of donor offspring. Moreover, s 53 simply provides that once a provider *learns* of the birth of a live offspring, the provider must take *all practicable steps* to obtain, from any person who knows of the donor offspring, information such as the date and place of the birth, the sex and the name of the donor-offspring and pass such information to the Registrar-General, who must keep indefinitely all such information. There is no legal obligation to notify the provider of such a birth.

It is against this background that the provisions regarding the accessing of such information are to be considered. Section 50 provides that donor offspring

---

[97] According to s 5, "provider":

(a) means a person who, in the course of a business (whether or not carried on with a view to making a profit), performs, or arranges the performance of, services in which donated embryos or donated cells are used; and

(b) includes a successor provider.

[98] Section 47.

[99] Section 48.

may access information about donors kept by providers and the Registrar-General. However, s 50 distinguishes between offspring over the age of 18 years and those under that age in terms of the extent of the information that they may access. Thus, only offspring over the age of 18 years may access identifying donor information.[100] Offspring under the age of 18 years may only access such donor information that is 'not identifying'. Nevertheless, the guardians of such offspring may access identifying information,[101] although the Act does not stipulate that such information is to be accessed on behalf of the offspring. Access to donor information, whether identifying or non-identifying, is subject to the proviso that such information will not be provided where the provider is satisfied, on reasonable grounds, that the disclosure is likely to endanger any person.[102] Equally, donor offspring may also access any information about themselves as kept by providers or the Registrar-General.[103]

Section 59 provides that donor offspring 18 years or older may consent (and may also cancel such consent) to the disclosure of identifying information to the donor.[104] The broader rights available to those over the age of 18 years regarding access to identifying information either about themselves or information that they may choose to make available to donors may be made available to those aged 16 or 17 years by way of a Family Court order where a Family Court judge is satisfied that it is in the best interests donor offspring to do so.[105] Unfortunately, children born from donations before the enactment of the HART Act will not share these rights,[106] although the Act does provide for the establishment of a voluntary register the provisions of which are governed by provisions similar to the legislatively mandated register.[107] This approach was welcomed by the Privacy Commissioner, who noted the concern expressed over the child's right to know his or her genetic origins being elevated over the donor's guarantee of privacy.[108] The Act also provides that

---

[100] Section 50(1). According to s 5, "identifying information", in relation to any person, means that person's name, address, or contact details; and includes any information that is likely to enable another person to ascertain that person's name, address, or contact details.

[101] Section 50(2).

[102] Section 50(4).

[103] Section 57.

[104] In the absence of the consent required under s 59, ss 60 and 61 only allow either providers or the Registrar-General, respectively, to tell the donor whether offspring has been born, and the sex thereof.

[105] Section 65.

[106] Section 43.

[107] Section 60.

[108] Office of the Privacy Commissioner, *Assisted Human Reproduction Bill, Report by the Privacy Commissioner to the Minister of Justice in Relation to Part 3 of the Assisted Human Reproduction Bill*, 1999, http://www.privacy.org.nz/people/assisted.html.

the Privacy Commissioner may investigate any complaints arising out of the holding or accessing of information regarding donors and their offspring.[109]

4.1.2. The Status of Children Amendment Act 2004

Any subsequent legal relationship between a child resulting from an AHR pregnancy and his or her parents is governed by Part 2 of the SCAA. Section 13 describes the purpose of the Act as follows:

(a) remove uncertainty about the status of children conceived as a result of AHR procedures; and
(b) replace the Status of Children Amendment Act 1987 with provisions that continue the effects of that Act (except for the status of a father without the rights and liabilities of a father), but also extend the status of parent to a woman living as a de facto partner of a birth mother.

Essentially, s 17 provides that the woman who becomes pregnant as a result of an AHR procedure is the legal mother of the child, irrespective of whether the child was conceived as a result of a donated ovum or embryo derived from a donated ovum. Section 18 outlines the rules about when the non-donor parent is to be regarded as a parent. To that end, s 18 provides that where the partner[110] of the woman who has undergone the AHR procedure has consented to that procedure, that partner becomes the parent of any child of the pregnancy. Sections 19 to 22 outline, more specifically, the rules about donors of genetic material. Thus, s 19 provides that where a woman is partnered,[111] the ovum donor or donor of an embryo derived from the ovum is not the parent of a child of that pregnancy unless she is the mother's partner at time of conception. Section 20 deals with the situation of a woman acting alone and provides that the non-partner ovum/embryo donor is not a parent unless she becomes the mother's partner after the time of conception. Sections 21 and 22 relate to donors of semen. Thus, according to s 21, where a woman is partnered and undergoes AHR procedure involving donated sperm, the sperm

---

[109] Section 66 Human Assisted Reproduction Act 2004.
[110] Section 14 of the Act defines "partner" as follows:

(a) in relation to a woman who is married and to whom paragraph (b) does not apply, means the woman's husband; and
(b) in relation to a woman ('woman A') who is married but is living with a man, or with another woman, as a de facto partner, means the man or other woman who is living with woman A as a de facto partner (and so does not mean woman A's husband); and
(c) in relation to a woman ('woman A') who is not married but is living with a man, or with another woman, as a de facto partner, means the man or other woman who is living with woman A as a de facto partner.

[111] According to s 14, "partnered woman" means a woman:

(a) is married; or
(b) is married, but is living with a man, or with another woman, as a de facto partner; or
(c) is not married but is living with a man, or with another woman, as a de facto partner.

donor is not, for any purpose, a parent of any child of the pregnancy. Section 22 relates to a non-partnered woman/woman acting alone[112] and, similarly to s 20, provides that the donor of the sperm will only become the parent of a child of that pregnancy where he becomes the partner of the woman after the conception. Sections 18, 21 and 22 will have effect irrespective of any conflict over paternity.[113] In relation to partnered women having undergone AHR involving donated genetic material, the partner's consent will be presumed unless there is evidence to the contrary.[114] With regard to parental rights and responsibilities, ss 23 and 24 of the Act provide that the rights and liabilities of a parent ensue in relation to donors (either of ova, embryos or sperm) who later become the partners of those women having become pregnant as a result of the AHR procedure in question. Equally, the child of any such pregnancy has the rights and liabilities of a child of such parent.

The effect of this legislation is that, save in those certain instances where the unpartnered woman becomes partnered to the donor, the individuals who donated the sperm and ovum and, who consequently are genetically related to the child, may have *no* legal relationship with the child. All legal rights and responsibilities towards the child lie with the birth mother and her consenting partner.[115] Therefore, this Act is primarily concerned with protecting the rights and interests of one set of adults, specifically the rights and interests of the mother and her partner. As such, current legislation tends to emphasise the rights and interests of the parents with, arguably, only passing reference to the rights of children.[116]

5. AHR and the Right to Identity in New Zealand – Advancing Openness or Discrimination

Although the moves towards greater openness in the area of AHR are to be welcomed, nonetheless, some aspects of the current legislative regime mean that, in reality, these moves do nothing to break down the tradition of secrecy that surrounds AHR or diminish the negative effects of such secrecy upon the "future

---

[112] Section 14 defines "woman acting alone" as a woman who:

(a) who is not a partnered woman; or
(b) who is a partnered woman, but has undergone an AHR procedure without her partner's consent.

[113] Section 26.
[114] Section 27.
[115] However, s 41 Care of Children Act 2004 makes provision for agreements to be made between parents and donors relating to contact between the donor or donors and the child, or to the role of the donor or donors in the upbringing of the child, or to both. Such agreements are not enforceable under the Act but may become the subject of a court order if one of the parties to the agreement makes an application to the court.
[116] With the exception of the rights and liabilities arising out of ss 20 and 22.

psychological security of children conceived pursuant to these processes".[117] Not only that, such aspects of the legislation allow for several avenues of discrimination against children born of AHR.

5.1. The Potential for Discrimination Remaining in Current Legislation

As the previous section indicates, current legislation is framed very much in terms of the rights and liabilities of adults, whether they are donors, or parents of donor-conceived offspring who have reached adulthood. From the perspective of children born of AHR, it is positive to note that donors may no longer remain anonymous. From the perspective of donors, the lack of anonymity is balanced somewhat by the lack of legal relationship with donor offspring. However, with regard to the rights of children born of AHR, the situation is not quite so positive as the balance of rights remains very much in favour of parents who are under no legal obligation to inform their children of the true nature of their genetic identity. The adult-orientated nature of the current AHR regime is reflective of the general discrimination that children suffer in many facets of society where such discrimination is inherently age-based, as such an approach is based upon the, often inaccurate, equation of lack of child equality with the lack of child capacity. The adult-orientated nature of the current AHR regime also differentiates between children in two further ways. First, children born of AHR are subject to the age-based distinctions provided for in the HART Act in terms of the ages that they must reach in order to access either non-identifying or identifying information regarding their genetic heritage. Second, the non-retroactive nature of the legislation differentiates between the ability of children born before and after the Act to access information regarding their genetic identity.

With regard to the issue of the lack of obligation upon parents to signal the true circumstance of the conception of their children, the practical reality of the current legislation is that the ability and extent to which donor-conceived offspring are able to exercise their right to identity continues to lie very much in the hands of their parents. A further reality is that a situation could arise where some children born of AHR will be in a better position to access such information and others will not, a situation which, given that it stems from parental control which may be exercised differently, may be considered to be further discrimination within a group that is arguably already discriminated against. The question to be considered is whether this balance of rights as between parent or child, which has the effect of limiting the right to identity of the latter, may be justified. The basis for parental control in this context is

---

[117] Caldwell and Daniels, supra note 4.

an echo of the more fundamental principle of paternalism which, in turn, may be regarded as a justification for parental control in such a highly sensitive area. Although national and international law also recognise paternalism, this recognition of parental rights is tempered by the need to recognise that the child's welfare and interests, and ultimately their rights, are to be regarded as a paramount consideration. This recognition is further added to by the need to take into account the Guiding Principles of the Convention on the Rights of the Child, namely, non-discrimination, evolving capacities, and ensuring the voice of the child is heard, principles which are also echoed in various aspects of domestic law.

A further aspect to the need to balance parental and child rights in this context is the extent to which the principles of non-discrimination and equality, which extend to discrimination based upon birth,[118] impact up the measure of States' discretion regarding their human rights obligations, so that phrases such as 'as far as possible', 'undertake to respect', and 'unlawful interference' should be interpreted so as to rank the child's right to identity, family and privacy above the privacy rights of his or her parents. This argument takes on added force when these fundamental principles are supplemented by the Guiding Principles of the Convention referred to above. Consequently, although a balance of rights as between parents and children must be recognised, any basis for denying children access to such information would have to be legitimate, proportionate and necessary in a democratic society in order to avoid claims of discrimination in the protection and exercise of the human rights in question. The current legislative regime governing AHR in New Zealand may be regarded as legitimising the preference accorded to parental rights. However, the test for discrimination does not stop with such legitimisation. The question remains to be considered as to whether the prioritisation of parental privacy over the child's right to identity serves an important and significant objective. As the legislative regime currently stands, the outcome of this objective is to prioritise parental rights, in particular, parental privacy rights, at the expense of the child's right to identity.[119] The prioritisation of parental rights seems very much at odds with a, albeit somewhat flawed, legislative regime which does not indicate a reason for such a prioritisation nor does such an approach sit well with a regime which is apparently designed to encourage openness as

---

[118] New Zealand legislation is silent on the matter.

[119] The striking of this balance in favour of parents was noted by Hammond J in *Hemmes v Young*, 8 March 2005, CA33/04, a recent Court of Appeal case arising out of the Adult Adoption Information Act 1985, when he concluded (at para 88):

> that international instruments, practice and jurisprudence have not yet reached the point where it can conclusively be said that adopted children possess a universal and internationally recognised right to know their biological parentage, *although the tide of opinion is flowing in that direction.* [emphasis added.]

well as to provide legal certainty. Accordingly, the significance and importance attached to this approach is not apparent and thus, it would seem that
parental control over any decision to inform their child as to their true genetic
heritage is discriminatory.

With regard to the further avenues for discrimination inherent in the current
regime, the first of these relates to age-based limitations that regulate when
children born of AHR may access information regarding their genetic heritage.
Of particular concern to the issue of whether the current age-based limitations
are discriminatory is the requirement that that child reach the age of 16 years
before they may access any information, identifying or non-identifying. It is also
of concern that identifying information is only available to those age 18 years
and over. Prior to the enactment of the current AHR legislation, the latter
age-based limitation was described as "the clearest of ripostes to children's
rights".[120] Justification for the age-based limitation of 16 years may be found
in s 21(1)(i) of the Human Rights Act, which prohibits age-based discrimination
but which, paradoxically, limits the bringing of such claims to individuals aged
16 years or older. Irrespective of the arguably arbitrary nature of legislation
which seeks to prohibit age-based discrimination but which is itself constructed
to limit the protection which it affords to those aged 16 years and older, there
would appear to be a discrepancy between setting the lower threshold for age-
based discrimination at 16 years and the restriction on accessing identifying
information at 18 years. The basis for such discrepancy is unclear, although
reference may undoubtedly be made to the less than fully autonomous nature
of the 16 year old, which allows some consideration of the need to apply an
interpretation of the interests and welfare of the child that is focused more on
protecting the child rather than securing increased autonomy.

Judicial decision-making of this kind was referred to in the previous chapter in relation to cases concerning the autonomy of individuals under the age
of 16 years to refuse to consent to medical treatment. Although the potentially
arbitrary nature of the age-based limitation in those cases was recognised, the
limitations were justified by reference to the severity of the consequences for
the children themselves should they be allowed to exercise their right to refuse
medical treatment. Any argument that the embargo on information that may
be accessed by donor-conceived children is aimed at meeting the important
and significant objective of providing for and protecting the child aged under
16 years because of his or her immaturity needs to be balanced against the
impact of the embargo, which may have severe consequences for the children in

---

[120] Freeman, supra note 5.

terms of their 'genealogical bewilderment' and perpetuating greater concern and anxiety regarding the nature of their genetic identity.[121] The view of the Health Select Committee which reported back to Parliament on the provisions of the proposed legislation recommended the removal of any age restriction on donor offspring accessing non-identifying information about the donor. However, the Committee did recommend that identifying information be made available at the age of 18 years.[122] A member of the Select Committee later explained the basis for this age limitation to Parliament as being in response to the large number of submissions made to it:

> In the end we [the Health Select Committee] decided that although genetic information could be obtained, donor offspring had to be of a certain maturity before they could handle information about the actual name of the donor.[123]

This explanation seems to be somewhat at odds with the rather more detailed analysis of age-based distinctions required by the Ministry of Youth Affairs recommendations to policy makers who seek to rely upon age-based distinctions.[124] In terms of international law, the principles of non-discrimination, best interests of the child, the evolving capacities of the child and the right of the child to have his or her voice heard needs to be taken into account in order to avoid any arbitrariness in the setting of age limits or definitions of maturity. These principles find some expression in the HART Act with its reference to the need to protect the dignity and rights of the child born of AHR.[125] Given that the age-based distinctions both withhold and limit access to the benefit of knowing one's genetic heritage, the use of the distinction remains to be justified.

The non-retroactive nature of the Act should serve to dissipate any potential for concern that may arise amongst donors whose privacy would have been guaranteed under the previous legislative regime. However, the non-retrospective

---

[121] This point, equally applicable to donor-conceived children, was also considered by Hammond J in *Hemmes v Young*, supra note 119, when he observed (at para 117) that:

adoption research has indicated that many adopted persons have a "deep" psychological need to know the true identity of those who brought them into this world. This because they must be enabled to place themselves in a social context, have a sense of continuity with their past, and what is sometimes called a "complete biography". (See Fortin *Children's Rights and the Developing Law* 2 ed 2003, at 383.)

[122] Health Select Committee, *Human Assisted Reproductive Technology Bill (195–2)*, Wellington: House of Representatives, 2004, at p 13, http://www.clerk.parliament.govt.nz/Content/SelectCommitteeReports/195bar2.pdf, as accessed on 21 March 2005.

[123] NZPD, Vol. 620, 6 October 2004, p 15932. http://www.clerk.parliament.govt.nz/Content/Hansard/Final/FINAL_2004_10_06.htm#_Toc85604856; http://www.clerk.parliament.govt.nz/hansard/Hansard.aspx, as accessed on 21 March 2005.

[124] Chapter 1, note 124.

[125] Section 3(a) HART Act.

nature of the HART Act also gives rise to discrimination-related concerns, as
a failure to extend the right to access identifying information to a category of
children born from donations before the legislation was enacted could amount
to discrimination if there was a failure to legitimate such differentiation in
treatment.[126] In *Rose & Anor v Secretary of State for Health Human Fertilisation and
Embryology Authority,* the English High Court sought to justify this differentiation on the grounds that:

> The donors donated the sperm voluntarily for the purposes of relieving the afflic-
> tion of infertility and on the clear understanding, if not promise, that their iden-
> tity would remain undisclosed forever. Any failure now to honour that long
> standing understanding, quite apart from being manifestly unfair to the donors,
> would drive a coach and horses through the A.I.D. system.[127]

The distinction between those born before the HFE Act and those born after
was further highlighted by Stephen Brown P, when he stated:

> the critical distinction between the two Claimants is that Ms Rose was born
> many years before any legislation was on the statute book when secrecy was very
> much the order of the day. EM was born afterwards; so some of its provisions
> are of direct relevance to her.[128]

The balance of rights could be struck more evenly in New Zealand if the
information to be accessed were to be limited to non-identifying information.
Harmonisation of rights as between pre-Act donors and their donor offspring
could be achieved under the terms of the Privacy Act 1993 and the Health
Information Privacy Code, making it feasible for both parties to obtain such
information with regard to each other, with each case being decided upon its
own merits.[129]

   On this analysis, failure to ensure these rights for all children born of AHR
would amount to discrimination. However, the potential for discrimination
could be further avoided if parents were legally obliged to inform their children of the circumstances of the child's conception or birth.

---

[126] The extension of this right to a footing equal to all donor-conceived offspring should be
distinguished from the ability to actually exercise the right which may be hampered by lack of
donor information.

[127] *Rose & Anor v Secretary of State for Health Human Fertilisation and Embryology Authority,* supra
note 82, at para 11.

[128] Ibid, at para 18.

[129] Right 6 of the Code allows the child both to obtain confirmation from the clinic/provider
that it holds information and to have access to it. This right must be balanced with s 29(1)(a) of
the Privacy Act which provides that such a request will be denied if "disclosure of the information would involve the unwarranted disclosure of the affairs of another individual or of a
deceased individual."

5.2. Advancing Children's Rights with Increased Openness

Limitations on the ability of donor-conceived children to exercise their right to identity was identified, in 2003, in the New Zealand Law Commission's Discussion Paper *New Issues in Legal Parenthood*.[130] Chapter 5 of the Discussion Paper focused on the issue of children and identity and included a series of questions some of which had particular significance to the right to identity of donor-conceived children. The potentially discriminatory aspects of the manner in which this right might be limited was identified both by the Law Commission[131] as well as in a subsequent NGO submission to the Commission on that matter. With regard to the underlying problem concerning the failure to signal their true genetic identity to donor-conceived children, the Law Commission asked whether the publicly available birth certificate of a donor-conceived child or child born of surrogacy should be annotated to indicate that a person named on it is not the genetic or gestational parent.[132] In response to this question, it was recommended that such annotations should be made.[133] Under the Status of Children Amendment Act 2004, reference to s 16 would be sufficient as it would indicate to the child in question that other individuals were involved in his/her conception.[134]

It was further recommended that the annotation should also be automatic and obligatory and it would oblige parents to inform their children of the circumstances of their conception or birth.[135] To make such an annotation optional could have the effect of denying to the child the ability to exercise his or her rights to identity and to respect for family/private life as the child's ability to exercise this right would be dependant on parental choice to make the indicating information available. With regard to the situation of children conceived

---

[130] New Zealand Law Commission, *New Issues in Legal Parenthood* (NZLC PP54) Wellington: NZLC, 2004. http://www.lawcom.govt.nz/Documents/Publications/PP54%20New%20issues%20in%20Legal%20Parent.pdf, as accessed on 1 March 2005.

[131] http://www.lawcom.govt.nz/Documents/Publications/SOP%20Parts/2PP54%20chapts%205–6.pdf, as accessed on 1 March 2005.

[132] Ibid, at 71. See, for a general discussion, 69–71.

[133] C Breen, *Submission on: The Right to Identity of Donor Conceived Children – Responses to Some Issues Raised in Chapter 5 of New Issues in Legal Parenthood*, Wellington, ACYA, 2004.

[134] Section 16 provides:

   (1) This Part applies in respect of a pregnancy referred to in any of sections 17 to 22,—
      (a) whether the pregnancy occurred before or after the commencement of this Part:
      (b) whether or not the pregnancy resulted from a procedure carried out in New Zealand.

   (2) This Part applies in respect of a child born of a pregnancy referred to in any of sections 17 to 22,—
      (a) whether the child was born before or after the commencement of this Part:
      (b) whether or not the child was born in New Zealand.

[135] Breen, supra note 133.

in surrogacy arrangements or private donor gamete conceptions, such children should be able to obtain information about their genetic parent(s) on an equal footing to other children born of AHR. Moreover, automatic annotation would place a positive obligation upon the State to ensure that the child's rights were respected. The Human Rights Commission, in a 1994 submission to MCHART, noted the variation in access to information in this area and, in supporting calls for a centralised register, it observed that AHR is "an area where children's rights should weigh heavily".[136] In addition, the automatically annotated publicly available birth certificate should be supplemented by a private certificate. Such an approach is preferable to the more common approach of a central register, as provided for in the HART Act, and such a certificate would amount to a true record of all the individuals involved in the child's conception.[137]

6. Conclusion

Although the rights of donor-conceived children are recognised, the current legislation does not give the principle of non-discrimination and equality with regards to the child born of AHR the recognition required in order to reflect national and international law and the law in other jurisdictions. The need for such child-orientated legislation makes the rights and interests of children resulting from AHR the paramount consideration, a consideration which, if applied to age-based distinctions, would also serve as a legal basis for removing the discrimination, both general and age-based, inherent in the current legislation in New Zealand. Furthermore, ideals of bi-culturalism infused with the cultural values of whakapapa underline the importance of greater openness to protect the interests of the child and the adult, both Maori and Pakeha alike. Such willingness is being encouraged amongst donors with the current approach provided for in the HART Act and the SCAA but, as the Law Commission Discussion Paper indicates, such provisions do not go far enough. Consequently, the legislation needs to be amended to avoid discrimination in all matters associated with AHR but especially with regards to the right of the child to know his or her identity.

---

[136] Human Rights Commission, *Submission of the Human Rights Commission to the Ministerial Committee on Assisted Reproductive Technologies,* Auckland, Human Rights Commission, 1994, at 10.

[137] Breen, supra note 133.

CHAPTER FOUR

THE CORPORAL PUNISHMENT OF CHILDREN IN NEW ZEALAND: THE POWER OF PARENTAL RIGHTS IN NEW ZEALAND

1. Introduction

The (im)balance between the rights of children and the rights of parents, and the role of the State in maintaining this (im)balance by virtue of the exercise of its legislative and judicial functions, is further exemplified, in the context of New Zealand, by s 59 of the Crimes Act 1961. According to s 59, the corporal punishment of children by their parents may be justified under the defence of domestic discipline, which permits the use of force in the correction of a child if the force used is reasonable in the circumstances. This defence of domestic discipline highlights the conflict inherent in New Zealand legislation between the comparatively recently-recognised concept of children's rights and the much older concept of parental rights. In many respects, modern New Zealand legislation and recent case law pertaining to children have sought to prioritise the rights of the child over those of parents by incorporating the standard of the best interests of the child into the decision-making process. However, the results of such attempts have been inconsistent in relation to corporal punishment in terms of the level of protection against violence that has been accorded to children. Section 59, both in substance and interpretation, presents more difficulties than it resolves. The courts not only have to grapple with the definition of what is "reasonable in the circumstances", they must also try to reconcile the lower level of protection arising out of s 59 with other legislation which is aimed at providing for and protecting children both generally and more specifically from domestic violence in order to avoid claims of discrimination as between children and adults. At the international level, New Zealand has also grappled with the inconsistency of its domestic laws with its obligations under international human rights law, an inconsistency that has been commented upon by both the UN Committee on the Rights of the Child and the UN Committee Against Torture.

The corporal punishment of children encompasses age discrimination in terms of the extent that it allows discriminatory treatment as between children and adults. Corporal punishment also encompasses the notion of age-based limitations, as the courts have made determinations as to the excessiveness of the force used in relation to the age of the child in question. It is argued in this

chapter that the defence of reasonable chastisement embodied in s 59 is discriminatory as there exists no clear justification for the difference in the level
of protection against assault as between adults and children that results from
the provisions of that section. To that end, Part 2 constitutes an overview of
some of the historical and philosophical background to corporal punishment.
This backdrop not only attempts to demonstrate the strong overlap between
some of the historical attitudes towards children alluded to in Chapter 1 and
corporal punishment but it also seeks to provide a backdrop to the current
debate concerning corporal punishment and the rights of children and parents.
Part 3 consists of a critique of some of the recent academic debate regarding
the corporal punishment of children. Although the focus of this section is New
Zealand academic debate, such debate mirrors much of the debate regarding
corporal punishment taking place in other jurisdictions. Part 4 provides an
overview of human rights treaty provisions that may be, and have been, interpreted as prohibiting corporal punishment. Part 5 returns to New Zealand and
provides an international and comparative analysis of New Zealand's stance
on the defence of domestic discipline in terms of comments made by the
Committee on the Rights of the Child. This part will also focus upon the consideration (or lack of) by the New Zealand courts of the notion of children's
rights in cases where s 59 of the Crimes Act is used to allow parental rights to
override those of the child.

2. The Corporal Punishment of Children: A Historical and Philosophical Framework

The infliction of corporal punishment upon children has been debated for
centuries. For example, in drawing a distinction between the differing modes
of child discipline, Seneca asserted that corporal punishment was appropriate
for those incapable of reason, including young children. Older children were
to be guided by the grant or withdrawal of praise or rewards thereby setting
the distinction between the discipline of children and the coercion of "honour-
less slaves".[1] Plutarch noted that philosophy taught men proper conduct, such
as "to be affectionate with children".[2] He advised against the corporal punishment of children, although, admittedly, he did draw a distinction between
those that were freeborn and those that were slaves, stating that:

> Children ought to be led to honourable practices by means of encouragement
> and reasoning, and most certainly not blows nor by ill treatment; *for it is surely*

---

[1] R Saller, *Patriarchy, Property and Death in the Roman Family*, Cambridge, CUP, 1994, 143.
[2] Plutarch, *De liberis educandis* (at 10), quoted in Saller, ibid, at 143.

agreed that these are fitting rather for slaves than for the freeborn; for so they grow numb and shudder at their tasks, partly from the pain of blows, partly also on account of the hybris. Praise and reproof are more helpful for the freeborn children than any sort of ill-usage, since the praise incites them towards what is honourable, and reproof keeps them from what is disgraceful.[3] [emphasis added]

On the other hand, the Medieval Christian philosopher, Augustine was of the view that no distinction should be drawn between the child and the slave as, in the worship of God, everyone sins and everyone is in servitude.[4] Sin provided the imperative for corporal punishment as corporal punishment "came to manifest paternal love as never before".[5] According to Augustine:[6]

> If anyone in the household opposes the domestic peace through disobedience, he is disciplined by word or by whip or by any other kind of just and legitimate punishment, to the extent that human society allows. Such discipline is for the profit of the one being disciplined so that he is readjusted to the peace from which he had departed.

The argument in favour of the whip was justified as being necessary to save sinning children from damnation and formed the basis of an argument that was to have a long history in later Christian Europe.[7] Thomas Aquinas was of the opinion that the status of children, as much as of slaves and of women, should be dealt with in separate categories. Consequently, justice was to be accorded in proportion to one's status as child, woman or slave. The justice to be apportioned to the child was to be based upon his status as the property of his father:

> a son belongs to his father, since he is part of him somewhat. . . . Hence a father is not compared to his son as to another simply, and so between them there is not just simply but a kind of just, called paternal.[8]

Such views were based on a society that were models of patriarchy in which the oldest ascendant male had supreme powers over his wife and children, and kinship relations generally passed through the male line.[9] The early medieval centuries saw no change in the patriarchal authority over the family that was

---

[3] Ibid, at 12.

[4] Augustine, *The City of God*, Book XIX, Chapter 15. Reprinted in MW Tkacz and D Kries (trans), *Augustine: Political Writings*, Indianapolis, Hackett Publishing, 1994, at 155–156.

[5] Saller, supra note 1, at 146.

[6] Augustine, supra note 4, Chapter 16, at 156–157.

[7] Ibid. Other Christian writers saw the need for moderation. Parents in some Christian societies valued children as continuations of themselves and so were loathe to punish them.

[8] Thomas Aquinas, *Summa Theologiae*, Part II, Book II, Question 57, Article 4. Reprinted in WP Baumgarth and RJ Regan (eds), *St. Thomas Aquinas: On Law, Morality, and Politics*, Indianapolis, Hackett Publishing, 1988, at 142–143.

[9] S Dixon *The Roman Family*, London, Johns Hopkins University Press, 1992, at 3.

vested in the husband and father.[10] The patriarchy of Reformation Europe was exacerbated by religious teachings that emphasised the subordination of a wife to her husband and the general inferiority of women to men.[11] Whilst the patriarchal legitimisation for political authority may have collapsed in the nineteenth century, as exemplified by the American and French Revolutions, on the whole law and custom still acknowledged the husband's sovereignty over his wife.[12] Consequently, until well into the twentieth century, power and authority over children continued to rest exclusively with the father, reflecting his dominant role in all family matters, as "the common law of England denied to a wife any legal right to the custody or care and control of her children: and the concept that a wife was a mere chattel whose identity merged into that of her husband was thereby reflected in the legal structure governing the most basic of human relationships".[13]

Whilst the right to inflict corporal punishment can be traced both historically and philosophically, such a journey through time and thought is illustrated by the belief that slaves, women and children were at best inferior and at worst mere chattels. Theoretically at least, the concepts and practice of slavery and the inferiority of women have suffered a demise with the emancipation of slaves and women and the advent of race and gender equality legislation. However, for some, the remnants of such beliefs remain as, with regard to the corporal punishment of children, they "defend the status quo"[14] and contend that "parents ought to be legally permitted to administer moderate corporal punishment for the purpose of correction".[15] In other words, parents should be allowed to maintain the legal right to discipline their children physically. The converse of this argument is that children should not have the right not to be physically disciplined. Such contentions favouring the corporal punishment of children by their parents not only fail to consider the merits of the argument regarding the retention of the defence of domestic discipline, they amount to an entrenchment of power on behalf of the majority that remains to be justified, and justified not only by the majority, in order to avoid being discriminatory. Moreover, such assertions constitute a view that, in the past,

---

[10] F Gies and J Gies, *Marriage and the Family in the Middle Ages*, New York, Harper & Row, 1987, at 54.

[11] J Harris, *The Family and Industrial Society*, Cambridge, CUP, 1983, at 143–144.

[12] M Abbot, *Family Ties: English Families 1540–1920*, London, Routledge, 1993, at 35.

[13] S Cretney, "'What Will the Women Want Next?' The Struggle for Power within the Family 1925–1975" (1996) 112 Law Quarterly Review, 110, 112.

[14] R Ahdar and J Allan, "Taking Smacking Seriously: The Case for Retaining the Legality of Parental Smacking in New Zealand" (2001) 1 NZ Law Review, 1 at 33.

[15] Ibid.

would have undermined the movement for the emancipation of women and, prior to that, the prohibition of slavery and which would currently form the basis for gender and race discrimination.

It is at this juncture that the accuracy of the comparison between race, gender and age discrimination has been questioned on the following bases. First, the temporary nature of the lesser levels of protection against assault that are based on transient characteristics (from a legal perspective), characteristics that cease to exist, from a legal perspective, upon reaching the age of majority. Second, the fact that all children are subject to the lesser levels of protection against assault, levels of protection that increase as the child matures. Third, the recognised differences between children and adults, differences that need to be taken into account not only to ensure the special safeguards and care to be accorded to the child, by reason of his or her physical and mental immaturity, differences which become increasingly blurred as the child evolves into the (young) adult, but also in order to avoid discrimination. As the merits of drawing a distinction between race and gender discrimination and age discrimination have been addressed in Chapter 1, the remainder of this chapter will focus upon revealing the discriminatory nature of s 59.

3. *Corporal Punishment of Children: Recent Academic Debate in New Zealand*

In New Zealand, the assertion that children do not have the right to be free from physical punishment constitutes the point of departure for a more recent analysis of corporal punishment. As elsewhere, it has been asserted that the framing of the discourse surrounding the corporal punishment of children in terms of "hitting" or "violence" rather than "smacking" is nothing more than the strategic choosing of a "some pejorative noun"[16] in order to win the debate on corporal punishment by adopting "the linguistic high ground".[17] In response, it may be argued equally that the persistent use of the seemingly innocuous term "smacking" to describe the reality of the "hitting" of children as a form of punishment is itself an attempt to at least colour the debate surrounding bodily punishment of children. It has also been contended that it is too crude to conflate "violence" with "smacking", particularly in terms of the message that smacking may send, which is that violence is a legitimate form of problem-solving.[18]

---

[16] Ibid, at 22.
[17] Ibid.
[18] Ibid, at 29.

It has been asserted that children should and can learn about the "vast moral difference"[19] between "legitimate authorities – the judiciary, parents, or teachers – who use punitive powers to punish wrongdoing, and children or private citizens going around beating each other".[20] Related academic debate also focuses on whether corporal punishment may be linked with child abuse.[21] However, inasmuch as the debate over which noun (or verb) is the most appropriate way to describe the hitting of children as a form of punishment detracts from the central argument over whether all hitting is abusive or illegitimate, so too does further exploration of the perceived links between child discipline and child abuse.[22] Such arguments detract from the assertion that the child has a *right* not to be subjected to corporal punishment irrespective of the competing claims as to the benefit or harm associated with the practice.

The adoption of a rights analysis highlights the unique or peculiar nature of the corporal punishment of children. If children have a ready grasp of the fact that a smacking from their parents does not entitle them to aggress offensively against their peers,[23] does this ready grasp of the peculiar nature of smacking derive from an equally ready grasp of their particular (inferior) position in society, or from the fact that they have been taught that hitting is wrong? In terms of the former, the principles of non-discrimination and equality suggest that children and adults should be regarded as being identical in terms of the right not to be hit. The denial to children of the right to physical integrity, without proper justification, is to accord them a lower status in society. This assertion is met with the counter-claim that if children and adults truly are to be accorded identical status in society and, as such, "if children have some purported right not to be hit, do they not also have some equivalent right not to be subject to false imprisonment and not to have their civil liberties withdrawn".[24] In other words, it is claimed that if children possess the right not to be hit, then alternative forms of punishment such as 'time out' or deductions from their pocket money, or the withdrawal of television privileges or being 'grounded' are equally invalid restrictions on a child's civil liberties. However, this assertion ignores the correlations that may be drawn between 'time out'

---

[19] Ibid, quoting D Benatar, "Corporal Punishment" (1998) 24 Social Theory and Practice 237, at 246.

[20] Ibid.

[21] Infra note 56.

[22] Other than those comments made by the Committee on the Rights of the Child, See, infra notes 52–55 and accompanying text.

[23] Ibid, at 31, quoting D Baumrind, "A Blanket Injunction Against Disciplinary Use of Spanking is Not Warranted by the Data" (1996) 98(4) Pediatrics 828, 829.

[24] Ibid.

and the adult equivalent of a prison sentence or false imprisonment, and between deductions from a child's pocket money and the fining of an adult. These correlations highlight the well-recognised and accepted fact that an individual's civil liberties or human rights are not absolute.

What is missing from the equation or correlation of punishments as between child and adult is that, in New Zealand at least, there is no 'adult version' of corporal punishment. No matter how much an adult has misbehaved, he or she will not be subject to physical punishment – his or her right to physical integrity will be maintained. This difference in treatment may be explained by reference to the distinction that may be drawn between the child and the adult. However, this 'difference' between children and adults becomes discrimination when the unequal protection of rights is posited on nothing more than the particular characteristics of such individuals. One characteristic or justification for the corporal punishment of children, in particular, tends to be advanced more than others and that is the perceived inability of the child to reason. If this is the distinction drawn, why does the law accord protection from any form of corporal punishment to those adults incapable of reason or even to those whose reasoning simply differs from our own?

However, as the preceding analysis indicates, as well as the analysis in Chapter 1, the child's perceived lack of reason or autonomy is intricately linked to the notions of paternalism and, in particular, parental rights. Although the balance of power as between parent and child has shifted to the extent that children are no longer to be regarded as being simply the property of their parents, the often very emotive discussion surrounding corporal punishment exemplifies much of the continuing tension emanating from the concept of children's rights and the threat that it is perceived as posing to the status quo of parental rights. The maintenance of parental rights is legitimate, especially when it is construed in terms of repelling unwarranted State intervention into family life, a construction that has found expression in the provisions of human rights instruments that seek to ensure the right to respect for family life as recognised from the Universal Declaration onwards. However, the interrelated concepts of parental rights, right to respect for family life and the maintenance of the distinction between the public and private sphere have not proven to be absolute either in international human rights law or in the provisions of domestic legislation that pertain to family life. As such, the notion of a balance of rights – underpinned by the principles of non-discrimination and equality – reasserts itself in terms of parental rights, as an aspect of the right to respect for family life. Equally, the child's right to be free from corporal punishment is an aspect of the overarching human rights concept of the right to physical integrity and in particular the right to be free from cruel, inhuman and degrading punishment.

4. Corporal Punishment as a Violation of the Child's Human Rights

Generally, the Universal Declaration,[25] the ICCPR,[26] the American Convention[27] and the European Convention[28] all contain provisions that can be broadly described as rights to bodily integrity or the right to "security of person", provisions that are arguably violated by the application of corporal punishment. These treaties also contain provisions regarding the right to personal privacy.[29] Equally, Article 12(1) of the ICESCR recognises the "right of everyone to the enjoyment of the highest attainable standard of physical and mental health".

However, it is with regard to the right to be free from cruel, inhuman or degrading punishment that the issue of corporal punishment most arises. In terms of the notion of the balance of rights as between parent and child, the maintenance of the status quo in favour of the former has been more apparent in the jurisprudence generated by the ICCPR and the European Convention with regard to the right to be free from cruel, inhuman or degrading punishment. To date, the discussion by the respective treaty monitoring bodies has been confined to issue of excessive corporal punishment of children which suggests that the right to be free from cruel, inhuman or degrading punishment does not apply equally and without discrimination.

To that end, Article 7 of the ICCPR forbids subjecting anyone to torture or to cruel, inhuman, or degrading treatment or punishment. In its General Comment 20, the Human Rights Committee stated that "the aim of the provisions of article 7 . . . is to protect both the dignity and the physical and mental integrity of the individual".[30] Consequently, States Parties are under a duty to provide everyone with protection by way of legislation or other avenues against the acts prohibited by Article 7, whether inflicted by people acting within their official capacity "or in a private capacity".[31] Furthermore, the Committee has observed that "no justification . . . may be invoked to excuse a violation of article 7 for any reasons".[32]

---

[25] Article 3, Universal Declaration of Human Rights, G.A. Res. 217A, (III) U.N. Doc. A1810 (1948).
[26] Article 9(1), International Covenant on Civil and Political Rights, U.N. G.A. Res. 2200 (XXI), 21 UN GAOR, Supp. (No. 16) 52, U.N. Doc. A16316 (1966).
[27] Article 5(1) American Convention on Human Rights, O.A.S. Treaty Series No. 36.
[28] Article 3(1), *European Convention for the Protection of Human Rights and Fundamental Freedoms*, 213 U.N.T.S., 221, no. 2889; Council of Europe, European Treaty Series, 4 November 1950, no. 5; Council of Europe, Collected Texts, Strasbourg (1987), 3–21.
[29] See the Universal Declaration, Article 12; ICCPR, Article 17(1)-(2); European Convention, Article 8(1); American Convention, Article 11(2)–(3).
[30] General Comment 20: Replaces General Comment 7 Concerning Prohibition of Torture and Cruel Treatment or Punishment (Article 7), U.N. Doc. HRI/GEN/1/Rev.2 (1996), at para 2.
[31] Ibid.
[32] Ibid, at para 3.

These observations become all the more pertinent as the Committee has stated that the prohibition in Article 7 is to relate:

> Not only to acts that cause physical pain but also to acts that cause mental suffering to the victim. In the Committee's view, moreover, the prohibition must extend to corporal punishment, including *excessive* chastisement ordered as punishment for a crime or as an educative or disciplinary measure. It is appropriate to emphasise in this regard that article 7 protects, in particular, children, pupils and patients in teaching and medical institutions.[33] [emphasis added]

Given that General Comments have often expanded the meaning of the rights contained in the ICCPR and that they are adopted by consensus, they constitute an important and authoritative source of interpretation of provisions of the Covenant.[34] Although Article 7 particularly emphasises excessive corporal punishment of children in teaching institutions, the General Comment states that Article 7 extends to individuals acting in a private capacity.[35] It has also been suggested that such an interpretation may be applied to the identical language of Article 5 of the Universal Declaration, given that the Covenant constitutes a legally binding codification of the principles of the Universal Declaration.[36]

One of the many criticisms levelled at international human rights treaties is the weakness of their enforcement mechanisms. However, the First Optional Protocol to the ICCPR contains fourteen articles granting important procedural rights to individuals to make complaints about breaches of their civil and political rights. These rights could be extended to a child who wishes to bring a complaint to the Committee that his or her rights are not being protected by a State Party that is failing to protect its children against excessive corporal punishment.

The Convention Against Torture (CAT), the Preamble of which indicates that it is meant to protect "all members of the human family",[37] prohibits torture[38] and cruel, inhuman or degrading treatment or punishment.[39] In 2004, the Committee Against Torture considered the issue of whether corporal

---

[33] Ibid, at para 5.

[34] M Nowak, "The Covenant on Civil and Political Rights" in R Hanski and M Suksi (eds), *An Introduction to the International Protection of Human Rights: A Textbook* (2nd ed), Turku/Abo: Institute for Human Rights, Abo Akademi University, 1999, 94.

[35] General Comment 20, supra note 30.

[36] S Bitensky, "Spare the Rod, Embrace Our Humanity: Toward a New Legal Regime Prohibiting Corporal Punishment of Children" (1998) 31 Uni of Michigan Journal of Law Reform 353, at 406.

[37] Convention Against Torture and Other Cruel, Inhuman or Degrading Treatment or Punishment, U.N. Doc. A/39/708 (1984), para 1.

[38] Article 1.

[39] Article 16.

punishment amounted to cruel, inhuman or degrading punishment in its consideration of New Zealand's State Party report.[40] In contrast to the Human Rights Committee's approach to date, the Committee Against Torture, in its Concluding Observations and Comments, recommended that New Zealand implement the recommendations made by the Committee on the Rights of the Child in 2003 regarding s 59. That latter body had recommended, *inter alia*, that New Zealand should not only amend legislation to prohibit corporal punishment in the home but that it should strengthen public education campaigns and activities aimed at promoting positive, non-violent forms of discipline and respect for children's rights to human dignity and physical integrity, while raising awareness about the negative consequences of corporal punishment.[41] Thus, the Committee Against Torture appears to be advocating a stricter interpretation of the right to be free from cruel, inhuman or degrading punishment that incorporates all corporal punishment rather than the interpretation adopted by the Human Rights Committee, with its focus on excessive corporal punishment. The Committee Against Torture's recommendation also goes some way to resolving the difficulty posed by the interrelationship between Articles 1 and 16 of the Convention, which state that the conduct prohibited must be undertaken "by or at the instigation of or with the consent or acquiescence of a public official or other person acting in an official capacity". Consequently, the public/private distinction regarding the implementation of human rights norms can no longer be said to exclude the physical punishment of children by their parents, as punishment now amounts to a violation of the provisions of CAT.

Whether the corporal punishment of children constitutes torture, or cruel, inhuman or degrading treatment or punishment was also considered by the European Court of Human Rights in its interpretation of Article 3 of the European Convention. Article 3 provides that "no one shall be subjected to torture or to inhuman or degrading treatment or punishment". Both the European Court of Human Rights and the former European Commission of Human Rights considered several cases and determined that, in certain circumstances, the corporal punishment of children violated the provisions of Article 3.[42]

---

[40] Third periodic reports of States parties due in 1999: New Zealand. 09/08/2002. CAT/C/49/Add.3. (State Party Report).

[41] CRC/C/15/Add.216, para 30.

[42] For example, in *Tyrer v United Kingdom* (1978) 2 EHRR 1 the Court considered that the judicial application of corporal punishment amounted to a violation of Article 3, noting that the Convention was "a living instrument which . . . must be interpreted in the light of present-day conditions" and that the standards that were currently accepted in European society were to be determinative rather than those that were prevalent when the Convention was initially adopted (at 10). In the context of discipline in schools, the Court said, obiter, that such discipline could amount to a violation of Article 3 as in *Campbell and Cosans v United Kingdom* (1982) 4 EHRR 293 and *Costello-Roberts v United Kingdom* (1993) 19 EHRR 112.

However, it was not until *A v United Kingdom*[43] that the Court considered whether the physical punishment of children by their parents amounted to a violation of the European Convention. This case involved the beating of a child by his stepfather. The applicant claimed that the beating reached a level of severity prohibited by Article 3. In addition, the applicant claimed that States Parties were required to take measures designed to protect individuals (including children) from ill-treatment by other private individuals, and that the defence of "reasonable chastisement" did not provide adequate protection to the applicant.

The Court recalled that ill-treatment had to attain a minimum level of severity to fall within the scope of Article 3.[44] It noted that the assessment of this minimum level was relative, depending on all the circumstances of the case, such as the nature and context of the treatment, its duration, its physical and mental effects, and, in some instances, the sex, age and state of health of the victim.[45] The Court found that the beating of the applicant, who was nine years' old at the time, with a garden cane that had been applied with considerable force on more than one occasion reached the level of severity prohibited by Article 3.[46] The Court was also asked to consider whether the State Party was to be held responsible, under Article 3, for the beating of the applicant by his stepfather.[47] The Court noted that children and other vulnerable individuals were particularly entitled to State protection, in the form of effective deterrence, against such serious breaches of personal integrity.[48] It found that the domestic law defence of "reasonable chastisement" did not provide the applicant with adequate protection against the acts prohibited by Article 3. Accordingly, the Court held that the State Party's failure to provide adequate protection constituted a violation of Article 3.[49] The judgment of the Court turned on the harshness of the punishment in the circumstances, an approach that suggests that the Court would not regard all corporal punishment of children as violating Article 3, regardless of the severity of the punishment.

Article 5(2) of the American Convention also prohibits torture or cruel, inhuman or degrading treatment or punishment. In somewhat of a contrast with the European Convention, the Inter-American Commission on Human Rights has commented that full observance of the American Convention entails ratification of the Convention on the Rights of the Child. This suggests that, with regard to the rights of the child, the more general provisions of the

---

[43] (1998) 27 EHRR 611.
[44] Ibid, at 618.
[45] Ibid.
[46] Ibid, at 620.
[47] Ibid.
[48] Ibid, at 622–623.
[49] Ibid, at 624.

American Convention should be interpreted in light of the more specific provisions of the Convention on the Rights of the Child. Consequently, the interpretation of the latter Convention as prohibiting corporal punishment means that Article 5 of the American Convention could also be interpreted as prohibiting the corporal punishment of children.

International human rights treaties provide a general framework against which to consider whether the corporal punishment of children constitutes a violation of international human rights norms. Arguments that these treaties do prohibit corporal punishment of children are supported by the inclusive language of the treaties, which apply to "everyone", in addition to the imposition of corporal punishment being inconsistent with the interpretation and implementation of certain core principles and provisions. However, the necessity of children-specific language to highlight the rights of the child over those of the parents (as has happened in a number of other matters relating to the rights of the child), as well as the unsuitability of the argument (in terms of the rights of the child) that only the exercise of excessive force can amount to cruel, inhuman or degrading punishment, requires that a stronger argument for corporal punishment constituting a violation of children's rights be sought elsewhere.

The Convention on the Rights of the Child contains several provisions that relate, both directly and indirectly, to the prohibition on the corporal punishment of children. However, the substantive provisions of the Convention are also to be interpreted in light of the Convention's Guiding Principles. Proponents of corporal punishment contend that Article 5 of the Convention justifies reasonable physical chastisement,[50] with its statement that:

> States Parties shall respect the responsibilities, rights and duties of parents or, where applicable, the members of the extended family or community as provided for by local custom, legal guardians or other persons legally responsible for the child, to provide, in a manner consistent with the evolving capacities of the child, appropriate direction and guidance in the exercise by the child of the rights recognised in the present Convention.

This argument was raised by the United Kingdom's delegation to the Committee on the Rights of the Child. The United Kingdom contended that "'normal' punishment within the family was regarded as a private matter, involving decisions which pertained to the rights and responsibilities of parents implied in article 5 of the Convention".[51] In response, the Committee stated that:

> It must be borne in mind, however, that article 19 of the Convention required all appropriate measures, including legislative measures, to be taken to protect

---

[50] Bitensky, supra note 36, at 395, note 200.
[51] Summary Record of the 205th Meeting, Comm. on the Rts. of the Child, U.N. Doc. CRC/C/SR.205 (1995), at para 70.

the child against, inter alia, physical violence. A way should thus be found of striking the balance between the responsibilities of the parents and the rights and evolving capacities of the child that was implied in article 5 of the Convention. *There was no place for corporal punishment within the margin of discretion accorded in article 5 to parents in the exercise of their responsibilities.* Other countries had found it helpful to incorporate a provision to that effect in their civil law. As had already been pointed out, it was in any case well-nigh impossible to assess objectively what constituted moderate corporal punishment.[52] [emphasis added]

The "appropriate measures" required by Article 19 relate to the obligations imposed upon States Parties by that article to:

Take all appropriate legislative, administrative, social and educational measures to protect the child from *all forms of physical or mental violence, injury* or abuse, neglect or negligent treatment, maltreatment or exploitation, including sexual abuse, while in the care of parent(s), legal guardian(s) or any other person who has the care of the child. [emphasis added]

The Committee has approached this issue of corporal punishment on two levels. First, the Committee has viewed Articles 5 and 19 as being interrelated. Consequently, whilst the plain and ordinary meaning of Article 19, read alongside the *travaux préparatoires,* may not explicitly extend to corporal punishment, the Committee has read Articles 5 and 19 together as prohibiting corporal punishment, thereby providing a fuller interpretation of the Convention. The linking of corporal punishment and violence has been criticised as being nothing more than an "activist" or "politically correct"[53] interpretation of the Convention by "the small, self-selecting body of people that makes up the Committee".[54] However, such a criticism not only fails to recognise the dynamic nature of law, both national and international, but also ignores both the standard-setting nature of the Convention and the spirit with which State Parties should accept their Convention obligations to implement and *advance* the rights of the child. Secondly, irrespective of the *merits* of the argument that to describe "smacking as a species of 'physical violence, injury or abuse' is to conflate two distinct phenomena",[55] the Committee stated that corporal punishment does not fall within the margin of discretion accorded to parents by Article 5 in the exercise of their responsibilities. It is irrelevant whether such punishment is pitched at the level of smacking or physical violence, and so allegations of "activist" interpretations in conflating smacking with violence or abuse are avoided or are ill-founded.

---

[52] Ibid, at para 72.
[53] Ahdar and Allan, supra note 14, at 32.
[54] Ibid.
[55] Ibid.

The provisions of Article 19 are not only underpinned by the child's right to life, as provided for in Article 6, but are also coloured by the right to survival and development contained in Article 6(2). The correlation between the provisions of Articles 6 and 19 and corporal punishment turns not only on the concern that such punishment may hinder the child's emotional development. It also turns on the perceived link between corporal punishment and child abuse.[56] As previously stated, this chapter refrains from an analysis of the merits of such arguments, as such an analysis would detract from the assertion that the child has a *right* not to be subjected to corporal punishment, irrespective of the competing claims as to the benefit or harm associated with the practice.

As the comments made by the Committee to the United Kingdom's delegation indicate, a balancing exercise has to be adopted in the interpretation of the various provisions of the Convention. This need for balance is also apparent from the drafting and final wording of Article 3. As such, the overall spirit and purpose of the Convention[57] make it clear that, in terms of the corporal punishment of children in the familial context, the recognition accorded to the rights of parents in Article 5 should not outweigh the overall goal of the Convention, which is to protect the rights of the child. The provisions of Article 19 should be interpreted to further this goal, so that a child who exercises his or her rights – rights that encompass all facets of the child's daily life – can exercise those rights with *appropriate* "direction and guidance". Such direction and guidance should exclude corporal punishment (which all acknowledge is bodily punishment[58]), irrespective of whether such punishment is framed in terms of 'smacking' or physical and mental violence or injury.

The provisions of Article 19 regarding the protection of the child from all forms of physical or mental violence or injury may have a direct correlation with the child's right under Article 24(1) "to the enjoyment of the highest

---

[56] The correlation between abuse and punishment has been considered by, amongst others, B Wood, "Children are People Too – Facilitating Social Change about Physical Punishment", presentation to the Public Health Association Conference (Auckland, July 2001), available at http://epochnz.virtualave.net/ paper_children_people_too.html; M Straus, "Corporal Punishment and Primary Prevention of Child Abuse" (2000) 24 Child Abuse and Neglect 1109 (for further research by Straus on this area see http://pubpages.unh.edu/~mas2/cp.htm); DM Fergusson and MT Lynskey, "Physical Punishment/Maltreatment During Childhood and Adjustment in Young Adulthood" (1997) 21(7) Child Abuse and Neglect 617; S Gerven, *The Religious Roots of Physical Punishment and the Psychological Impact of Physical Abuse* New York, Alfred A Knopf, 1991. See also, in general, *Global Initiative to End All Corporal Punishment of Children*, available at http://endcorporalpunishment.org. The link (or lack of it) between child abuse and corporal punishment is also discussed by Ahdar and Allan, supra note 14, at 21–30.

[57] Elements of the spirit and purpose may be found in the language of the Preamble and in the Guiding Principles contained in Articles 2, 3, 5 and 12.

[58] Ahdar and Allan, supra note 14, at 22.

attainable standard of health". Similarly to the obligations imposed by Article 19, Article 24(2) provides that "States Parties shall pursue full implementation of this right". It is also worth noting that the Convention requires State Parties to "take all effective and appropriate measures with a view to abolishing traditional practices prejudicial to the health of children".[59]

Article 28(2) contains the only direct reference to the discipline of children, and merely states that:

> States Parties shall take all appropriate measures to ensure that school discipline is administered in a manner consistent with the child's human *dignity* and in *conformity* with the present Convention. [emphasis added]

Once again, this provision should be interpreted in a manner consistent with the spirit of the Convention, the Guiding Principles and Articles 19 and 24. The Committee has taken such an approach, interpreting Article 28(2) as requiring States Parties to proscribe corporal punishment in schools.[60]

Finally, Article 37(a) provides that:

> States Parties shall ensure that no child shall be subjected to torture or other cruel, inhuman or degrading treatment or punishment.

This provision could be interpreted as setting a higher threshold of physical or mental injury that must be suffered by the child, a threshold that has correlations with the question whether the corporal punishment applied was excessive and went beyond the bounds of reasonable chastisement. The judgment of the European Court in *A v United Kingdom*[61] provides some support to the contention that corporal punishment constitutes a violation of Article 37(a). In some respects, Article 37(a) stands alone in a discussion of whether the Convention prohibits corporal punishment, because the articles considered above may be interpreted as proscribing any corporal punishment. Article 37(a) does not necessarily do so, since it does not proscribe less severe punishment. But, in terms of the setting of a threshold of injury, it may be that Article 37(a) should be read in a manner similar to the other Convention provisions that purport to deal with corporal punishment.

---

[59] Article 24(3). The New Zealand Family Court implicitly recognised this right in *Ausage v Ausage* [1998] NZFLR 72, distinguishing *Erick v Police* 7/3/85, Heron J, HC Auckland M 1734/84, which had had regard to the harsher disciplinary regime for children in Niue. In *Ausage* Judge Somerville said that "the degree of force which might be reasonable to apply for the purposes of correction under s 59 does not differ according to ethnic or religious belief" (at 79).

[60] Concluding Observations regarding the United Kingdom (CRC/C/15 Add.34 (1995)) at para 16.

[61] (1998) 27 EHRR 611.

In its consideration of State Party reports, the Committee has, on numerous occasions, expressed particular concern over corporal punishment and its inconsistency with the principles and provisions of the Convention.[62] The dialogue between the Committee on the Rights of the Child and New Zealand, with respect to s 59, indicates that the Committee favours a narrower approach given its repeated recommendation that s 59 be repealed. The issue was subject to some commentary by the Committee when it considered New Zealand's initial report[63] during its fourteenth session in 1997. The Committee raised the issue on a number of occasions, noting that:

> The worst abuse often took place in the family. Compliance with article 19 of the Convention so as to prevent all forms of abuse would, however, require some very strong legislation. New Zealand legislation allowed a degree of violence regarded as reasonable in the circumstances. The risk of that approach was that it was arbitrary and introduced the notion that violence against children might be permissible in some situations.[64]

The New Zealand response to this expression of concern was "that social and educational measures were taken to protect children against violence in

---

[62] See, e.g., its Concluding Observations regarding Ireland (CRC/C/15/Add.85 (1998)), in which the Committee expressed its concern about the lack of legislative prohibition of corporal punishment within the family, which, in the Committee's opinion, contravened the principles and provisions of the Convention (para 16). It suggested that the State Party take all appropriate measures, including those of a legislative nature, to prohibit and eliminate the use of corporal punishment within the family. It also suggested that awareness-raising campaigns be conducted to ensure that alternative forms of discipline are administered in a manner consistent with the child's human dignity and in conformity with the Convention (para 39). Similarly, in the Concluding Observations regarding the United Kingdom (CRC/C/15/Add.34 (1995)), the Committee recommended that physical punishment of children in families be prohibited in the light of the provisions set out in Articles 3 and 19 of the Convention. In connection with the child's right to physical integrity, as recognised by the Convention, namely in Articles 19, 28, 29 and 37, and in the light of the best interests of the child, the Committee suggested that the State Party consider undertaking additional education campaigns. The Committee said (at para 31) "Such measures would help to change societal attitudes towards the use of physical punishment in the family and foster the acceptance of the legal prohibition of the physical punishment of children." Finally, in its Concluding Observations with regard to Zimbabwe (CRC/C/15/Add.55 (1996)) the Committee expressed its concern at the acceptance in the legislation of the use of corporal punishment in school, as well as within the family. It stressed the incompatibility of corporal punishment, as well as any other form of violence, injury, neglect, abuse or degrading treatment, with the provisions of the Convention, in particular Articles 19, 28(2) and 37 (para 18). The Committee has also made statements in its concluding observations that generally condemn corporal punishment of children, but without any special reference to the family context. See, e.g., its Concluding Observations regarding Sri Lanka (CRC/C/15/Add.40 (1995)), at paras 15 and 32.

[63] CRC/C/28/Add.3, 12/10/1995.

[64] Summary Record of the 364th meeting: New Zealand, CRC/C/SR.364, 23/1/97, at para 78.

general"[65] but that the government of the time had not reached a consensus on the repeal of s 59.[66] In its Concluding Observations the Committee expressed "its concern at the authorisation provided by section 59 of the Crimes Act to use physical force against children as punishment within the family".[67] To that end, the Committee recommended that New Zealand:

> Review legislation with regard to corporal punishment of children within the family in order to effectively ban all forms of physical or mental violence, injury or abuse.[68]

The potential for conflict between the legality of corporal punishment and New Zealand's obligations under the Convention re-emerged with the publication of New Zealand's periodic report to the Committee.[69] The periodic reports, which States Parties are required to submit to the Committee under Article 44(1)(b), are supposed to conform to the Committee's *General Guidelines Regarding the Form and Contents of Periodic Reports*. In relation to corporal punishment, the *Guidelines* require States Parties to indicate all appropriate legislative, administrative, social and educational measures taken pursuant to Article 19. In particular, the *Guidelines* require States Parties to indicate in their periodic reports:

> Whether legislation (criminal and/or family law) includes a prohibition of all forms of physical and mental violence, including corporal punishment, deliberate humiliation, injury, abuse, neglect or exploitation, inter alia within the family, in foster and other forms of care, and in public or private institutions, such as penal institutions and schools.[70]

New Zealand's response was that s 59:[71]

> Provides sufficient protection through:
> - The fact that section 59 does not sanction any form of violence or abuse against children.
> - The provisions of the Children, Young Persons, and Their Families Act 1989 provide protection when abuse is substantiated.

This interpretation echoes the attempts by the judiciary to reconcile the apparent conflict between these two Acts by excluding force used by a parent

---

[65] Summary Record of the 365th meeting: New Zealand, CRC/C/SR.365, 4/4/97, at para 13.
[66] Ibid.
[67] Concluding Observations of the Committee on the Rights of the Child: New Zealand, CRC/C/15/Add.71, 24/1/97, at para 16.
[68] Ibid, at para 29.
[69] Ministry of Youth Affairs, *Children in New Zealand. United Nations Convention on the Rights of the Child* Second Periodic Report of New Zealand (2000).
[70] CRC/C/58 (1996), at para 88.
[71] *Children in New Zealand*, supra note 69, at para 79.

by way of correction from the definition of "violence".[72] This interpretation suggests that the hitting of a child across the legs and face would not constitute violence, especially when it does not result in physical injury such as marking or bruising.[73] This distinction was reiterated by a New Zealand representative in 2003, when she stated:

> that Section 59 of the Crimes Act 1961 did not legitimise the use of physical force against children but provided a defence for the use of such force under certain circumstances. The Government had given careful consideration to its options under Section 59, taking into account the diversity of views surrounding the issue and its desire to ensure full compliance with the Convention. The Cabinet had recently decided to defer further consideration of the issue until December 2005 and to embark in the meantime on a public education strategy on alternatives to physical punishment. As Section 59 did not specify what constituted reasonable force, it was likely that court decisions would change over time to reflect changes in public attitudes.[74]

This approach to the issue of corporal punishment continued to worry to the Committee on the Rights of the Child, as evidenced by the concern expressed by the Committee, in 2003, that despite a review of legislation, New Zealand has still not amended s 59 of the Crimes Act 1961. While it welcomed the Government's public education campaign to promote positive, non-violent forms of discipline within the home, the Committee emphasised that the Convention required the protection of children from all forms of violence, which includes corporal punishment in the family, and which should be accompanied by awareness-raising campaigns on the law and on children's rights to protection.[75] Accordingly, the Committee recommended that New Zealand:

a) Amend legislation to prohibit corporal punishment in the home;
b) Strengthen public education campaigns and activities aimed at promoting positive, non-violent forms of discipline and respect for children's right to human dignity and physical integrity, while raising awareness about the negative consequences of corporal punishment.[76]

Accordingly, treaty monitoring bodies seem to be moving away from an analysis of corporal punishment which focuses upon finding violations of the child's right to be free from cruel, inhuman and degrading punishment only where the physical force used to discipline is excessive. Rather, the prohibition on

---

[72] *T v T* 9/7/99, Judge Robinson, FC Auckland FP 004/919/90.

[73] *Steyn v Brett* [1997] NZFLR 312.

[74] Committee on the Rights of the Child (2003), Second periodic report of New Zealand (continued) CRC/C/SR.897, at para 47.

[75] Committee on the Rights of the Child (2003), Concluding Observations of the Committee on the Rights of the Child: New Zealand, CRC/C/15/Add.216, at para 29.

[76] Ibid, at para 30.

cruel, inhuman or degrading punishment seems to extend to the corporal punishment of children without qualification.

The effect of the latter development is two-fold. First, in this particular context, it resolves the hitherto exacerbating effect of the perceived distinction between the public and private spheres upon the already problematic interrelationship between domestic and international law. This distinction had been used to place actions by private individuals, which otherwise could be considered to be human rights violations, beyond the protection offered by human rights instruments, on the ground that violations of the latter are generally applicable only to actions involving the State. It had equally been argued that it is the rejection of this distinction between the public and the private that has formed the general theoretical basis for the international human rights movement.[77] However, such a rejection of the public/private divide is now clearly exemplified by the expanded interpretation of the various provisions of the human rights treaties as discussed in *A v United Kingdom*.[78] This analysis along with the recent comments regarding physical punishment made by the Committee Against Torture provide some of the clearest examples of the application of international human rights norms to the private sphere. The second effect of the changing focus away from excessive force and the consequent extension of the prohibition of cruel, inhuman or degrading punishment to include all corporal punishment is more in line with the fundamental principles of non-discrimination and equality that provide that human rights protection is to be accorded to all without (unjustifiable) distinction.

New Zealand has ratified, amongst other human rights treaties, the ICCPR and the first Optional Protocol, the ICESCR, CAT, and the United Nations Convention on the Rights of the Child. In addition, New Zealand has sought to incorporate the principles and provisions of the Declaration and the ICCPR with the passing of the New Zealand Bill of Rights Act 1990. However, the above analysis indicates that by retaining s 59 on its statute books, New Zealand is failing to meet its international obligations regarding the rights of the child both in terms of the prohibition on cruel, inhuman and degrading punishment and the principles of non-discrimination and equality. The question that arises is whether such a finding can be regarded as having any impact within the domestic sphere.

It has been argued that as long as the majority of the New Zealand public supports the corporal punishment of children, there is no democratic basis for

---

[77] R Eisler, "Human Rights: Towards An Integrated Theory for Action" (1987) 9 Human Rights Quarterly 287, at 290.

[78] European Court of Human Rights, 23 September 1998.

the abolition of corporal punishment and, as a correlation, New Zealanders
are free to ignore international obligations requiring the abolition of the
parental right of corporal punishment.[79] Although it may be correct to view
international human rights treaties, such as the ICCPR and the Convention on
the Rights of the Child, as instruments of international law which do not bind
New Zealand courts, nevertheless, such treaties do provide a context in which
current social and legal standards may be set, thereby providing a standard
according to which ambiguous domestic legislation may be interpreted.[80]
Accordingly:

> if a statute touches on the subject-matter of the treaty, its interpretation can be
> influenced by the principle that the legislature is unlikely to have legislated in a
> manner contrary to its international obligations.[81]

Although the views of the Committee on the Rights of the Child are not legally
binding on New Zealand courts, it is not accurate to state that a rejection of
the Committee's views is entirely without consequence. It is to this aspect of
New Zealand's international obligations that the judiciary have made explicit
reference. It has equally been argued that a State Party (such as New Zealand)
may interpret an article of the Convention on the Rights of the Child in a
manner inconsistent with any interpretation that may be advanced by the
Committee on the Rights of the Child, because the Committee is not an
authoritative interpreter of the Convention.[82] This assertion may be true to
the extent that the opinions of treaty-monitoring bodies are "a reliable guide
to the Committee's thinking and set out its understanding of what particular
articles require of state parties"[83] and are no more binding on domestic courts
than the treaties themselves. However, such a dismissive approach to the significance of New Zealand's obligations under international law does not seem

---

[79] Adhar and Allan, supra note 14, at 8. The authors use a 1993 survey as a basis for this
assertion. In terms of their assertion that Maori and Pacific Islanders strongly favour corporal
punishment, it is worth noting that a Hamilton-based Samoan High Chief recently stated that
smacking children was not part of Samoan culture and that high-profile cases where custom
had been used as an excuse for violence had "disgraced the whole country": "Culture Claims
'a Disgrace'" *Waikato Times*, 3 November 2001. Similarly, a past president of the Maori
Women's Welfare League acknowledged that there had been a change in attitude towards
smacking, and said that the Annual Conference of the League has "stressed that Maori were to
stop harming their children": "Maori League Looks to New Ways of Parenting" *New Zealand
Herald*, 25 September 2000.
[80] G Austin, "The UN Convention on the Rights of the Child – and Domestic Law" 1(4)
Butterworths Family Law Journal (1994), 63.
[81] J Burrows, *Statute Law in New Zealand*, Wellington, Butterworths, 1992, at 238.
[82] Ahdar and Allan, supra note 14, at note 61, quoting a letter to the authors from Professor
Malcolm Evans, Professor of Public International Law at the University of Bristol.
[83] Ibid.

to be reflected in the jurisprudence of the New Zealand courts. In spite of the fact that the ability of the judiciary to incorporate international principles is governed by the primacy of New Zealand domestic law over international law,[84] the judiciary have had recourse to consider international norms when interpreting ambiguous statutes or when filling gaps in the common law.[85] For example, in *Wellington District Legal Services Committee v Tangiora*, Keith J referred to:

> . . . the presumption of statutory interpretation that so far as its wording allows legislation should be read in a way which is consistent with New Zealand's international obligations, eg *Rajan v Minister of Immigration* [1996] 3 NZLR 543 at p 551. That presumption may apply whether or not the legislation was enacted with the purpose of implementing the relevant text . . .[86]

Justice Keith also said that "use of the international provisions to assist the reading of the national text does not expressly depend on the existence of relevant international obligations".[87]

This relationship between international law and domestic obligations was considered more recently by Thomas J in his minority judgment in *Attorney-General v E*.[88] This case considered New Zealand's obligations under the United Nations Convention relating to the Status of Refugees 1951 and the Protocol Relating to the Status of Refugees 1967. According to Thomas J:

> It cannot be thought that these obligations were undertaken half-heartedly or tongue-in-cheek. They are to be given effect. When, therefore, the actions of the state . . . conflict with this country's international obligations it is the clear duty of the Court to ensure that those obligations are observed.[89]

---

[84] Austin, supra note 80. In other words, "if a statute touches on the subject-matter of the treaty, its interpretation can be influenced by the principle that the legislature is unlikely to have legislated in a manner contrary to its international obligations": Burrows, *Statute Law in New Zealand* (1992) supra note 81, at 230. Nevertheless, there have been several cases where this has been explicitly recognised. For example, in *Auckland Healthcare Services v T* [1996] NZFLR 670, 671, Patterson J referred to Article 6 of the UN Convention on the Rights of the Child, which placed New Zealand, as a State Party to the Convention, under an obligation to recognise that every child has an inherent right to life and stated that Parties shall ensure to the maximum extent the survival and development of the child. Similarly, in *Auckland Healthcare Services v L* [1998] NZFLR 998, 1003 the Court took into account the provisions of Article 3(1) of the Convention on the Rights of the Child in conjunction with the provisions pertaining to the right to life in Article 6(1) of the ICCPR.

[85] S Joseph, J Schulz and M Castan, M, *The International Covenant on Civil and Political Rights: Cases, Material and Commentary*, Oxford, OUP, 2000, 9.

[86] [1998] 1 NZLR 129, 137, quoting from *New Zealand Air Line Pilots' Association Inc v Attorney-General* [1997] 3 NZLR 269, 289 (CA).

[87] Ibid.

[88] [2000] 3 NZLR 257.

[89] Ibid, at 273.

Such observations may not amount to an explicit statement that New Zealand must *defer* either to its international human rights treaty obligations, or to the views of the respective treaty monitoring bodies as interpreter of these obligations. For example, the Human Rights Committee, the monitoring body of the ICCPR, has been described as being the pre-eminent interpreter of that treaty.[90] Although the Committee is not a judicial body its views are strong indicators of the legal obligations incurred by States Parties upon ratification of the Covenant. Nevertheless, they are indicative of the necessary relationship between a State Party and a human rights treaty monitoring body that results from ratification. Consequently, inasmuch as a rejection by a State Party of the views of the Human Rights Committee indicates bad faith towards its Covenant obligations,[91] rejection of the views of the Committee on the Rights of the Child is an indication of bad faith on the part of New Zealand towards its obligations under the latter Convention.[92]

The New Zealand judiciary has increasingly paid attention to international treaty norms, and has made specific reference to the provisions in the Convention on the Rights of the Child, with varying degrees of success in protecting the rights of the child.[93] Although the advances made in terms of international human rights law regarding corporal punishment are to be welcomed, as is the judiciary's reliance on international norms, it is rather disappointing that such moves do not incorporate an analysis of the prohibition on discrimination. The issue of corporal punishment remains equally problematic in terms of the domestic law, where some aspects of the distinction between the public and private spheres continue to form the basis for differential, and arguably discriminatory, levels of protection from violence as between children and adults. The issue of corporal punishment in relation to domestic law will be addressed in the ensuing analysis.

---

[90] Joseph, Schultz and Castan, supra note 85, at 14–15; Nowak, supra note 34, at 96–97.
[91] Nowak, ibid, at 96–97.
[92] By virtue of Article 44 of the Convention on the Rights of the Child, New Zealand is required:

  1. . . . to submit to the Committee, through the Secretary-General of the United Nations, reports on the measures they have adopted which give effect to the rights recognized herein and on the progress made on the enjoyment of those rights:
  (a) Within two years of the entry into force of the Convention for the State Party concerned;
  (b) Thereafter every five years.

  2. Reports made under the present Article shall indicate factors and difficulties, if any, affecting the degree of fulfilment of the obligations under the present Convention. Reports shall also contain sufficient information to provide the Committee with a comprehensive understanding of the implementation of the Convention in the country concerned.

[93] *Tavita v Minister of Immigration* [1994] 2 NZLR 257; *Auckland Healthcare Services v L* [1998] NZFLR 998, 1001; *Auckland Healthcare Services v T* [1996] NZFLR 670, 671.

5. Discrimination or Differentiation? Section 59 within the Framework of New Zealand Domestic Legislation

Section 59 of the Crimes Act 1961 provides:

(1) Every parent of a child and, subject to subsection (3) of this section, every person in the place of the parent of a child is justified in using force by way of correction towards the child, if the force used is reasonable in the circumstances.

(2) The reasonableness of the force used is a question of fact.

(3) Nothing in subsection (1) of this section justifies the use of force towards a child in contravention of section 139A of the Education Act 1989.

Section 59 provides specific statutory protection against criminal prosecutions and civil liability for child assault and other charges. The protection offered to parents (and, consequently, the limited protection offered to children against physical injury) by s 59 is an anomaly in a number of respects.

First, within the terms of the section itself, s 59(3) relates to the prohibition by s 139A of the Education Act 1989 of corporal punishment in early childhood centres or registered schools unless the person administering the punishment is a guardian of the child. On the one hand, this provision has positive implications as it constitutes evidence of changing societal values regarding the appropriateness of the physical punishment of children. On the other hand, s 59(3) of the Crimes Act and s 139A of the Education Act seem to accord even greater legitimacy to the corporal punishment of children by their parents. Second, within the framework of the Crimes Act itself, s 59 is discriminatory in that it provides unequal legal protection and redress against the application of force as between adults and children. For example, in terms of the use of force and injury suffered, s 195 of the Crimes Act, relating to the offence of cruelty to a child, states that cruelty constitutes "wilfully ill-treating . . . the child . . . in a manner likely to cause him unnecessary suffering, actual bodily harm or injury to health". However, this section does not prevent the exercise of force by way of correction,[94] which indicates that children may be subjected to "necessary" suffering, actual bodily harm and injury to health. Similarly, in terms of the use of force, the protection provided by s 59 may be contrasted with the provisions of s 196 of the Crimes Act. Section 196 concerns the assault of one person by another person, with assault being defined in terms of the intentional application of force.[95] "Force" has been given a wide interpretation that does not necessarily include violence[96] and that does

---

[94] RJ Robertson, FB Adams, JN Finn, R Mahoney, *Adams on Criminal Law*, Wellington, Brookers, 2001, at 422.

[95] Section 2(1) Crimes Act 1961.

[96] *Police v Raponi* (1989) 5 CRNZ 291, 296.

not turn on the amount of force used,[97] so that "mere touching can amount
to an assault . . . a pat on the bottom . . . can be an assault".[98] Section 59, in
speaking of "reasonable force", indicates that some degree of force may be
suffered by a child (since only excessive injury amounts to an unreasonable
use of force by way of correction). By contrast, a mere pat or even an appre-
hension of the infliction of force by one adult upon another can attract a criminal sanction.[99] In many respects, the anomalous character of s 59 constitutes
one of the last remnants of the distinction between the public and private
spheres. Although societal or governmental interference in family life and the
private sphere has never been seen to be encouraged, it has, nevertheless,
come to be recognised as being commonplace. Section 59 provides prime evidence of the artificiality of this distinction at the level of domestic law.

Section 59 is also an anomaly in terms of the broader legal framework relating to State intervention in instances where violence is alleged. For example,
the Domestic Violence Act 1995 (DVA) has been described as forming "the
backbone of the argument against corporal punishment of children",[100] although
the Act does not refer specifically to corporal punishment. Section 3(1) of the
Act defines domestic violence as being "violence against that person by any
other person with whom that person is . . . in a domestic relationship" and s 3(2)
defines "violence" as including "physical abuse" but does not define what
amounts to physical abuse. However, s 3(4) provides that a single act may
amount to abuse for the purposes of s 3(2). The overall aim of the Act is set
out in s 5(1), which provides:

> The object of this Act is to reduce and prevent violence in domestic relationships
> by—
>
> (a) Recognising that domestic violence, in *all its forms*, is unacceptable behaviour;
> and
> (b) Ensuring that, where domestic violence occurs, there is effective legal protec-
> tion for its victims. [emphasis added]

The apparent conflict between the DVA and s 59 was considered by Fisher J
in the High Court case of *Sharma v Police*.[101] Justice Fisher had to consider the

---

[97] *Police v Bannin* [1991] 2 NZLR 237; 244.
[98] *Police v Raponi*, supra note 96, at 296.
[99] Section 196 Crimes Act 1961.
[100] C Hall, "Child Abuse v Domestic Discipline" (1998) Youth Law Review (November) 10.
[101] [2003] 2 NZLR 473; [2003] NZFLR 852. Mrs Sharma had obtained a temporary protection
order against Mr Sharma, the appellant, the purpose of which was to prevent Mr Sharma from
physically abusing either herself or her nine-year-old son who was the complainant. Mrs Sharma
had asked her son to retrieve some items from the house that they used to share with the appellant. When the child refused to replace a particular item and instead pulled a face at the appellant,
the latter slapped the complainant in the head as well as hitting him twice in the legs.

question of whether the defence of child discipline would be available to a person against whom a protection order had been obtained under the DVA. Although he stated that he would have expected the DVA to exclude expressly a s 59 defence,[102] he found the statutory wording to require otherwise. According to Fisher J, the breach of a protection order contrary to ss 19(1)(a) and 49(1)(a) of the DVA would be an act for which anyone can be punished under any other enactment, and it followed that the child discipline defence offered by s 59 of the Crimes Act would be available to a defendant in such circumstances. Such an interpretation of the law was strengthened, in his opinion, by the fact that this type of offence would be committed only if the defendant was responsible for physically abusing the protected person.[103] According to Fisher J:

> So long as s 59 of the Crimes Act remains part of the general law of this country it might be difficult to categorise reasonable force for child discipline as "physical abuse" in the absence of an express provision on the point in the Domestic Violence Act.[104]

Thus, it was with regret that Fisher J accepted that the DVA left a child discipline defence open even where a protection order was in force for the specific purpose of protecting the complainant against the defendant and that the defence was open to the appellant in the case at hand.[105] Although Fisher J's analysis is to be applauded, it is somewhat unfortunate that he did not further explore the discriminatory nature of the lower level of protection against violence to be afforded to children under the DVA, given that the purpose of this Act is to reduce and prevent violence in domestic relationships.

A final example of State intervention is s 14 of the Children, Young Persons, and Their Families Act 1989 (CYPFA), which relates to the granting of care and protection orders in instances of alleged violence against children. The interrelationship between this Act and s 59 was considered in *Re the Five M Children*.[106] Judge Inglis referred in detail to Fisher J's judgment in *Sharma* that there was no conflict between s 59 and the relevant provisions of the DVA. This allowed Judge Inglis to hold that, provided that the force used by Mrs C was by way of correction and reasonable in the circumstances, there would be no conflict between the provision of the CYPFA and s 59.[107] In reviewing the facts that gave rise to the corporal punishment of the children

---

[102] Ibid, at para 9.
[103] Ibid, at para 10.
[104] Ibid, at para 11.
[105] Ibid, at para 12. Fortunately, the defence failed on the facts as Fisher J concluded that the force used in the circumstances was not reasonable.
[106] [2004] NZFLR 337.
[107] Ibid, at paras 43–45.

involved, he found that s 59 prevailed. Given that the Department chose not to press the point, Judge Inglis was able to dispose of the potential legal conflict matter arising from a rigid application of Departmental policy and the complete legal protection provided by s 59 to Mrs C. However, in drawing the discussion to a close – and perhaps giving an indication of the delicate nature of the balance between the two pieces of legislation – he referred to the evidence of the psychologist who had interviewed the children and who, in Inglis J's opinion, had made the valid point that:

> it could be unwise to use physical discipline on children who need recovery from the psychological damage created by their previous experiences in a physically and emotionally abusive home. Indeed that reasoning could readily enough be extended by saying that any foster parent, dealing with children with that kind of past experience of neglect, deprivation and physical abuse from a parent, should realise that any form of punishment could be misunderstood by such a child, and that if needed it should be seen clearly by the child as necessary correction, not as a sign of dislike, indifference or rejection.[108]

Similarly, s 59 of the Care of Children Act 2004, which replaces s 16B of the Guardianship Act 1968, requires the Court to determine on the evidence whether allegations of violence are proved in any proceedings relating to an application for an order relating to the custody of, or access to, a child.[109] The dichotomy between the above legislative provisions, which seek to protect the child from family violence, and s 59 was recognised in a Family Court Judge's observation that:

> By retaining s 59 of the Crimes Act and enacting s 16B, the legislature on the one hand is gaining the support of those in the community who do not want corporal punishment, their view being satisfied by s 16B, but at the same time retains the support of those who consider corporal punishment appropriate by retaining s 59.[110]

According to the Judge, the only way to resolve "the apparent conflict between the two sections must be to exclude from the definition of 'violence' force used by a parent by way of correction . . .".[111] This point was revisited in *Bonnar v Fischbach*[112] when Judge Boshier referred to the definition of 'violence' as

---

[108] Ibid, at para 48.
[109] See, e.g., *Spence v Spence*, infra note 141, and accompanying text.
[110] *T v T* 9/7/99, Judge Robinson, FC Auckland FP 004/919/90, 9.
[111] Ibid.
[112] [2001] NZFLR 925. The applicant contended that s 16B of the Guardianship Act applied because the respondent psychologically abused and damaged their children and that this abuse is contemplated within the scope of s 16B, and that this should result in only supervised access by him to the children. The respondent denied such violence saying that he had merely disciplined them on occasions which did not amount to "violence" as defined by s 16A of the Guardianship Act.

specifically defined in s 16A of the Guardianship Act[113] as meaning physical abuse or sexual abuse, and offered the following definition of 'abusive behaviour':

> "Abusive" must be a clearly wrong use of physical force. Mere use of physical force or unwise use of force, is insufficient. The level and appropriateness of physical force alleged to have occurred, must bring it within a range that is plainly unacceptable.[114]

There is a overlap in current legislation between s 59 of the Crimes Act and the object and purpose of the DVA that gives rise to some concern, in spite of the assertion that the provisions of both Acts were not to be regarded as "not so inconsistent with or repugnant to each other, such that s 59 is deemed be repealed by the later statute".[115] This assertion downplays the object of the DVA, which is to render all forms of domestic violence unacceptable. Such an overlap between the statutes arises out of the failure of the DVA to refer to the disciplining of children or to define "physical abuse", a legislative gap that allows s 59 to be used in determining what amounts to domestic violence. As such, the broader legislative framework of State intervention in instances of family violence stops short of domestic discipline, as the ensuing judicial interpretation of the relevant statutory provisions demonstrate.

The interpretation of the above statutory provisions is a question of balance: whether force used was reasonable, and whether the "self-same act was either an obviously just act of parental correction or an act of revenge".[116] Striking the right balance is "a matter of degree and will depend in large measure on what can be perceived to be the current social view at any given time".[117] The current social view in New Zealand is that some degree of physical punishment is acceptable, despite New Zealand's international legal obligations suggesting otherwise. The question of reasonableness has been considered by the courts on a number of occasions but with scant reference to New Zealand's more general obligations under international human rights law, let alone the Convention on the Rights of the Child. An overview of the current social view may be gleaned from some recent judicial thinking regarding corporal punishment.

Steyn v Brett[118] concerned an application for a protection order under s 9 of the DVA. Judge Grace had to determine whether a father slapping his fourteen-year-old daughter across the cheek with an open hand, and hitting her legs,

---

[113] As replaced by s 58 of the Care of Children Act.
[114] *Bonnar* v Fischbach, supra note 112, at para 48.
[115] *Ausage v Ausage* [1997] NZFLR 72, 76.
[116] *R v Drake* (1902) NZLR 478, 487, per Edwards J.
[117] *Kendall v Director of Social Welfare* (1986) 3 FRNZ 1, 12.
[118] [1997] NZFLR 312.

amounted to domestic violence requiring a protection order. Judge Grace was
of the opinion that the parties were in a domestic relationship, thereby satisfying the provisions of s 3(1). He noted that s 3(4) provides that a single act or
incident may amount to abuse, and that the Court was bound by the High
Court's decision in *Erick v Police*[119] that the domestic discipline of children did
not amount to the physical abuse of children.[120] Judge Grace noted that social
attitudes towards domestic discipline had changed in New Zealand in recent
years, and that the DVA was indicative of current social attitudes. However,
he was of the opinion that the protection of the DVA could not be invoked in
the case at hand because the applicant had provoked her father into hitting
her. He observed that "this is not a case where the respondent has slapped the
applicant for no apparent reason",[121] that the applicant had acted neither
calmly nor rationally, and that the respondent's behaviour was merely a spon-
taneous reaction to such behaviour.[122] Furthermore, he was of the opinion
that since the applicant did not require any medical treatment and no bruising or marking arose from the "incident", the slapping of the applicant across
the cheek did not constitute physical abuse for the purposes of s 3(2)(a) of the
DVA (although he did concede that the behaviour of the respondent was
inappropriate).[123]

Similarly, *Ausage v Ausage*[124] was concerned with the application of a protection order under the DVA. Somewhat uniquely, the Court considered some
of the relevant provisions of the Convention on the Rights of the Child, including Article 5 regarding the rights and responsibilities of parents, Article 14(2)
relating to the rights and responsibilities of parents to provide direction and
guidance to the child in the exercise of the child's right to freedom of thought,
conscience and religion, Article 19 regarding the child's right to protection
from all forms of violence, and Article 24(3) regarding the abolition of traditional practices prejudicial to the health of the child. Having had regard to
these provisions, Judge Somerville concluded that "one of the prime objectives of the Convention is to protect all children, regardless of race, colour, *sex*
or religion"[emphasis added].[125] Unfortunately, he declined to be drawn into
the debate whether physical discipline amounted to physical or mental violence, preferring instead to conclude that "the degree of force which might be
reasonable to apply for the purposes of correction under s 59 does not differ

---

[119] 7/3/85, Heron J, HC Auckland M 1734/84.
[120] *Steyn v Brett*, supra note 118, 316.
[121] Ibid, at 317.
[122] Ibid.
[123] Ibid.
[124] [1998] NZFLR 72.
[125] Ibid, at 79.

according to ethnic background or religious belief".[126] He concentrated solely on the issue of whether the degree of force used was reasonable and noted that, in determining whether it was or not, the Court should have regard to:[127]

- The age and maturity of the child
- Other characteristics of the child, such as physique, sex and state of health
- The type of offence
- The type and circumstances of punishment.

The Court found that the hitting and punching of the applicant in the middle of the night whilst she was in bed on one occasion when she was aged sixteen, as well as the striking of the applicant across the face causing injury when she was aged seventeen, amounted to domestic violence and went beyond the limit of reasonable force in s 59.

The Court's recognition of the applicability of the Convention on the Rights of the Child in *Ausage* invites further consideration of the conflict between the question of reasonableness in domestic law and the provisions of the Convention. Of the four considerations suggested by Judge Somerville for determining whether the force used is reasonable, the first is a violation of both the spirit and purpose of the Convention, as it focuses on the age of the child, thereby violating the principle of equality to be accorded to all children. The second violates the spirit, purpose and Article 2 of the Convention, as well as all other human rights treaties, in considering the sex of the child as being relevant to the degree of force used. The third consideration (type and circumstances of the punishment) would seem to be based upon the first two considerations because if the type and circumstances of the punishment are dependent upon the age and sex of the child it permits age-based and gender-based discrimination and so falls foul of the requirements of dignity and equality. Thus, Somerville J's analysis fails to take into account not only the Guiding Principle of non-discrimination and equality contained in Article 2 of the Convention, it also seems to disregard the principles of non-discrimination to be found in domestic human rights legislation, particularly with regard to gender discrimination given the limited application to age discrimination.[128]

Similarly, the extent to which the rights of parents are prioritised over those of the child may be observed in the ensuing determination by Judge Somerville of the law of New Zealand as:

> In inflicting punishment the parent must act in good faith, having a reasonable belief in a state of facts which would justify the application of force. In such a

---

[126] Ibid.
[127] Ibid, at 80.
[128] Section 19 New Zealand Bill of Rights Act 1990; s 21 Human Rights Act 1991.

case the parent would be protected from liability even though the factual position as he reasonably believes it to be is not actually the case. The purpose of the
punishment must therefore be both subjectively and objectively reasonable.[129]

Nowhere in his judgment does Judge Somerville refer to what is arguably the
most significant of the Guiding Principles of the Convention, namely the principle contained in Article 3(1) requiring that "In all actions concerning children . . . undertaken by . . . courts of law . . . the best interests of the child shall
be a primary consideration". Instead the Judge seems to give primary consideration to the rights and interests of the parents, and the reasonableness of the
punishment, in determining whether the parents could avail themselves of the
protection provided by s 59.

The question of domestic discipline has arisen also under the s 14 of the
Children, Young Persons, and Their Families Act 1989, which relates situations in which children may be in need of care and protection. In *In Re I, T,
M & J*,[130] Judge Moss considered the question of the reasonableness of the
punishment in terms of whether a weapon or instrument was used, and observed
that "generally where a weapon is used that factor will move the incident of
punishment across the line from reasonable discipline into physical abuse".[131]
In that case children had been struck by their father either with sticks or by
blows to the face with his hand. The children suffered both physical injury and
emotional distress. The question that the Court had to consider was whether
"the physical disciplining of the children, is such that the children are physically
harmed or abused and as a result of that, in need of care and protection".[132]

Judge Moss relied heavily on the judgment of Judge Somerville in *Ausage*,
and drew on his summary that "in order to be lawful the punishment must be
both subjectively and objectively reasonable".[133] He also adopted the formulation of the standards set by the American Academy of Paediatrics, which
defined spanking as "Physically non-injurious, intended to modify behaviour
and administered with the open hand to the extremities or buttocks".[134] Judge
Moss concluded that the incidents of punishment suffered by the children could
not be justified by s 59, that they were serious incidents of physical abuse that
were likely to reoccur and that, as a result, State intervention in the form of a
care and protection order under s 14 was warranted.[135]

---

[129] *Ausage v Ausage*, supra note 124, 80.
[130] [2000] NZFLR 1089.
[131] Ibid, at 1100.
[132] Ibid, at 1099.
[133] Ibid, at 1100.
[134] Ibid, at 1099.
[135] Ibid, at 1101–1103.

Whether domestic discipline constituted child abuse was most recently considered by the New Zealand courts in *Spence v Spence*,[136] which concerned an application for custody and access. Section 16B of the Guardianship Act 1968[137] required the courts to consider, in determining whether to grant custody or access to the party against whom the allegations of violence have been made, the following:

- The nature and seriousness of the violence used;
- How recently the violence occurred;
- The frequency of the violence;
- The likelihood of further violence occurring; and
- The physical or emotional harm caused to the child by the violence.

Judge Johnston reviewed the relevant statutory provisions (including the DVA, the Guardianship Act and s 59 of the Crimes Act) and several judicial decisions regarding the interpretation of reasonable force (including *Kendall*,[138] *Ausage*[139] and *T v T*[140]). The children in question had been hit by their father with a variety of instruments which had resulted in bruising, welts and marks. The father acknowledged that the younger the children were, the more often they were hit, and he admitted to striking one of his children when she was only eight or nine months old.[141] According to Judge Johnston such punishment "involved force excessive in the circumstances"[142] upon children who were too young to understand that they had done something wrong or to adjust their behaviour. The force used was:

> excessive, unreasonable and abusive. It was . . . violence. It is used by a person in power to control others who are in no position to defend themselves, offer any resistance, or express any view.[143]

In some respects a distinction should be drawn between *Steyn* and *Ausage*, on the one hand, and *In Re I, T, M & J* and *Spence*, on the other, in that both the Care of Children Act (to the extent that it replaces the Guardianship Act in this context) and the Children, Young Persons, and Their Families Act are aimed at balancing the protection of children with the maintenance of familial relationships, a balance that underpins both domestic and international law regarding child protection. The discrepancy in the protection resulting

---

[136] [2001] NZFLR 275.
[137] The legislative forerunner to the Care of Children Act 2005.
[138] *Kendall v Director of Social Welfare*, supra note 117.
[139] *Ausage v Ausage*, supra note 124.
[140] *T v T* 9/7/99, Judge Robinson, FC Auckland FP 004/919/90.
[141] *Spence v Spence*, supra note 136, 277–283.
[142] Ibid, at 286.
[143] Ibid.

from a discriminatory interpretation of the DVA is less apparent. However, although the courts in *In Re I, T, M & J* and *Spence* were very clear in their determinations that the force used was excessive and constituted physical abuse, that the decision whether the children were in need of protection was partly dependent upon a determination whether the force used could be *justified* is a misguided shibboleth. The sole question should be whether the acts in question were sufficiently violent to warrant care and protection orders.

Case law indicates that juries are more prepared to accept that s 59 offers a defence even in cases where the force used is excessive, where implements are sometimes used to administer the discipline, and where physical marks are left on the child's body. This lack of consistency may be seen in a District Court case, where a jury decided that a father had been within his rights to strike his 12-year-old daughter with a hosepipe after she had interrupted him in the course of an argument with her sister, even though the 'smack' caused injury in the form of a welt on her back.[144] A jury also found a couple who disciplined the nine-year-old son of one of the couple with a bamboo stick not guilty of assault, after having heard evidence about the boy's history of bad behaviour.[145] Similarly, a father who smacked his son with a piece of wood about 30 centimetres by two centimetres about six or eight times, leaving linear bruises visible for several days, was found by a jury to have used reasonable force.[146] These cases surely lead one to question the assertion that, the defence of reasonable justification does not apply to "clear-cut instances of physical abuse . . . [that] fall outside the protection of s 59",[147] on the basis that the behaviour that is beyond "the pale" of s 59 is somewhat less than clear cut. Similarly, these cases also demand reconsideration of the assertion that:[148]

> Those on the other side of the debate have to rely on instances of the horrific, to slide insouciantly from legal smacking – a smack on the bottom to improve behaviour and inculcate discipline – to bashing over the head with a vacuum cleaner, or some such other clear instance of what is illegal *according to today's law* (and according to the vast preponderance of those who today smack their children). [emphasis added]

As such, juries, as representatives of the New Zealand population, seem to regard s 59 as providing protection for actions beyond "a smack on the bottom". The lower level of protection provided to children against assault and abuse is all too apparent from the above cases. Although it is argued that s 59 does not

---

[144] "Father Acquitted in Pipe Beating" *New Zealand Herald*, 3 November 2001.
[145] "Parents Not Guilty of Assault Over Bamboo Stick Beating" *New Zealand Herald*, 6 September 2001.
[146] "Smacking Father Used Reasonable Force – Jury" *The Dominion*, 23 February 2001.
[147] Ahdar and Allan, supra note 14, at 6.
[148] Ibid, at 7.

provide a defence to "the mop handle to the head sort of abuse that is already illegal"[149] it is difficult to distinguish between this type of illegal discipline and examples of the hosepipe and bamboo stick to the back varieties of parental discipline which have been regarded as justifiable levels of parental discipline.

Interpretations of s 59 in conjunction with the provisions of other Acts suggest that a degree of violence against children is acceptable. The point of departure is that there must be significant infliction of physical suffering upon the child before the courts determine that a parent has gone beyond the protection offered by s 59. Therefore, in terms of the criminal law, domestic violence and child protection legislation, the corporal punishment of children is a matter of degree – some physical discipline does not amount to assault, domestic violence or does not trigger care and protection orders. An analysis of the provisions of s 59 and its interrelationship with other legislation that focuses solely on whether the punishment was excessive or not does not allow for any discussions of whether the difference in the level of protection from any assault and violence as between children and adults is justifiable. There seems to be an implicit understanding that this difference is justifiable because it derives from a more general prioritisation of parental rights over those of children. This implicit justification is legitimised, legislatively speaking at least, by s 59 which expressly prioritises the right of parents to inflict corporal punishment upon their children over the right of such children to be free from such punishment, a right which more recently is being framed in terms of the right to be free from cruel, inhuman or degrading punishment. However, the question remains, irrespective of the existence of s 59, as to whether the different levels of protection, or the prioritisation of parental rights over children, between children and adults can be justified – whether it serves an important and significant objective which is rational and proportionate.

As the previous sections indicate, both international human rights law and New Zealand domestic law recognise the right to respect for family life and the rights that flow therefrom. In terms of children's rights the family unit is the object of particular protection because of the recognition that, in general, the rights and interests of the child are best served from within this family unit. This recognition also forms the basis for resisting State intervention and the maintenance of the public/private divide. The preservation of such concepts could amount to important and significant objectives which justify the tipping of the balance of rights in favour of parents. Thus, in terms of Dickson CJ's test in *Oakes*,[150]

---

[149] Ibid, at 7–8.
[150] *R v Oakes* [1986] 1 SCR 103 (SCC) [1986] 1 SCR 103; 1986 CanLII 46 (SCC), http://www.canlii.org.ezproxy.waikato.ac.nz:2048/ca/cas/scc/1986/1986scc7.html as viewed on 7 February 2005, at paras 69–70.

the protection to be accorded to the family unit and the importance of the role of parents within this unit is of sufficient importance within a free and democratic society to override some of the rights of children within that family unit. The wording of s 59, even its actual existence, would appear to be a means of giving explicit recognition to this balance and arguments in favour of its retention have focussed very much upon the upholding of these concepts. In spite of the recognition of these concepts as a sufficiently significant objective, the ensuing limitations on children's rights must satisfy a proportionality test. Thus, according to *Oakes*, the question remains as to whether the provisions of s 59 constitute measures that have been designed carefully to achieve this objective. In other words, are the provisions rationally connected to the objective? Unsurprisingly, the wording of s 59 does not make a (rational) connection between the right of parents to discipline their children and the legal protection that is accorded to the family unit. Judicial consideration of the statute has not focused directly upon the rationality of the objective as its focus has continued to be upon the degree of force used in the circumstances. It is perhaps arguable that the requirement for 'reasonable force' is an implicit recognition of this requirement for a rational connection.

The focus on the question of whether the force used, by both judges and juries alike, gives rise to consideration of both the second and third aspects of the proportionality test – which is that the measures adopted and their effects, even if rationally connected to the objective, must impair the rights or freedoms of children as little as possible. The debate at the national and international level ranges across whether corporal punishment amounts to a limitation of the rights of the child – whether that right is expressed in terms of the child's right to bodily integrity, the right to be free from abuse, or the right not to be subject to cruel, inhuman or degrading punishment – or whether such punishment needs to be excessive in order to trigger these rights and freedoms. However, the decisions in recent New Zealand cases must raise questions over whether the measures provided for in s 59, and perhaps more significantly given the various levels of actual bodily injury that have been inflicted upon children, constitute minimal impairment of the rights of children. It must be highly questionable as to whether the effect of the legal measures in s 59 which ultimately have been to justify the punishment of children with a beating from a hosepipe or a piece of wood, is rationally connected to the objective of securing the right to respect for family life and the related notion of resistance to State intervention into family life. Thus, in terms of the measures adopted in s 59 and particularly as a consequence of their effects, the different levels of protection from violence as between adults and children cannot be justified and, accordingly, should be regarded as discriminatory.

6. Conclusion

In terms of New Zealand's social policy regarding children and their rights, the statutory defence of domestic discipline is anomalous. New Zealand has signaled its acceptance of international obligations, obligations that render the corporal punishment of children unlawful. New Zealand has taken a number of steps towards trying to (re)educate New Zealanders about the use of corporal punishment, and has mounted a number of campaigns to educate the population on other means of discipline.[151] However, the message sent by the continued presence of s 59 on the statute books undermines any initiatives that the government may undertake, as it allows for a degree of violence to be used against children as a tool in the childrearing. The repeal of s 59 would not render the corporal punishment of children illegal. Whether such repeal would have a significant impact in reducing the rate of child abuse in New Zealand remains to be seen. However, it would go some way to redressing the imbalance between children's rights and parental rights, which is nothing more horrific than bringing the rights of children in line with the rights accorded to, if not enjoyed by, all other members of society.

---

[151] Such initiatives have come from both governmental and non-governmental organisations. For governmental initiatives, see the Office for the Commissioner for Children, which has published a significant amount of material, including: Office for the Commissioner for Children, *Think About it: Is Hitting Your Child Really a Good Idea?* Wellington, OCC, 2001; Office for the Commissioner for Children, *Hitting Children is Unjust*, Wellington, OCC, 2001; GM Maxwell and J Carroll-Lind, *The Impact of Bullying on Children*, Wellington, OCC, 1997; GM Maxwell and J Carroll-Lind, *Children's Experiences of Violence*, Wellington, OCC, 1996; B Wood, *Hey! We Don't Hit Anybody Here*, Wellington, OCC, 1996; I Hassall, *Hitting Children – Unjust, Unwise and Unnecessary* Wellington, OCC, 1993; B Wood, *Living in a No-Hitting Family: Children are Family Members Too: A Teaching Resource Kit*, Wellington, OCC, 1994; G Maxwell, *Physical Punishment in the New Zealand Home, Occasional Paper No 3*, Wellington, OCC, 1994. See also *Parenting Without Hitting/Smack-Free Zone/Wahi Patu Kore*, Information from "Alternatives to Smacking" Campaign, Department of Child, Youth and Family Services, Wellington. For non-governmental initiatives, see B Wood, *Submission to the Minister of Justice, Minister of Social Services and Minister of Youth Affairs from EPOCH New Zealand on Repeal or Amendment of Section 59 Crimes Act 1961*, 2001, available at http://epochnz.virtualave.net/paper_submission_section_59.html.

CHAPTER FIVE

TAKING LIBERTIES: THE DETENTION
OF THE AT-RISK CHILD IN IRELAND

1. Introduction

This chapter examines the protection accorded to the rights of those Irish
children who have been identified by the Irish courts as being children who
may for a multitude of reasons be regarded as being children at risk. In such
circumstances, these children become subject to State intervention where the
State exercises its *parens patriae* jurisdiction, a jurisdiction that is both constitutionally and legislatively mandated. This right of State intervention to secure
the welfare of children at risk should come accompanied, one would assume,
with a concomitant obligation to ensure that the State will in fact secure that
welfare. However, in terms of the reality of the extent to which the Irish State
meets these obligations, it has been stated that:

> when one examines what has been happening over the last few years, one cannot
> but be left with a sense of dismay. It is no exaggeration to characterise what has
> gone on as a scandal.[1]

The scandal referred to is that of the almost total failure of the State to secure
the rights of a portion of its citizens who are in need of special care, care which
often takes the form of containment and treatment in order to secure the welfare of the child. Where the State has managed to respond to the requirement
of containment and treatment, the response has varied from placing the child
in establishments that range from bed and breakfasts to penal institutions. It is
those instances of the confinement of at-risk children in penal institutions that
raise issues of age discrimination as both national and international law prohibit the detention of individuals in penal institutions where such detention is
not as a consequence of the committing of a criminal act. However, the lack
of care facilities for at-risk children has left the Irish courts with no option but
to order such detentions.

This chapter considers the State's obligation to secure the welfare and best
interests of the child and the extent to which this obligation may be, and has
been, used to justify differential treatment. Similarly to the issue of the child's
right to medical treatment considered in Chapter 2, this chapter considers

---

[1] *D.B. v The Minister for Justice* [1999] 1 IR 29, 43, Kelly J.

whether the principle of the best interests of the child should trump the principle of non-discrimination and equality. To that end, it examines whether the
Irish State in seeking to exercise its *parens patriae* mandate to protect and provide for at risk, non-offending children could have feasibly justified age-based
discrimination in the form of detention of such children in penal institutions.
In the context of the issue raised in this chapter, the principle of the best interests of the child is subject to the principles of non-discrimination and equality.
Although the protection of and provision for the child may be regarded as an
important and significant objective, the means used to achieve this objective
must be rational and proportionate in order to justify such differential treatment. Unlike the matters considered in Chapter 2, however, the limitations
considered in this chapter have derived from the failure of the Irish State, in
the form of the Government, to provide suitable alternate care facilities. It was
this failure that placed the Irish State in violation of both its obligations under
domestic and international law, violations that were recorded not only by the
domestic courts but also at the international level.

Part 2 of this chapter outlines the protection afforded to the at-risk child by
the Irish Constitution and legislative framework. Part 3 considers the manner
in which the Irish courts have interpreted such protection. Part 4 outlines the
standards of protection to be afforded to children at risk by international
human rights law. This chapter concludes with an analysis of the interrelationship between the principles of the welfare of the child and non-discrimination
thus highlighting the need to strike the appropriate balance between them in
order to avoid violations of the rights of the (at-risk) child.

2. Constitutional and Legislative Protection of the Rights of the At-Risk Child in Ireland

2.1. Constitutional Protection

The constitutional protection accorded to the rights of the at-risk child is
derived from a number of the provisions of the Constitution of Ireland 1937.
At a general level, Article 40.1 provides that all citizens shall, as human persons, be held equal before the law. However, Article 40.1 also states that the
provision allows the State, in its enactments, to have due regard to differences of
capacity, physical and moral, and of social function.[2] The State's regard for such
differences is balanced by the provisions of Article 40.3.1 which provides that:

> The State guarantees in its laws to respect and, as far as practicable by its laws,
> to defend and vindicate the personal rights of the citizen.

---

[2] *Bunreacht na hEireann*, Dublin, Government Stationery Office.

The manner in which these rights are to be defended is provided for in Article 40.3.2, which requires the State to "in particular, by its laws protect these rights as best it may from unjust attack". Finally, Article 40.4.1 states "No citizen shall be deprived of his liberty save in accordance with the law."

More particularly, in terms of the rights of the at-risk child, Article 42.4.1 provides that:

> The State shall provide for free primary education . . . and, *when the public good requires it, provide other educational facilities or institutions*. . . . [emphasis added]

In terms of the rights of the at-risk child, Article 42.5 is the most significant provision of the Constitution as it not only empowers the State to intervene into family life in order to protect more fully the rights of the child, but it also provides that such intervention must always be with due regard for the natural and imprescriptible rights of the child. It is against this background of constitutional protection and State intervention that the statutory provisions regarding at-risk children will now be considered.

2.2. *Legislative Protection*

The Child Care Act 1991 is the central piece of legislation in relation to children at risk in Ireland. The long title of the Act describes it as "an Act to provide for the care and protection of children and for related matters thereby clarifying the nature and scope of the powers and duties of the health boards in relation to child care practice." Section 3 of the Child Care Act 1991 sets out the duties of a health board in relation to the care and protection of children residing in its administrative area where a child is defined as a person under the age of 18 years other than a person who is or has been married.[3] To that end, s 3 provides:

1. It should be a function of every health board to promote the welfare of children in its area who are not receiving adequate care and protection.
2. In the performance of this function, a health board shall—
   (a) take such steps as it considers requisite to identify children who are not receiving adequate care and protection and co-ordinate information from all relevant sources relating to children in its area;
   (b) having regard to the rights and duties of parents, whether under the Constitution or otherwise—
      (i) *regard the welfare of the child as the first and paramount consideration*, and;
      (ii) in so far as is practicable, give due consideration, having regard to his age and understanding, to the wishes of the child;
   and

---

[3] Section 2 Child Care Act, 1991. Section 8(2) of the Act specifies the categories of children who are to be considered, in particular, as not receiving adequate care and protection.

    (c) have regard to the principle that it is generally in the best interests of a child to be brought up in a family.

Section 4(1) of the Act provides that:

> Where it appears to a health board that a child who resides or is found in its area requires care or protection that he is unlikely to receive unless he is taken into its care, it shall be the duty of the health board to take him into its care under this section.

Section 4(3) outlines the duties of a health board where the board takes a child into care as "(a) subject to the provisions of this section, to maintain the child in its care so long as his welfare appears to the board to require it and while he remains a child . . .". Section 5 of the Act provides health boards with the authority to deal with homeless children as follows:

> Where it appears to a health board that a child in its area is homeless, the Board shall enquire into the child's circumstances, and if the Board is satisfied that there is no accommodation available to him which he can reasonably occupy, then, unless the child is received into care of the Board under the provisions of this Act, the Board shall take such steps as are reasonable to make available suitable accommodation for him.

Section 16 of the Act imposes a duty upon the health board to institute proceedings:

> Where it appears to a health board with respect to a child who resides or is found in its area that he requires care or protection which he is unlikely to receive unless a court makes a care order or a supervision order in respect of him, it shall be the duty of the health board to make application for a care order or a supervision order, as it thinks fit.

Once a child has been taken into care, s 36 of the Act requires that:

> (1) . . . the health board shall provide such care for him, subject to its control and supervision, in such of the following ways as it considers to be in *his best interests* —. . .
>   (b) by placing him in residential care (whether in a children's residential centre registered under Part VIII in a registered home maintained by the health board or in a school or other suitable place of residence), or . . .
>   (d) by making such other suitable arrangements (which may include placing the child with a relative) as the health board thinks proper. [emphasis added]

In so far as it is relevant to at-risk children, s 38 provides that:

> 1. A health board shall make arrangements with the registered proprietors of children's residential centres or with other suitable persons to ensure the provision of an adequate number of residential places for children in its care;
> 3. A health board may, with the approval of the Minister, provide and maintain a residential centre or other premises for the provision of residential care for children in care.

Until the passing of 1991 Act, the Children Act 1908, in addition to the Irish Constitution, had provided the legislative framework for the care and protection of children. In spite of the fact that the 1991 Act repealed a number of sections of the Children Act 1908, s 58 of the 1908 Act continues to be the governing piece of legislation by which at-risk children come before the courts. Section 58(4) of the Children Act 1908 states:

> Where the parent or guardian of a child proves to a petty sessional court that he is unable to control the child, and that he desires the child to be sent to an industrial school under this Part of this Act, the court, if satisfied on inquiry that it is expedient so to deal with the child, and that the parent or guardian understands the results which will follow . . ., may order him to be sent to a certified industrial school: . . .

It is this piece of legislation that has given rise to considerable judicial attention as regards the powers of the State to intervene in order to promote and protect the at-risk child. Accordingly, there is considerable legislative provision in place which empowers the Irish health boards to act to protect the rights and welfare of the at-risk child. Unfortunately, although the Irish Parliament recently passed the Children Act 2001, which was designed to repeal the 1908 Act, to date, only a very few of the provisions of the 2001 Act have actually come into force and so current child care and protection measures continue to be based on the provisions of the 1908 and 1991 Acts. Consequently, the effectiveness of the health boards' powers continue to be based upon legislation that is almost a century old. Nevertheless, whilst such intervention has spawned considerable judicial consideration of the effect and manner of such intervention upon the rights of the at-risk child, as the following section demonstrates, neither the decisions of the Courts nor the legislative framework have much effect in the face of the Government's failure to provide secure accommodation to best ensure the rights and interests of the at-risk child.

3. Judicial Interpretation of the Constitutional and Legislative Protection Afforded to the At-Risk Child

3.1. F.N. v Minister for Education

The case of *F.N. v Minister for Education*[4] was the first of a number of cases in which the inherent jurisdiction of the High Court to direct the detention of

---

[4] [1995] 1 IR 409, http://80-www.lexisnexis.com.au.ezproxy.waikato.ac.nz:2048/cui/uni-login/default.htm?login.asp?uni=waikato, as accessed on 18 November 2002. The applicant was born on 6 May 1982. He was placed in the care of the Eastern Health Board on 18 October 1982. His mother died in 1990 but had no contact with him from 1983. The identity of his father was unknown. The Health Board placed the applicant in foster care in October 1982 where he

children on an interlocutory basis was first recognised.[5] In delivering his reserved judgment, Geoghegan J noted that the case related to application for relief by way of judicial review in the form of a declaration that the respondent Minister failed to protect and vindicate the applicant child's rights under Articles 40.3 and 42 of the Constitution. In addition, an order of mandamus was sought to direct the respondents to protect and vindicate the constitutional rights of the applicant by providing not only secure accommodation for the applicant but also providing for the religious and moral, intellectual, physical and social education of the applicant. In November 1994, the District Court had made an order pursuant to s 58(4) of the Children Act 1908, on the application of the Health Board, directing the applicant to be sent to a named certified industrial school. However, the principal of that school refused to admit the applicant, which he was legally entitled to do. The result was that there were no facilities that could provide a child with special treatment, attention and education which, to be effective, would have to contain an element of containment or detention. In response to this situation, Geoghegan J noted that:

> the remarkable fact is that an Act passed before the first world war with a few modern amendments is the only Act on the statute book which even attempts to deal with the problems encountered by this child.[6]

In rejecting an assertion by counsel for the respondent to the effect that while better care services and facilities, including education facilities for children such as the applicant, were highly desirable as a matter of policy, there was no constitutional obligation on the State to provide services beyond what is at present provided so as to cater for the very special needs of somebody like the applicant, Geoghegan J stated:

> It is remarkable that as far back as 1908 before ever a written Constitution was thought of and before modern ideas and knowledge about child development

---

remained until January 1994. At this point he was placed a residential home due behavioural problems. This placement proved unsuccessful, and pursuant to an order of court the applicant was placed in an Assessment Centre for a short period. The applicant subsequently stayed in Health Centres where he remained during the day and from where he was then taken to bed and breakfast accommodation provided Health Board. Psychiatric examination and assessment of the applicant had concluded that that F.N. had hyperkinetic conduct disorder, and required a period of time in a secure unit which could contain him safely while confronting his behaviour.

   [5] *F.N.* was followed by a number of further High Court decisions: *G.L. v Minister for Justice* (Unreported, High Court, Geoghegan J, 24 March 1995); *D.T. v Eastern Health Board* (Unreported, High Court, Geoghegan J, 10 February 1995); *D.D. v Eastern Health Board* (Unreported, High Court, Costello P., 3 May 1995); *P.S. v Eastern Health Board* (Unreported, High Court, Geoghegan J, 27 July 1995); *S.C. v Minister for Education* (Unreported, High Court, McGuinness J, 20 December 1996).

   [6] *F.N. v Minister for Education*, supra note 4, at 4.

and child problems had emerged, the legislature thought fit to make special statutory provisions for the care and upbringing of unruly children.[7]

Geoghegan J proceeded to consider decisions by the Supreme Court, particularly those decisions in which the constitutional rights of the child, in general, had been vindicated. First, he referred to the Supreme Court decision of *G. v An Bord Uchtala*[8] in which O'Higgins CJ had stated that:

> Having been born, the child has the right to be fed and to live, to be reared and educated, to have of the opportunity of working and of realising his or her full personality and dignity as a human being. These rights of the child, (and others which I have not enumerated) must equally be protected and vindicated by the State. . .[9]

The Supreme Court had further noted, in *G. v An Bord Uchtala*, that normally these duties would be carried out by the parents, nevertheless, in special circumstances the State had to take on the obligation. Geoghegan J also drew attention to that fact that the vindication by the State of a child's constitutional rights had been further elaborated upon by the Supreme Court in two further cases,[10] and having regard to the principles enunciated in these cases, he took the view that:

> where there is a child with very special needs which cannot be provided by the parents or guardian there is a constitutional obligation on the State under Article 42, s. 5 of the Constitution to cater for those needs in order to vindicate the constitutional rights of the child.[11]

In more recent years, the Irish courts have been faced with the challenge of determining the extent to which the Constitution could be interpreted to protect the rights of the at-risk child. Despite the fact that the courts have determined that the relevant constitutional provisions, as more clearly expressed in legislative provisions, are to be interpreted to extend to cover the rights of such children, a difficulty remains as the Irish Government continues to fail to protect these recognised rights.

3.2. *T.D. v Minister of Education and Others*

The Irish Supreme Court has dealt with the issue of the failure of the State to protect the constitutional rights of at-risk children. In the case of *T.D. v Minister*

---

[7] Ibid, at 5.
[8] [1980] IR 32.
[9] Ibid, at 56.
[10] *In Re The Adoption (No 2) Bill, 1987* [1989] IR 656 and *M.F. v Superintendent Ballymun Garda Station* [1991] 1 IR 189.
[11] *F.N. v Minister for Education*, supra note 4, at 6.

of Education,[12] the respondents had appealed a decision of the High Court in which the trial judge, Kelly J, had ordered them to take all steps necessary to facilitate the building and opening of a number of specified secure and high support units, stating:

> I have come to the conclusion that in the absence of an appropriate undertaking on the part of the Minister the time has now come for this court to take the next step required of it under the Constitution so as to ensure that the rights of troubled minors who require placement of the type envisaged are met.

> The order that I propose making will ensure that the Minister, who has already decided on the policy, lives up to his word and carries it into effect. I am neither dictating nor entering into questions of policy. But if the court is to keep faith with its own obligations under the Constitution and with the minors with whose welfare it is concerned the injunctions sought must be granted.[13]

The bases of the appeal were, first, that the applicants lacked *locus standi* and, second, that the High Court did not have the power to make the order that it did as the order effectively sought to compel the Minister to use his executive powers and, as a consequence of issuing this order, the High Court had entered into questions of policy in violation of the principle of separation of powers. In the process of considering these matters, the Supreme Court also considered the rights of at-risk children. To that end, the rights of the applicant minors were defined by Keane CJ as:

---

[12] *T.D. v Minister of Education,* Judgment of the Irish Supreme Court of 17 December 2001, as accessed on www.irlii.org, 25 October 2002. The appeal was the culmination of a lengthy sequence of such cases in the High Court, where the Court had been asked to ensure that the State discharged what had been claimed to be its constitutional obligation to provide for the accommodation needs of children with particular problems. The Supreme Court noted that, since the judgment and order had its origins in the first of the cases in the title, *T.D.*, it was convenient to set out the facts of that case at the outset. The applicant was born on 9 January 1983 and at the time of the Supreme Court case was aged 18 years. At the date of the judgment and order in the High Court, he was aged 17. He started his schooling in Goldenbridge National Schools, Dublin. He attended the Phoenix Park Special School for pupils with emotional disturbance for one year from 1990. He was then placed in Warrenstown House, an Eastern Health Board residential unit which also provided educational facilities, from May 1991 to September 1992. He attended St. Laurence O'Toole Special School until June 1995, but did not return in September as it was alleged that he was being bullied by other pupils. On 19 November 1996, the District Court made an order pursuant to s 58(4) of the Children Act 1908 as a result of which he was placed in St. Laurence's, Finglas, Dublin. Thereafter he was placed in a number of different institutions. At the date of the hearing in the High Court, he was living with his parents in Inchicore. The appellant sought an order of mandamus directing the respondents to provide for appropriate education suitable to the needs of the applicant in a suitable educational establishment. Ibid, at paras 1–4.

[13] *D. (T.) v Minister for Education* [2000] IEHC 21; [2000] 3 IR 62; [2000] 2 ILRM 321 (25 February, 2000), www.irlii.org, as accessed on 25 October 2002, at paras 68–69.

a right to be placed and maintained in secure residential accommodation so as to ensure, so far as practicable, his or her appropriate religious and moral, intellectual, physical and social education.[14]

Chief Justice Keane observed that the Constitution did not recognise such a right and, to the extent that it existed, it had to be classified as one of the unenumerated personal rights guaranteed under Article 40.3.1 of the Constitution, a construction that had been adopted previously by the High Court and the Supreme Court in *Ryan v The Attorney General*.[15] Chief Justice Keane also referred to O'Higgins CJ's observations on the rights of the child in *G. v An Bord Uchtala*, in which O'Higgins CJ had stated:

> The child also has natural rights. . . . Having been born, the child has the right to be fed and to live, to be reared and educated, to have the opportunity of working and of realising his/her full personality and dignity as a human being. These rights of the child (and others which I have not enumerated) must equally be protected and vindicated by the State. In exceptional cases the State, under the provisions of Article 40.5 of the Constitution, is given the duty, as guardian of the common good, to provide for a child born into a family where the parents fail in their duty towards that child for physical or moral reasons.[16]

Chief Justice Keane also noted that the rights of the child had also been recognised by the Supreme Court in *In Re: The Adoption (2) Bill 1987*, when Finlay CJ had stated that Article 42.5 also imposed the following obligations upon the State:

> In the exceptional cases envisaged by that section where a failure in duty has occurred, the State by appropriate means shall endeavour to supply the place of the parents. This must necessarily involve supplying not only the parental duty to educate but also the parental duty to cater for the other personal rights of the child.[17]

According to Keane CJ, this general recognition of the rights of the child was given particular expression with regard to the rights of the at-risk child by Geoghegan J in *F.N. v The Minister for Education and Others*. In that case, the Judge expressed the view that the right claimed on behalf of the applicant in that case – broadly similar to the right asserted on behalf of the applicants in the present case – was one of the unenumerated rights of children which parents were obliged to protect and uphold, and that their failure to do so rendered that case an exceptional case within the meaning of Article 42.5, in which the State was obliged to uphold and protect the right.[18]

---

[14] *T.D. v Minister of Education*, supra note 12, at para 57.

[15] *Ryan v The Attorney General* [1965] IR 294.

[16] *G. v An Bord Uchtala*, supra note 8, as quoted in *T.D. v Minister of Education*, supra note 12, at para 60.

[17] *In Re: The Adoption (2) Bill 1987*, supra note 10, as quoted in *T.D. v Minister of Education*, supra note 12, at para 61.

[18] *T.D. v Minister of Education*, supra note 12, at para 61.

Such rights, in Keane CJ's opinion, arose from the special position of children as being dependant on their parents. He was also of the view that the applicants in these and similar cases, because of behavioural problems deriving from various causes, clearly required special treatment in secure units and, as a result, they clearly constituted exceptional cases in which the State was under a duty to ensure that that their right to such treatment was upheld.[19] In his judgment, Keane CJ held that the State had an obligation to protect the rights of the at-risk child, he recognised that the High Court did have the power to hold that the State was violating the constitutional rights of the child, and found that the applicant children did in fact have *locus standi*. In spite of these findings, the Chief Justice held that the High Court was not empowered to dictate to the respondent the manner in which those rights should be protected as to do so would be a violation of the constitutionally-mandated separation of powers.[20]

In contrast, Denham J, the sole dissenting judge, stated that the constitutional rights of the applicant children were in issue as a consequence of the action or lack of action of the respondents.[21] She was of the opinion that the circumstances of these cases were exceptional and noted that there were circumstances in which a court had a duty to intervene to protect constitutional rights. Because of the exceptional circumstances of the cases at hand, Denham J was satisfied that the High Court did in fact have a jurisdiction to make the mandatory orders that were the subject of the appeal to the Supreme Court. Given the fact that the High Court was continuing to review the situation in addition to the fact that the respondents had an expressed and implied right to apply to the court, Denham J was satisfied that the order in question was necessary in the circumstances to vindicate the rights of the applicant children. Accordingly, in Denham J's opinion:

> By such an order the people's institutions of state may, on balance, achieve a vindication of the children's constitutional rights. In the circumstances the use of a mandatory order directing the Minister to take all necessary steps and do all things necessary to facilitate the building and opening of the named high support units (the provision of which the Minister had previously indicated to the court was already in hand), was consistent with the obligation of the court to vindicate constitutional rights.[22]

In dismissing the appeal, Denham J stated that given the exceptional circumstances of these cases it was within the jurisdiction of the High Court to make

---

[19] Ibid, at para 68.
[20] Ibid, at paras 79–80.
[21] Ibid, at para 105.
[22] Ibid, at para 163.

the mandatory order which she believed was a proportionate response in the exceptional circumstances to protect the rights of the applicants.[23]

3.3. D.G. v The Eastern Health Board and Others

The constitutional rights of the at-risk child had previously been considered by the Supreme Court in *D.G. v The Eastern Health Board and Others*,[24] in which the applicant (a minor) brought an appeal against a High Court order that he be detained in a penal institute for a period of three weeks.[25] According to

---

[23] Ibid, at para 164.

[24] [1997] 3 IR 511. http://80-www.lexisnexis.com.au.ezproxy.waikato.ac.nz:2048/cui/uni-login/default.htm?login.asp?uni=waikato, as accessed on 19 November 2002.

[25] The applicant was born in July 1980 and had been in the care of the respondent health board since 1984. In 1996, the applicant was sent to a secure unit in the United Kingdom by the first respondent during which time he was convicted of criminal offences and was sentenced to nine months detention. Before the completion of that sentence the applicant was transferred to St. Patrick's Institution, Dublin. In March 1997, the applicant was released from St. Patrick's Institution without there being any accommodation available to him. The applicant was subsequently placed in hostel accommodation at two different locations, both of which proved respectively unsuitable and unable to accommodate him. On 27 June 1997, the matter came before Kelly J in the High Court who summarised the matter as follows:

> This is yet another case in which the court is called upon to exercise an original constitutional jurisdiction with a view to protecting the interests and promoting the welfare of a minor. The application arises because of the failure of the State to provide an appropriate facility to cater for the particular needs of this applicant and others like him. It is common case that what is required to deal with his problem is a secure unit where he can be detained and looked after. No such unit exists in this State and even if one did, there is no statutory power given to the court to direct the applicant's detention there. Such being the case, and in the absence of either legislation to deal with the matter or the facilities to cater for the applicant, I have in the short term to do the best that I can with what is available to me.

Justice Kelly continued by summarising the history of the applicant, which he described as quite appalling. According to Kelly J, the applicant:

1. was not mentally ill;
2. had a serious personality disorder;
3. was a danger to himself;
4. was a danger to others;
5. had a history of criminal activity and violence;
6. had a history of arson;
7. had in the past absconded from non-secure institutions;
8. had failed to cooperate with the first respondent and its staff; and
9. had failed to cooperate in the carrying out of a psychiatric assessment upon him in the past.

Faced with these circumstances, Kelly J was of the opinion that there were four options available to him:

1. do nothing;
2. direct the applicant's continued detention in the hostel accommodation in which he had been most recently placed
3. order the applicant's detention in the Central Mental Hospital, or
4. order the applicant's detention in St. Patrick's Institution.

Justice Kelly ordered that the applicant be detained in St. Patrick's Institution, a penal institution, for a three-week period.

Hamilton CJ, the issues which arose on appeal were first, whether the High Court had jurisdiction to order the detention of the applicant; second, if the High Court had such jurisdiction, whether the jurisdiction extended to making an order directing the detention of the applicant in a penal institution; and finally, and perhaps most significantly for the purposes of this analysis, whether the High Court jurisdiction had been properly exercised by the trial judge given the applicant's contention that the detention order violated his constitutional right not to be deprived of his liberty save in accordance with the law, in addition to those unenumerated rights that had identified by Higgins CJ in *G. v An Bord Uchtala* which the applicant also claimed to have been violated.

After finding that the High Court did have jurisdiction to make the order that its jurisdiction had been properly exercised, Hamilton CJ proceeded to consider the constitutional rights of the child as identified by the applicant. Although he recognised that the High Court's detention order conflicted with the applicant's constitutional right to liberty, Hamilton CJ, nonetheless, dismissed the appeal stating:

> It is clear from a consideration of the judgment of the learned trial judge that he recognised that the paramount consideration for him was the welfare of the child . . . The welfare of the applicant took precedence over the right to liberty of the applicant. There is ample evidence to support his finding in that regard.[26]

Whilst three of the other Supreme Court Judges also dismissed the appeal on similar grounds, Denham J provided the sole dissenting judgment and, in spite of the fact that she was of the opinion that the High Court judge was correct in taking the view that he had to vindicate the applicant's constitutional rights by ensuring, as best he could, the promotion of the child's welfare, she, nonetheless, held that the decision to detain the applicant in a penal institution breached a number of his constitutional rights. With regard to the child's right to liberty, Denham J held that the High Court was required to act in accordance with the Constitution. She observed that:

> A deprivation of liberty by being placed in a child's residential institution brings into consideration the differences of capacity, physical and moral, and of social function. It also encompasses the fundamental right of the child to his welfare and to his right to education. It is a harmonising of children's conflicting rights of welfare and liberty. However, detention in a penal institution is not such a harmony.[27]

In terms of the child's moral welfare, Denham J was of the view that the containment of a child in an institution for the welfare of children could not be compared to the detention of a child in a penal institution. As such, the detention order

---

[26] *D.G.*, supra note 24, at 9.
[27] Ibid, at 16.

had violated the applicant's moral welfare as it resulted in him being placed in a punishment institution when he had not been charged or convicted of an offence.[28] Justice Denham's dissenting judgment continued with the observation that an order to detain an adult in a penal institution in such circumstances would amount to preventative detention, which was unconstitutional. As such, the child was not being accorded treatment equal to that of an adult. She recognised, however, the Constitution clearly envisaged that differences in equality between individuals were affected by differences in capacity. Accordingly, the mere fact that such an order could not be made of an adult did not per se render it unconstitutional as the rationale for such loss of equality by the child was that this loss of liberty was based upon securing the welfare of the child. However, according to Denham J, such a rationale could not apply here:

> A deprivation of liberty by placement in a child care institution carries with it the concept of the welfare of the child. A prison does not. Thus the inequality suffered by the child by being placed in a penal institution in such circumstances relative to the position of an adult is unconstitutional, the applicant's right to equality has been breached by this order.[29]

She further noted that the detention order had violated the child's rights to bodily integrity and his social welfare. According to Denham J, the courts were under a duty to protect and vindicate the applicant's constitutional rights as to his person and welfare including the right to life, to protection of the person, to liberty, bodily integrity, and equality. Although the State had the constitutional obligation to supply the place of the parents, this duty was to be exercised with due regard for the rights of the child. Denham J recognised the difficult position that the High Court judge had been in and she recognised that the Court was unable to conjure up a secure accommodation unit.[30] However, she also noted that the responsibility to provide such accommodation did not lie with the courts, rather it was a statutory obligation imposed upon the respondent. In spite of her recognition of such difficulties, Denham J allowed the appeal as she remained:

> satisfied that the detention order is a step too far, an invasion of the child's rights as to moral, intellectual, physical and social welfare, to order his detention in a penal institution in the stated absence of appropriate accommodation. Also, it is a breach of his right to liberty, equality and bodily integrity.[31]

The structuring of Denham J's analysis in terms of the High Court order as constituting a violation of the applicant's unenumerated constitutional rights

---

[28] Ibid.
[29] Ibid, at 16.
[30] Ibid, at 18.
[31] Ibid.

in general and as constituting a violation of his constitutional right to liberty, equality and bodily integrity resonates strongly with certain provisions of international human rights law. Unfortunately, neither the High Court nor the Supreme Court took into account Ireland's international human rights obligations in their consideration of the issues raised by the failure of the Irish State to provide secure units for at-risk children. This failure to refer to international human rights law is indicative of the Court's assessment of the significance of Ireland's international obligations, as epitomised by the Supreme Court in *Doyle v The Commissioner of An Garda Siochana* where the relationship between Irish domestic law and the provisions of the European Convention was stated to be as follows:

> Ireland takes the dualistic approach to its international obligations and the European Convention is not part of the domestic law of Ireland (see *In re 0 Laighleis* [1960] IR 93). The Convention may overlap with certain provisions of Irish Constitutional law and it may be helpful to an Irish court to look at the Convention when it is attempting to identify unspecified rights guaranteed by Article 40.3 of the Constitution. Alternatively the Convention may, in certain circumstances, influence Irish law through European Community law. But the Convention is not part of Irish domestic law and the Irish court has no part in its enforcement.[32]

Nevertheless, both Keane CJ and Denham J have both recognised the role that Ireland's international obligations may play. For example, in *O'C.(J.) v D.P.P.*, Keane CJ stated that he assumed "that our laws are to be expounded in the context of the State's international obligations including the European Convention on Human Rights. . ."[33] Similarly, in *Kelly v O'Neill*, Denham J noted that whilst the European Convention on Human Rights was not part of the domestic law in Ireland, she was in no doubt that "the jurisprudence of the European Court on Human Rights may provide helpful guidelines (at least when the balance to be struck between the protection of the due administration of justice and freedom of expression was to be considered)."[34] Finally, in *Norris v The Attorney General*,[35] Henchy J stated that:

> the touchstone of constitutionality must be held to reside solely in our Constitution. That does not mean that this Court is not open to the persuasive influence that may be drawn from decisions of other courts, such as the European Court of

---

[32] [1999] 1 IR 249, as viewed in Lexis July 2002.http://80www.lexisnexis.com.au.ezproxy.waikato.ac.nz:2048/cui/unilogin/default.htm?login.asp?uniwaikato.

[33] 2000 IESC 58, 146.

[34] 1999 IESC 81; [2000] 1 IR 354; 2000 1 ILRM 507 (2 December 1999), at para 68.

[35] [1984] IR 36. The plaintiff subsequently brought his case to the European Court of Human Rights and was successful in his claim that Irish legislation which criminalised homosexual activity violated his rights under Article 8.

Human Rights, which deal with problems similar or analogous to that now before us.

As such, it is appropriate to consider the approach of the European Court to the issue of the at-risk child.

4. *The Rights of the At-Risk Child in International Human Rights Law*

4.1. *D.G. v Ireland*

The decisions of the Irish courts to order the detention of D.G. in a penal institute were successfully appealed by the applicant in the European Court of Human Rights. The European Court found Ireland to be in violation of its obligations under the European Convention on Human Rights.[36] The basis of the finding was that whilst the Irish courts could order a child to be detained in order to protect his or her welfare, they could not order such a child to be detained in a penal institution where that child had not committed any crime.

The basis of the applicant's complaint was that he was detained, without charge or conviction, in St. Patrick's penal institution between 27 June and 28 July 1997 in violation of Articles 3, 5, 8, 13 and 14 of the Convention. In particular, the applicant complained that his detention in St. Patrick's from 27 June to 28 July 1997 was neither in accordance with a procedure prescribed by law nor for the purposes of educational supervision nor of bringing him before any competent legal authority within the meaning of Article 5(1)(d) of the Convention. Furthermore, the applicant complained that the general failure to provide appropriate accommodation and care constituted a violation of his rights under Article 5(1) and concluded his submission by stating that Ireland had delayed significantly in putting in place appropriate facilities for children with the applicant's needs pursuant to its identified constitutional obligations set out in numerous domestic cases.[37]

In considering D.G.'s application, the Court referred to its decision in *Bouamar*[38] in which it had held that a brief period of detention in prison pending placement for education elsewhere did not breach Article 5(1)(d) of the European Convention. The Court recognised that D.G.'s detention was an interim custody measure and, as such, it was necessary for his assessment and containment given the danger he posed to himself and others. It also recognised that the detention was preliminary to a future regime of accommodation and

---

[36] *D.G. v Ireland*, Judgment of 16 May 2002.
[37] Ibid, at paras 66–71.
[38] *Bouamar v Belgium*, Judgment of 29 February 1988, Series A no. 129.

supervised education, in spite of the fact that the State was not obligated, at that time, to provide educational supervision to persons over 16 years of age. Therefore, according to the Court, in contrast to the situation in *Bouamar*, D.G.'s detention was not fruitless as it was ultimately aimed at the facilitation of his educational supervision. Moreover, the applicant's period of detention was kept to a minimum and was significantly shorter than that in the *Bouamar* case. Furthermore, the facilities in St. Patrick's were superior to those available in *Bouamar*.[39]

Nevertheless, the Court was of the opinion that the applicant was deprived of his liberty within the meaning of Article 5(1) from 27 June to 28 July 1997.[40] The Court recalled that, for the purposes of the Convention, any such detention had to be lawful both in domestic and Convention terms and stated that there had to be a relationship between the ground of permitted deprivation of liberty relied upon and the conditions of that detention.[41] In response to the Irish Government's contention that the applicant was detained on the grounds of educational supervision within the meaning of Article 5(1)(d), the Court considered whether the applicant's detention in fact complied with the conditions that were imposed by that sub-section. It noted that the applicant had turned 17 years of age during the impugned period of detention and therefore could no longer have been required to attend school. However, the Court also noted that Article 5(1)(d) referred to the educational supervision of minors and that s 2(1) of the Child Care Act 1991 had defined minors to be persons under the age of 18 years. Therefore, since the applicant was a minor throughout the relevant period, the only question that remained for the Court to decide was whether the detention was lawful and for the purpose of educational supervision as per its decision in *Bouamar*,[42] within the meaning of Article 5(1)(d).[43]

The Court concluded that, given the decisions of the High and Supreme Courts, the High Court orders were lawful for the purposes of domestic law as the High Court had exercised its inherent jurisdiction, which had been well-established by the Court's jurisprudence, to protect a minor's constitutional rights.[44] As to whether the orders were lawful for the purposes of the Convention, the Court recalled its decision in *Bouamar* in which it found that:

---

[39] *D.G v Ireland*, supra note 36, at para 68.
[40] Ibid, at para 73.
[41] Ibid, at para 75.
[42] *Bouamar*, supra note 38, at para 50. Bouamar was a minor at the time he was detained in a remand prison nine times (a total of 119 days during a period of 291 days) as a preliminary measure to ensure his placement under educational supervision.
[43] *D.G. v Ireland*, supra note 36, at para 76.
[44] Ibid, at para 77.

the confinement of a juvenile in a remand prison does not necessarily contravene sub-paragraph (d), even if it is not in itself such as to provide for the person's educational supervision.[45]

Nevertheless, in *Bouamar*, the Court ultimately held that:

> The detention of a young man in a remand prison in conditions of virtual isolation and without the assistance of staff with educational training cannot be regarded as furthering any educational aim. . . . [it concluded] that the nine placement orders, taken together, were not compatible with sub-paragraph (d). Their fruitless repetition had the effect of making them less and less lawful under sub-paragraph (d), especially as Crown Counsel never instituted criminal proceedings against the applicant in respect of the offences alleged against him.[46]

This aspect of the *Bouamar* judgment allowed the Court to conclude that if the Irish State chose a constitutional system of educational supervision implemented through court orders to deal with juvenile delinquency, it was obliged to put in place appropriate institutional facilities which met the security and educational demands of that system in order to satisfy the requirements of Article 5(1)(d).[47] The Court did not consider that the detention of the applicant in St. Patrick's was for the purposes of educational supervision.[48] According to the Court, St. Patrick's was a penal institution and the applicant was subjected to its disciplinary regime. The educational and other recreation services were entirely voluntary and the applicant's prison file did not indicate that the applicant had received any instruction during his detention. Most importantly, in the Court's opinion, the High Court was convinced that St. Patrick's could not guarantee the applicant's constitutional educational rights nor could it provide the special care that he required.[49]

The European Court noted that the High Court had considered detention in St. Patrick's to be the best of four inappropriate options and that, accordingly, the applicant's detention there should be temporary.[50] However, the question remained as to whether the applicant's detention in St. Patrick's constituted an interim custody measure for the purposes of an educational supervisory regime which was followed speedily by the application of such a regime. Again, the Court took into account the circumstances in which the applicant was held and concluded that the applicant's detention in June and July 1997 could not be considered to have been an interim custody measure preliminary

---

[45] *Bouamar*, supra note 38, at para 50.
[46] Ibid, at paras 52–53.
[47] *D.G. v Ireland*, supra note 36, at para 79.
[48] Ibid, at para 81.
[49] Ibid.
[50] Ibid.

to a regime of supervised education. According to the Court, the first two detention orders of the High Court were not based on any specific proposal for his secure and supervised education and that the third order was based on a proposal for temporary accommodation which, in any event, turned out to be neither secure nor appropriate and which inevitably led to yet another order of the High Court detaining the applicant in St. Patrick's. In the Court's opinion, even if it could be assumed that the applicant's detention from February 1998 was sufficiently secure and educationally appropriate, this order was put in place more than six months after his release from St. Patrick's in July 1997.[51] Accordingly, the Court concluded that the applicant's detention in St. Patrick's between 27 June and 28 July 1997 was not compatible with Article 5(1)(d) of the Convention and, since no other basis for justifying the applicant's detention had been advanced, the Court found that the applicant had been detained in breach of Article 5(1).[52]

4.2. The Rights of the At-Risk Child under International Human Rights Standards

As the above decision of the European Court of Human Rights indicates, Ireland's policy of placing at-risk children in penal institutions for their own protection and irrespective of the fact their placement there is not as a consequence of being charged and convicted of any crime is a violation of a number of international human rights norms. For example, Article 3 of the Universal Declaration[53] states that "Everyone has the right to life, liberty and security of person." Article 5 of the Declaration states that "No one shall be subjected to torture or to cruel, inhuman or degrading treatment or punishment." Finally, Article 9 states that "No one shall be subjected to arbitrary arrest, detention or exile."

These norms contained in the Universal Declaration were reiterated in, and given a legal basis by Article 7 of the ICCPR.[54] The meaning of this provision was further explored by the Human Rights Committee in its General Comment 20, wherein the Committee noted that:

> article 7 of the International Covenant on Civil and Political Rights is to protect both the dignity and the physical and mental integrity of the individual.[55]

---

[51] Ibid, at para 84.
[52] Ibid, at para 85.
[53] Universal Declaration of Human Rights, G.A. Res. 217A, (III) U.N. Doc. A1810 (1948).
[54] International Covenant on Civil and Political Rights, U.N. G.A. Res. 2200 (XXI), 21 UN GAOR, Supp. (No. 16) 52, U.N. Doc. A16316 (1966).
[55] Human Rights Committee, General Comment 20: *Replaces general comment 7 concerning prohibition of torture and cruel treatment or punishment (Art. 7): 10/03/92*, at para 2.

Moreover, the Committee noted that:

> The prohibition in article 7 is complemented by the positive requirements of article 10, paragraph 1, of the Covenant, which stipulates that all persons deprived of their liberty shall be treated with humanity and with respect for the inherent dignity of the human person.[56]

The Committee further noted that "The text of article 7 allows of no limitation."[57] Article 9(1) of the Covenant is most pertinent, with its statement that:

> Everyone has the right to liberty and security of person. No one shall be subjected to arbitrary arrest or detention. No one shall be deprived of his liberty except on such grounds and in accordance with such procedures as are established by law.

The Human Rights Committee further explored the obligations inherent in Article 9(1) in its General Comment 8[58] and stated that Article 9:

> paragraph 1 is applicable to *all deprivations of liberty*, whether in criminal cases or in other cases such as, for example, mental illness, vagrancy, drug addiction, educational purposes, immigration control, etc.[59] [emphasis added]

The Committee also noted that whilst some of the provisions of Article 9 only applied to people against whom criminal charges had been laid, nonetheless, the other provisions of Article 9 did apply to other situations in which a person might be detained:

> in particular the important guarantee laid down in paragraph 4, i.e. the right to control by a court of the legality of the detention, applies to all persons deprived of their liberty by arrest or detention.[60]

The provision contained in Article 10 is similarly significant for the rights of at-risk children with its statement that "All persons deprived of their liberty shall be treated with humanity and with respect for the inherent dignity of the human person."[61]

The human rights norms contained in the more general human rights instruments have been incorporated into the child-specific provisions of the

---

[56] Ibid.

[57] Ibid, at para 3.

[58] Human Rights Committee, General Comment 8: *Right to liberty and security of persons (Art. 9) 30/06/82*.

[59] Ibid, at para 1.

[60] Ibid. Article 9(4) provides that "Anyone who is deprived of his liberty by arrest or detention shall be entitled to take proceedings before a court, in order that court may decide without delay on the lawfulness of his detention and order his release if the detention is not lawful."

[61] This principle is reiterated in the Body of Principles for the Protection of All Persons under Any Form of Detention or Imprisonment, adopted by General Assembly resolution 43/173 of 9 December 1988. Principle 8 states, Persons in detention shall be subject to treatment appropriate to their unconvicted status. Accordingly, they shall, whenever possible, be kept separate from imprisoned persons.

Convention on the Rights of the Child.[62] The significance of this Convention for at-risk children is also apparent from the best interests principle contained in Article 3. This Guiding Principle of the best interests of the child is one of a number of principles which underpin the interpretation to be given to the Convention's provisions, including those that are particularly pertinent to the at-risk child. To that end, Article 20 of the Convention states that:

1. A child temporarily or permanently deprived of his or her family environment, or in whose own best interests cannot be allowed to remain in that environment, shall be entitled to special protection and assistance provided by the State.
2. States Parties shall in accordance with their national laws ensure alternative care for such a child.

Article 37 of the Convention reiterates the provisions of general human rights treaties with its statement that:

States Parties shall ensure that:

(a) No child shall be subjected to torture or other cruel, inhuman or degrading treatment or punishment. . . .
(b) No child shall be deprived of his or her liberty unlawfully or arbitrarily.[63]

The provisions of the Convention on the Rights of the Child, as well as the more general human rights treaties are also to be found at the level of regional human rights treaties. Similarly to Article 37 of the Convention on the Rights of the Child, Article 3 of the European Convention on Human Rights also prohibits torture or inhuman or degrading treatment or punishment[64] whilst, as previously noted, Article 5(1) prohibits arbitrary arrest or detention.

The provisions Articles 3 and 5 of the European Convention have been further developed by the Council of Europe with its European Convention for the

---

[62] United Nations Convention on the Rights of the Child, UN Doc. A/44/736, (1989), UNGA Doc. A/Res/44/25 of 5 December, (1989) 28 I.L.M., 1448, (1989).

[63] Article 37 continues by providing that:

(c) Every child deprived of liberty shall be treated with humanity and respect for the inherent dignity of the human person, and in a manner which takes into account the needs of persons of his or her age. In particular, every child deprived of liberty shall be separated from adults unless it is considered in the child's best interest not to do so and shall have the right to maintain contact with his or her family through correspondence and visits, save in exceptional circumstances;
(d) Every child deprived of his or her liberty shall have the right to prompt access to legal and other appropriate assistance, as well as the right to challenge the legality of the deprivation of his or her liberty before a court or other competent, independent and impartial authority, and to a prompt decision on any such action.

[64] European Convention for the Protection of Human Rights and Fundamental Freedoms, 213 U.N.T.S., 221, no. 2889; Council of Europe, European Treaty Series, 4 November 1950, no. 5.

Prevention of Torture and Inhuman or Degrading Treatment or Punishment.[65] This Convention establishes a European Committee for the Prevention of Torture and Inhuman or Degrading Treatment or Punishment which shall, by means of visits, examine the treatment of persons deprived of their liberty with a view to strengthening, if necessary, the protection of such persons from torture and from inhuman or degrading treatment or punishment.[66] According to the Explanatory Report which accompanies this Convention:

> The notion of deprivation of liberty for the purposes of the present Convention is to be understood within the meaning of Article 5 of the European Convention on Human Rights, as elucidated by the case-law of the European Court and Commission of Human Rights.[67]

The Convention may become particularly relevant to the Irish at-risk child as Article 30 provides that:

> Visits may be organised in all kinds of places where persons are deprived of their liberty, whatever the reasons may be. The Convention is therefore applicable, for example, . . . where minors are detained by a public authority.[68]

To that end, the framework of international human rights law provides extensive protection against arbitrary detention and the violation of other human rights that may flow from such detention, but is a further protective framework for the at-risk child which the Irish State currently has chosen to ignore.

5. Discriminatory Detention of the At-Risk Child

This chapter considers the rights of the Irish child that derive both from national and international law. These rights are underpinned by the Irish Constitution and it is these constitutional rights that constitute the point of

---

[65] European Convention for the Prevention of Torture and Inhuman or Degrading Treatment or Punishment (ETS no. 126).

[66] Ibid, Article 1.

[67] *Explanatory Report*, European Convention for the Prevention of Torture and Inhuman or Degrading Treatment or Punishment (ETS no. 126), at para 24. Paragraph 25 continues by stating that any lawful and unlawful deprivation of liberty arising in connection with Article 5 is immaterial in relation to the committee's competence. Paragraph 25 sets out the rather limited competence of the Committee wherein the Committee:

> shall not perform any judicial functions: its members will not have to be lawyers, its recommendations will not bind the state concerned and the committee shall not express any view on the interpretation of legal terms. Its task is a purely preventive one. It will carry out fact-finding visits and, if necessary, on the basis of information obtained through them, make recommendations with a view to strengthening the protection of persons deprived of their liberty from torture and from inhuman or degrading treatment or punishment.

[68] Ibid, at para 30.

departure for an analysis of the rights of the at-risk child in Ireland. Perhaps in somewhat of a contrast to the issues considered in the previous two chapters, a reasonably coherent framework of legal protection is in existence and the Irish courts have relied upon it to determine, often quite unequivocally, that the rights of the at-risk child in Ireland have been violated by the slow pace of the Government's provision of alternate care and confinement facilities. To that end, the courts have determined that the rights contained in the Constitution are not absolute and must be interpreted with reference to differences of capacity as between individuals, and in the context of children's rights, this differential treatment extends to differences in capacity that are age based. That said, the State must, nonetheless, balance the recognition of difference of capacity with its Constitutional obligation to defend and vindicate the personal rights of its citizens, including those of its children and, in the context of this Chapter, the rights of its at-risk children. The Constitution allows for State intervention to ensure the rights of the child, where such intervention is based upon protecting the natural and imprescriptible rights of the child and where it is based upon securing the welfare of the child. Where necessary, the constitutional rights of the child may be limited in order to secure his or her welfare. In terms of the at-risk child, the courts have determined that these constitutionally-based limitations, which have found expression in Irish legislation, place an obligation upon the State to provide care and confinement facilities. It is at this point that the discriminatory practice occurs as the welfare of non-offending at-risk children is sought to be ensured by confining such children in penal institutions, a limitation on the rights of the child that cannot be justified.

There are two levels of discrimination in operation with regard to the at-risk child. First, there is the actual confinement of such children in penal institutions that in the case of an adult would amount to preventative detention and would be unconstitutional. Thus, there is the difference in the extent to which the right to liberty is protected as between children and adults. This difference was justified in the Irish courts by the need to give preference to the welfare of the child over the right to liberty of the child, that the detention of the child served an important and significant objective. However, as previous chapters demonstrate, the basis for differential treatment does not stop with the identification of an important and significant objective. The measures adopted and the effects of those measures must also be considered in order to determine whether they are rationally and proportionally connected to the stated objective. It was these aspects of the test for discrimination that the majority of the Supreme Court failed to consider in *D.G. v The Eastern Health Board*. As a consequence, the majority's determination that such differential treatment was justifiable is not thoroughly grounded and does not serve as a satisfactory justification for the detention of at-risk children in penal institutions. Fortunately, Denham J advanced a more balanced analysis in her dissenting opinion in which the tests of rationality and proportionality were considered with considerable conscientiousness so that no further analysis is required here.

Second, there is the judicial consideration of the justification of the detention of at-risk children in penal institutions. Both the Irish courts and the European Court of Human Rights noted that the orders made were based ultimately upon the lack of alternate care facilities. Thus, the second level of discrimination suffered by at-risk children in Ireland derived from the limited extent, practically speaking, to which the courts, operating as an organ of the State, were going to be able to vindicate the personal rights of a certain portion of its citizens. No reasonable justification for this argument has been advanced by the Irish State. In terms of a broader analysis of the human rights of the child, the impact of a lower threshold for the detention of at-risk children is not confined to the fundamental principles of non-discrimination and equality. In spite of the fact that the requirement for flexibility is implicit in the best interests standard, flexibility should not equate with a lesser quality of protection or, in this context, a lower standard by which the best interests of such children was deemed to be achieved. Thus, unjustifiably different levels of protection were accorded to that subset of Irish at-risk children that were most in need of a much higher level of protection. Thus, in this Chapter the age discrimination issues do not derive directly from gaps in the law, rather they derive from the discriminatory conduct of the State in failing to give such legal protection a practical application.

6. *Conclusion*

The failure of the Irish State to provide secure accommodation for at-risk children is all the more concerning in light of the range of domestic and international provisions that are violated as a consequence of this failure, violations which have been recognised by both the Irish courts as well as the European Court of Human Rights. Whilst the State may seek some leverage in its arguments that it is not bound by the provisions of international law, it remains bound by its constitutional provisions to vindicate the rights of all its citizens including the at-risk child. Furthermore, both Ireland's Constitutional and international obligations are founded on the principles of non-discrimination and equality. The role of the judiciary in protecting fundamental rights is stymied by the persistent failure of the State to uphold these rights. Whilst the State may (rightly) contend that the concept of separation of powers is fundamental to a functioning democracy and that the Judiciary have no role to play in the implementing of policy, this is somewhat of a hypocritical stance to take as the Executive continues to undermine the democratic values, implicit in which are the principles of non-discrimination and equality, that it seeks to and is legally obliged to uphold.

CHAPTER SIX

AGE DISCRIMINATION AND THE RIGHTS OF IRISH-BORN CHILDREN OF ASYLUM SEEKERS

1. Introduction

Until recently, Irish Constitutional law and Irish legislation dictated that children born in the Republic of Ireland were automatically granted Irish citizenship. These provisions had been interpreted in light of the Constitutional guarantee regarding the protection of the family unit with the result that the non-EU national parents and families of children born in Ireland generally qualified for Irish residency. However, recent changes to the Constitution, to be accompanied by legislative change, have removed the automatic right to citizenship and any Constitutional protection that might ensure. The removal of automatic citizenship rights puts Ireland in line with other EU and non-EU States. It is also in line with a recent decision of the Irish Supreme Court, *Lobe v Minister for Justice, Equality and Law Reform,*[1] which emphasised the need to protect the 'integrity' of the Irish asylum system and held that the immigrant parents of Irish-born children were not entitled to remain in the State. The recent change in legislation is not retrospective and, consequently, the Supreme Court decision continues to affect those children born before the automatic right to citizenship was removed. The decision has the effect limiting the citizenship rights of such children since it may give rise to the *de facto* deportation of Irish children as a consequence of the deportation of their non-national parents. This state of affairs underscores the paternalistic aspect of children's rights where children as rights-holders may depend on their parents, or more particularly upon the ability of their parents to exercise their parental rights, to facilitate the exercise of their rights as children. In this context, any actions that limit parental rights have to be weighed against the impact of such limitations on the rights of their children in order to determine whether limitations on the rights of the latter are justifiable and amount to no more than legitimate differentiation. Failure to assess such an impact presents issues of age discrimination in its broader sense, because such failure does not factor in (extreme) youth when it acts to curtail the capacity to exercise one's rights. Rather, in the case at hand,

---

[1] [2003] IESC 3 (23 January 2003) http://www.bailii.org.ezproxy.waikato.ac.nz:2048/ie/cases/IESC/2003/3.html, as viewed 27 April 2005.

age – as it relates to lack of capacity – was employed to override the constitutionally granted rights of citizenship and the protection afforded by this right.

   Part 2 of this chapter will provide an overview of the rights of children born
of asylum seekers both in domestic and international law. Part 3 contains a
critical analysis of the extent to which the rights of children born of non-
nationals in general are protected under international human rights law, with
specific reference to the jurisprudence of the European Court of Human Rights.
Part 4 considers the legal protection accorded to the Irish-born child as both
an autonomous rights-holder as well as a member of the family unit under
Irish law. Part 5 critiques the above-mentioned Supreme Court decision to
deport the non-national parents of Irish-born children, finding that, at best, it
disregards the rights of the child and, at worst, it discriminates against the
Irish-born children of non-residents.

2. *International Human Rights Protection for Children Born of Asylum Seekers*

As indicated in Chapter 1, the general principles of non-discrimination and
equality are to be extended to children. These fundamental human rights principles are to be read in conjunction with the General Principles that underpin
the Convention on the Rights of the Child and they should inform any discussion regarding the rights of the child. This section applies these principles to the
situation of children of asylum seekers and highlights the specific human rights
standards that have to be met.

2.1. *The Right of the Child to Respect for Family and Private Life*

As indicated in Chapters 1 and 3 in particular, international human rights law
accords special protection to the child, with such special protection naturally
underpinning the right of the child to respect for family and private life. The
more general human rights provisions regarding the child's right to respect for
family and private life have previously been outlined in Chapter 3 in relation
to the child's right to identity. Those provisions of the Convention on the
Rights of the Child relating to the child's right to respect for family life were
also considered in Chapter 3. However, further protection has been accorded
to the family unit and the child's place within that unit by the Preamble to the
Convention on the Rights of the Child, which states that the States Parties to
the Convention are:

> Convinced that the family, as the fundamental group of society and the natural
> environment for the growth and well-being of all its members and particularly
> children, should be afforded the necessary protection and assistance so that it can
> fully assume its responsibilities within the community,

> Recognizing that the child, for the full and harmonious development of his or her personality, should grow up in a family environment, in an atmosphere of happiness, love and understanding, . . .

This provision is further supported by Article 5 of the Convention with its recognition of the responsibilities, rights and duties of parents to provide appropriate direction and guidance in the exercise by the child of the rights recognised in the Convention. This recognition is further supported by Article 16 of the Convention with its statement that:

> 1. No child shall be subject to arbitrary or unlawful interference with his or her . . . family . . .
> 2. The child has the right to the protection of the law against such interference. . .[2]

As many of the previous chapters indicate, the rights of the child, in international human rights law, are to be viewed independently from his or her membership of a family environment. Nevertheless, the above treaties indicate that the rights (and interests) of the child are often best protected by maintaining the child within his or her family. Thus, the protection afforded to the rights of the child with regard to the right to respect for family life, in particular, is significant to any discussion of the protection of the rights of children born of refugees. It is recognition of this particular aspect of children's rights that underpins the ensuing discussion on the rights of children born of asylum seekers, a class of rights-holder that has been recognised by the provisions of various international human rights treaties.

Although the Convention Relating to the Status of Refugees 1951[3] does not deal specifically with the issue children's rights, Article 24(3) of the ICCPR does state that every child has the right to acquire a nationality.[4] The issue of the right of a child to nationality in addition to the right to an on-going relationship with his or her parents is considered in Article 7 of the Convention on the Rights of the Child, which states:

> 1. The child shall . . . have the right from birth . . . the right to acquire a nationality and, as far as possible, the right to know and be cared for by his or her parents.
> 2. States Parties shall ensure the implementation of these rights in accordance with their national law and their obligations under the relevant international instruments in this field, . . . [5]

---

[2] United Nations Convention on the Rights of the Child, UN Doc. A/44/736, (1989), UNGA Doc. A/Res/44/25 of 5 December, (1989) 28 I.L.M., 1448, (1989).

[3] Convention Relating to the Status of Refugees 1951,189 UNTS 137.

[4] International Covenant on Civil and Political Rights, U.N. G.A. Res. 2200 (XXI), 21 UN GAOR, Supp. (No. 16) 52, U.N. Doc. A16316 (1966).

[5] Convention on the Rights of the Child, supra note 2.

The right of the child to a continued relationship with his or her family is considered in Article 9(1) of the Convention, which states:

> States Parties shall ensure that a child shall not be separated from his or her parents against their will, except when competent authorities subject to judicial review determine, in accordance with applicable law and procedures, that such separation is necessary for the best interests of the child.[6]

However, it is Article 10(1) of the Convention, in particular, which deals with the issue of family reunification and which imposes the following obligations upon States Parties:

> In accordance with the obligation of States Parties under article 9, paragraph 1, applications by a child or his or her parents to enter or leave a State Party for the purpose of family reunification shall be dealt with by States Parties in a positive, humane and expeditious manner. States Parties shall further ensure that the submission of such a request shall entail no adverse consequences for the applicants and for the members of their family.[7]

The rights accorded to the child born of asylum seekers are derived from and must be viewed against a broad framework of human rights standards. In sum, international human rights law dictates that the child born of an asylum seeker has the right to a family life, a right which must be implemented to secure the best interests of the child and which must be accorded to the child without discrimination of any kind.

3. *The Rights of Children Born of Asylum Seekers under the European Convention of Human Rights*

It is the European Court of Human Rights, as the monitoring body of the European Convention on Human Rights, which is one of the primary sources of jurisprudence on international human rights law regarding the rights of refugees (and their children). The Court has had to determine in a number of cases whether deportation orders violated the right to respect for family life as provided for in Article 8(1) or whether such orders were legitimate in terms of the limitations accorded to those rights by virtue of Article 8(2). Thus, the Court has engaged in determinations as to whether such orders are illegitimate, and therefore discriminatory, or whether they amount to differential treatment that is legitimate in the circumstances. In so doing, it has had to balance the provisions of the Convention with the principle of the margin of appreciation,

---

[6] Ibid.
[7] Ibid.

which recognises that a State has the right to control the entry of non-nationals into its territory, itself a principle well-recognised in international law. The jurisprudence of the Court indicates that a deportee is required to establish a substantial connection with the deporting state in order to establish a prima facie infringement on his or her rights.[8] On the part of the deporting State, however, it has to establish that the deportation order is 'in accordance with the law' and is in pursuit of 'legitimate interests' and 'is necessary in a democratic society.' Accordingly, the Court has had to examine the facts of each case in order to determine whether the State has "struck a fair balance between the relevant interests".[9]

This balancing of the right to respect for family life and the right of a State to control the entry of non-nationals into its territory was first considered by the European Court in the case of *Abdulaziz, Cabales and Balkandali v United Kingdom*.[10] The applicants claimed, inter alia, that their rights under Article 8 had been violated. In noting that the case was concerned with the relationship between family life and immigration, the Court, nevertheless stated that it could not:

> ignore . . . that, as a matter of well-established international law and subject to its treaty obligations, a State has the right to control the entry of non-nationals into its territory.[11]

According to the Court, "the duty imposed by Article 8 (art. 8) cannot be considered as extending to a general obligation on the part of a Contracting State . . . to accept the non-national spouses for settlement in that country".[12] The Court also noted that the applicants had not shown that there were any obstacles to establishing family life in their own or their husbands' home countries or that there were special reasons why that could not be expected of them. The Court ultimately held that there "was accordingly no 'lack of respect' for family life and, hence, no breach of Article 8. . ."[13] and that, in the circumstances, "the United Kingdom was not obliged to accept Mr. Abdulaziz, Mr. Cabales and Mr. Balkandali for settlement. . .".[14]

---

[8] M Janis, R Kay, and A Bradley, *European Human Rights Law: Text and Materials* (2nd ed), Oxford, Oxford University Press, 1998, at 258.

[9] *Dalia v France*, 19 February 1998, Reports, 1998-I, para 52.

[10] Judgment of 28 May 1985, Series A, No. 194 (1985). The applicants were lawfully and permanently settled in the UK. Their respective husbands were refused permission to remain with or join them in the UK under British immigration rules in force at the time.

[11] Ibid, at para 67.

[12] Ibid, at para 68.

[13] Ibid, at para 69.

[14] Ibid, at para 71.

However, in the *Berrehab* case,[15] the Court had to consider a situation where The Netherlands was attempting to deport a Moroccan national (the first applicant) who had been married to a Dutch national and was the father of a young child with Dutch nationality (the second applicant).[16] In finding that that there was a violation of Article 8(1), the Court then had to consider whether the violation was justified by the provisions of Article 8(2).[17] The Court focused on whether the refusal was necessary in a democratic society[18] and, to that end, had to consider whether 'necessity' implied that the interference corresponded to a pressing social need and, in particular, whether it was proportionate to the legitimate aim pursued.[19] As to the extent of the interference, the Court noted that there had been very close ties between Mr Berrehab and his daughter for several years and that the refusal of an independent residence permit and the ensuing expulsion threatened to break those ties. According to the Court, "the effect of the interferences in issue was the more serious as Rebecca needed to remain in contact with her father, seeing especially that she was very young".[20] Consequently, the Court found that that a proper balance had not been achieved between the interests involved, and that the deportation of Mr Berrehab was disproportionate as between the means employed and the legitimate aim pursued and could not be considered as being necessary in a democratic society and therefore constituted a violation of Article 8.[21]

---

[15] *Berrehab v The Netherlands*, Judgment of 21 June 1988, Series A, No. 138, (1988).

[16] Although Mr Berrehab was separated from the child's mother, he maintained close contact with his daughter. The applicant had subsequently been issued with a deportation order on the basis that he was no longer married to his Dutch wife, which had been the reason why he had been allowed to remain in the Netherlands, ibid, at para 10. The applicants asserted that "the applicability of Article 8 . . . in respect of the words right to respect for . . . private and family life did not presuppose permanent cohabitation. The exercise of a father's right of access to his child and his contributing to the cost of education were also factors sufficient to constitute family life." (at para 20) In agreeing with the applicants' assertion, the Court stated that it did not "see cohabitation as a sine qua non of family life between parents and minor children. . . and noted that a relationship arising out of a lawful and genuine marriage – such as that contracted by Mr and Mrs Berrehab – has to be regarded as family life" (at para 21). The Court further stated that it followed from the concept of family upon which Article 8 was based that: "a child born of such a union is ipso jure part of that relationship; hence, from the moment of the child's birth and by the very fact of it, there exists between him and his parents a bond amounting to family life, even if the parents are not then living together." Ibid.

[17] Ibid, at para 22.

[18] Ibid, at para 27.

[19] Ibid, at para 28.

[20] Ibid, at para 29.

[21] Ibid. Similarly, in *Beldjoudi v France*, Judgment of 26 March 1992, Series A, No. 234-A (1992), Mr Beldjoudi had been convicted of a number of offences and had been issued with a deportation order on the ground that his presence on French territory was a threat to public order. He had been born in France and was of Algerian descent. Along with his parents and sibling, he lost his claim to French nationality because he had not made a declaration recognising French

The issue arose again in *Mehemi v France*[22] when the Court found that the applicant's relationship with his wife and children amounted to family life and that this right had been interfered with as a result of his deportation. Whilst it found that the order was made in accordance with the law and that it had a legitimate aim, the Court had to consider whether the order was 'necessary in a democratic society' or whether it amounted to an interference with the exercise of the applicant's right to respect for his private and family life that was markedly disproportionate to the aims pursued.[23] According to the Court, its task was to ascertain "whether the measure in issue struck a fair balance between the relevant interests, namely the applicant's right to respect for his private and family life, on the one hand, and the prevention of disorder or crime, on the other".[24] Noting the destructive effect of drugs on people's lives, the Court recognised the reasons why the French authorities had shown great firmness with regard to those actively contributing to the spread of that scourge.[25] According to the Court the fact that the applicant participated in a conspiracy to import a large quantity of hashish counted heavily against him. However, on the other hand, the Court took into account the applicant's lack of links with Algeria, the strength of his links with France and above all the fact that the order for his permanent exclusion from French territory separated him

---

nationality in accordance with the Evian Agreements of 1962 regarding the independence of Algeria from France. Mr Beldjoudi and his wife claimed that all their family ties, social links, cultural connections and linguistic ties were in France and claimed that there were no exceptional circumstances that could justify deportation. In balancing the interests of those involved, the Court took into account the French authorities' claim that Mr. Beldjoudi's long criminal record of very serious crimes required his deportation on the grounds of public order. The Court equally noted that such a deportation would have a very severe impact on Mr Beldjoudi's family life. According to the Court, "the applicant did not seem to have any links with Algeria apart from that of nationality", ibid, at para 77. "In addition, he had been married to a French woman for almost twenty years, and uprooting her like this could cause her great difficulty in adapting, and there might be real practical or even legal obstacles, . . . and the interference in question might therefore imperil the unity or even the very existence of the marriage", ibid, at para 78. Accordingly, the Court found that "Having regard to these various circumstances, . . . the decision to deport Mr Beldjoudi, if put into effect, would not be proportionate to the legitimate aim pursued and would therefore violate Article 8 . . .", ibid, at para 79. Similar decisions were reached in *Moustaquim v Belgium*, Judgment of 18 February 1991, Series A, No. 193, (1991) and *Nasri v France*, Judgment of 13 July 1995, Series A, No. 324 (1995).

[22] Judgment of 26 September 1997, *Reports* 1997-VI, 1971. The applicant who had been born in France, had lived there more than 30 years prior to enforcement of permanent exclusion order, and who was the father of three minor children of French nationality whose mother he had married. After being convicted of drug offences, the French authorities ordered the permanent exclusion of the applicant from French territory on the ground that public-policy considerations preclude the presence within French territory of an alien engaged as a principal in the offence of drug trafficking, ibid, at para 11.

[23] Ibid, at paras 30–31.

[24] Ibid, at para 35.

[25] Ibid, at para 37.

from his minor children and his wife.[26] Consequently, the Court considered that the permanent exclusion order was disproportionate to the aims pursued and that, accordingly, there had been a breach of Article 8.[27]

Moreover, in *Dalia v France*[28] the Court held that the refusal by France to lift an exclusion order made against the applicant constituted an interference with her right to respect for her family life under the provisions of Article 8(1), a right that had been established by the birth of her son in France.[29] However, it remained for the Court to determine whether the exclusion order combined with a refusal to lift it satisfied the conditions of Article 8(2).[30] The Court was satisfied that the order was made in accordance with the law[31] and that it had a legitimate aim.[32] In terms of whether the deportation was necessary in a democratic society the Court acknowledged that the right of States Parties to deport aliens convicted of criminal offences must be "justified by a pressing social need and, in particular, proportionate to the legitimate aim pursued. . .".[33] The Court noted that Mrs Dalia relied mainly on the fact that she was the mother of a French child but that this vital family link had been formed when

---

[26] Ibid.

[27] Ibid. This emphasis on family rights contrasts with the earlier decision in *Boughanemi v France* Judgment of 24 April 1996, Reports-II, 573. In determining whether the deportation of the applicant on the grounds of public order amounted to a violation of Article 8, the Court acknowledged that Mr Boughanemi lived with a French woman in France as man and wife and formally recognised – admittedly not until 5 April 1994 – her child who was born on 19 June 1993. Nevertheless, according to the Court, "The concept of family life on which Article 8 . . . is based embraces, even where there is no cohabitation, the tie between a parent and his or her child, a tie which had not been broken in this instance." Ibid, at para 35. The Court stated that:

> Its task consists of ascertaining whether the deportation in issue struck a fair balance between the relevant interests, namely the applicant's right to respect for his private and family life, on the one hand, and the prevention of disorder or crime, on the other.

Ibid, at para 42. The Court distinguished the present facts from those of the circumstances of *Moustaquim, Beldjoudi,* and *Nasri.* The Court attached particular importance to the fact that Mr Boughanemi's deportation had been decided after he had been sentenced to a total of almost four years' imprisonment, non-suspended, three of which were for living on the earnings of prostitution with aggravating circumstances. The seriousness of that last offence and the applicant's previous convictions counted heavily against him. Accordingly, the Court did not find that the applicant's deportation was disproportionate to the legitimate aims pursued and there was no violation of Article 8. Ibid, at paras 43–45.

[28] *Dalia v France,* supra note 9, which concerned an Algerian national living in France against whom a permanent exclusion order had been made on the basis of her conviction for drug dealing. The applicant, who had given birth to a child in France, claimed that the refusal of the French authorities to lift the exclusion order interfered with her private and family life and contravened Article 8 of the Convention.

[29] Ibid, at para 45.

[30] Ibid, at para 46.

[31] Ibid, at para 47.

[32] Ibid, at para 48.

[33] Ibid, at para 52.

she was in France illegally and that she could not be unaware of the resulting insecurity. Consequently, the Court was of the opinion that this factor could not, therefore, be decisive. Furthermore, the Court noted that the exclusion order made as a result of her conviction was a penalty for dealing in heroin and the fact that Mrs Dalia took part in drug trafficking weighed heavily in the balance. In contrast to its decision in *Mehemi*, the Court concluded that that the refusal to lift the exclusion order made against the applicant could not be regarded as disproportionate to the legitimate aim pursued and that, therefore, there had been no violation of Article 8.[34]

In the case of *Ciliz v The Netherlands*,[35] the Court reiterated its position that a bond amounting to family life within the meaning of Article 8(1) existed between the parents and the child born from their marriage-based relationship and that this was the case in the present application. Such a relationship clearly existed in the present case although the relationship between the parents following their separation was not as harmonious with respect to the matter of the father's access to his child as in the case of *Berrehab*.[36] In the view of the Court, the events subsequent to the separation of the applicant from his wife did not constitute exceptional circumstances capable of breaking the ties of 'family life' between the applicant and his son.[37]

The Court also reiterated its view that regard must be had to the fair balance that had to be struck between the competing interests of the individual and of the community as a whole, and, in both contexts, the State enjoyed a certain margin of appreciation. In the instant case, the State had both a positive obligation to ensure that family life between parents and children could continue after divorce and a negative obligation to refrain from measures which could cause family ties to rupture.[38] According to the Court, the domestic authorities were in the process of acquitting themselves of the former obligation to the extent that in the proceedings relating to the establishment of a formal access arrangement

---

[34] Ibid, at paras 54–55. This approach echoed the earlier judgment of *C v Belgium*, Judgment of 7 August 1996, Reports 1996-III 915, in which the applicant had fathered a child in Belgium thereby creating a tie between parent and child which had not been broken. In spite of this, the applicant's criminal record weighed against his claim to the right to respect for family life and was also outweighed by the State's interest in maintaining public order. Accordingly, the Court found that there was no violation of Article 8, ibid, at paras 25–36.

[35] Judgment of 11 July 2000, (No 29192/95). The applicant, a Turkish national, had lost his residency rights as a result of his divorce from his wife who was Dutch resident, and was obliged to leave The Netherlands. He contested the expulsion proceedings. At the same time, he sought to obtain access to his son who had been born during his marriage but was deported before he was able to arrange an access agreement. Ibid, at paras 8–38.

[36] Ibid, at paras 59–60.

[37] Ibid.

[38] Ibid, at paras 61–62.

the feasibility and desirability of access were being examined. However, the decision not to allow the applicant continued residence and his subsequent expulsion frustrated this examination and it was for this reason that the Court viewed the case as one involving an allegation of an 'interference' with the applicant's right to respect for his 'family life'.[39] The Court had no difficulty in accepting that the decision to refuse the applicant continued residence in The Netherlands had a basis in domestic law and that it served a legitimate aim within the meaning of Article 8(2).[40]

In determining whether an interference was 'necessary in a democratic society', the Court took into account the margin of appreciation that has been left to the Contracting States. It recalled that the Convention did not, in principle, prohibit States from regulating the entry and length of stay of aliens but reiterated that, whilst Article 8 contained no explicit procedural requirements, the decision-making process leading to measures of interference must be fair and such as to afford due respect to the interests safeguarded by Article 8.[41] To that end, the Court referred to previous judgments in which it had stated that:

> What . . . has to be determined is whether, having regard to the particular circumstances of the case and notably the serious nature of the decisions to be taken, the parents have been involved in the decision-making process, seen as a whole, to a degree sufficient to provide them with the requisite protection of their interests. If they have not, there will have been a failure to respect their family life and the interference resulting from the decision will not be capable of being regarded as 'necessary' within the meaning of Article 8. . . .[42]

In sum, the Court considered that the decision-making process concerning both the question of the applicant's expulsion and the question of access did not afford the requisite protection of the applicant's interests as safeguarded by Article 8. The interference with the applicant's right under this provision was, therefore, not necessary in a democratic society. Accordingly, there had been a breach of that provision.[43]

---

[39] Ibid.

[40] Ibid, at paras 64–65.

[41] Ibid, at para 66.

[42] Ibid. See, *W v United Kingdom*, Judgment of 8 July 1987, Series A no. 121, 28 and 29, §§ 62 and 64; and *McMichael v United Kingdom*, Judgment of 24 February 1995, Series A no. 307-B, 55, § 86.

[43] According to the Court, the authorities not only prejudged the outcome of the proceedings relating to the question of access by expelling the applicant when they did, but, and more importantly, they denied the applicant all possibility of any meaningful further involvement in those proceedings for which his availability for trial meetings in particular was obviously of essential importance. It stated that when the applicant eventually obtained a visa to return to the Netherlands for three months in 1999, the mere passage of time had resulted in a *de facto* determination of the proceedings for access which he then instituted and that the authorities, through their failure to co-ordinate the various proceedings touching on the applicant's family rights, have not, therefore, acted in a manner which has enabled family ties to be developed, ibid, at paras 71–72.

The issue arose again more recently in the case of *Sen v The Netherlands*.[44] In reiterating the approach adopted in previous decisions, such as *Gül*,[45] the Court noted that the provisions of Article 8 had to be weighed against the freedom of the State in matters of immigration. In determining whether there had been a violation, the Court had to take into account the particular circumstances of the case. To that end, the Court noted Sinem Sen's young age when the application was first made, the fact that she had spent her whole life in Turkey and that she had strong linguistic and cultural links with that country and that she still had relatives there.[46] However, the applicants had settled in The Netherlands as a couple for many years, they had been legally resident there, two of their three children had been born and raised there and had very strong ties with the country of their birth and very few ties with their country of origin, other than that of nationality, and that the lack of ties constituted one of the major obstacles to the family returning to live in Turkey. As such, bringing Sinem to The Netherlands constituted the best course of action for developing a family life in light of her young age and the preference for her integration into the family unit of her parents. In leaving the parents no choice but to either give up the life that they had built up for themselves in The Netherlands or give the chance of being with their daughter, the Court concluded that The Netherlands had failed to strike a fair balance between the applicants' interest and their own interest in controlling immigration and held that there had been a violation of Article 8.[47]

---

[44] Judgment of 21 December 2001. The three applicants, all Turkish nationals, complained that their right to respect for family life had been infringed by the Dutch authorities refusal to grant a residence permit to Sinem Sen, the third applicant, and allow her to join her parents, the first two applicants, in The Netherlands. In considering whether the Dutch authorities had a positive obligation to allow Sinem to live with her parents in The Netherlands and so maintain and develop their family life, the Court reiterated the need for a fair balance to be struck between the positive and negative obligations arising from Article 8(2). Ibid, at paras 31–32.

[45] *Gül v Switzerland*, Judgment of 19 of February 1996, Reports 1996-I 159.

[46] Ibid, at paras 37–39.

[47] Ibid, at paras 40–41. This case can be contrasted with the difficult circumstances of an earlier case *Gül v Switzerland*, Judgment of 19 of February 1996, Reports 1996-I 159. The applicant was a Turkish national who, at the time of the case, lived with his wife in Switzerland. The applicant had lived with his wife and their two sons in Turkey until 1983 when he travelled to Switzerland, where he applied for political asylum. The applicant's wife joined her husband in Switzerland, after having severely burned herself during an epileptic fit. In September 1988 Mrs Gül gave birth to her third child, in Switzerland. As Mrs Gül still suffered from epilepsy, she could not take care of the baby, who was placed in a home in Switzerland, where she has remained ever since. In February 1989 Mr Gül's application for political asylum was rejected by the Swiss authorities. In 1990 Mr and Mrs Gül were granted a residence permit on humanitarian grounds and then unsuccessfully sought permission to bring their son Ersin, who had always lived in Turkey, to Switzerland. The applicant appealed this decision on the basis that it was impossible to return to Turkey because of his wife's precarious state of health and the

In essence, the reasoning of European Court of Human Rights was initially premised on the recognition that States Parties have the right of control over their immigration and asylum laws. Where this right overlaps with the provisions of Article 8, the Court also recognised that the right to respect for family life is not an absolute right and that it may be circumscribed by the State. However, such intervention must satisfy the provisions of Article 8(2). The case law referred to above indicates that the main issue to be determined with regard to Article 8(2) is whether the measures taken are legitimate to the aims pursued and are necessary in a democratic society. In the Court's opinion, once the applicant can establish 'family ties' within a State Party, the interests of that family (including those of the child as a part of the family unit) must be balanced with those of the State to regulate its immigration policy. However, as the above case law suggests, those instances in which a State may interfere with the right to respect for family life on immigration grounds must go some way beyond the simple threshold requirement of a State's right to regulate the entry of aliens into its territory. Even in cases where the applicant's criminal activities have posed a threat to 'public order' the impact upon family life of the deportation order remains to be considered, as demonstrated by the contrasting judgments of *Dalia* and *Mehemi*. Thus, the concept of the balance to be struck as between competing rights referred to in Chapter 1 is made explicit by the jurisprudence of the European Court of Human Rights in relation to immigration matters and the rights of the child.

---

length of time he had lived abroad, the family could be brought back together only in Switzerland. He argued that both Article 8 of the European Convention on Human Rights, guaranteeing the right to respect for family life, and the United Nations Convention on the Rights of the Child gave the two boys the right to join their parents in Switzerland. Ibid, at paras 6–23. The Court reiterated that the boundaries between the State's positive and negative obligations under Article 8 did not lend themselves to precise definition and regard must be had to the fair balance that has to be struck between the competing interests of the individual and of the community as a whole and that, in both contexts, the State enjoyed a certain margin of appreciation. In noting that the case concerned not only family life but also immigration, the Court observed that the extent of a State's obligation to admit to its territory relatives of settled immigrants would vary according to the particular circumstances of the persons involved and the general interest, and reiterated the point that, as a matter of well-established international law and subject to its treaty obligations, a State had the right to control the entry of non-nationals into its territory. The Court's task was to determine the truth of the assertion that moving the applicant's son to Switzerland would be the only way for the applicant, Mr Gül, to develop family life with his younger son, Ersin. Although the Court admitted that it would not be easy for the Güls to return to Turkey, it was of the opinion that there were, strictly speaking, no obstacles preventing them from developing family life in Turkey. According to the Court, that possibility was all the more real because Ersin had always lived there and had therefore grown up in the cultural and linguistic environment of his country. The Court distinguished *Berrehab* on that point. Having regard to all these considerations, and while acknowledging that the Gül family's situation was very difficult from the human point of view, the Court found that Switzerland had not failed to fulfil the obligations arising under Article 8. Ibid, at paras 39–43.

4. The Rights of Irish-Born Children of Asylum Seekers

Ireland has ratified a number of international treaties and has consequently undertaken a raft of international obligations with regard to the rights of children, in general, and those born of refugees, in particular.[48] In addition, membership of the European Union permits all residents of the European Union freedom of movement across the European Union. The interrelationship (or lack thereof) between Irish domestic law and international law has previously been considered in Chapter 5. However, the distinction between the legal effects of international law and domestic law in terms of asylum seekers was reiterated most recently in the Supreme Court case of *Lobe, Osayande and Others v Minister for Justice*.[49] Denham J reiterated the point made by Smyth J in the High Court when he stated that the Dublin Convention had the same status within domestic law as any other international instruments, such as the European Convention on Human Rights, in that it did not form part of the domestic law of the State,[50] Accordingly, Ireland is not bound by its international obligations and, in essence, the rights of Irish-born refugee children are to be governed solely by the provisions of the Irish Constitution. Nevertheless, the interpretation of these constitutional rights may be tempered by reference to the jurisprudence of the European Court of Human Rights.

At the domestic level, the rights of all children born in Ireland derive from a number of sources which are constitutional and statutory in nature.

4.1. Constitutional Protection

Until recently, Article 2 of the Irish Constitution used to grant automatic citizenship to all children born in Ireland:

> It is the entitlement and birthright of every person born on the island of Ireland, . . . to be part of the Irish nation. This is also the entitlement of all

---

[48] Ireland has ratified both International Covenants and the Convention on the Rights of the Child. Ireland has also acceded to the Convention relating to the Status of Refugees. In terms of the Council of Europe, Ireland has ratified the European Convention on Human Rights. Finally in terms of the European Union, Ireland has also ratified the Convention Determining the State Responsible for Examining Applications for Asylum Lodged in One of the Member States of the Community, Dublin, 15 June 1990.

[49] *Lobe*, supra note 1.

[50] Ibid, at para 197. Justice Smyth's assertion was based on the Supreme Court's decision in *Toma Adam v The Minister for Justice and Others* (unreported 5/4/2001), as reported in http://www.firstlaw.ie/, FL4321, p 15, which was, in turn, based upon the Supreme Court decision of *Doyle v The Commissioner of An Garda Siochana* [1999] 1 IR 249, as viewed in Lexis in July 2002 http://80www.lexisnexis.com.au.ezproxy.waikato.ac.nz:2048/cui/unilogin/default.htm?login. asp?uniwaikato. However, the Dublin Convention is now in force and given that it is part of European Union law it has direct effect on Irish legislation.

persons otherwise qualified in accordance with the law to be citizens of
Ireland.[51]

However, the rights contained in this provision have been restricted by the
Twenty-Seventh Amendment of the Constitution Bill. Prior to this, there was
no constitutional guarantee to Irish citizenship, apart from that contained in
Article 9(1), which confirmed citizenship on all of those born in Ireland before
1937 when that Constitution was enacted to the earlier 1922 version. Prior to
the Twenty-Seventh Amendment, Article 9 of the Constitution had stated that
citizenship matters would be determined by the Irish Parliament which subsequently passed the Irish Nationality and Citizenship Act 1956. The 1956 Act
was amended in 2001, to reflect the amendments to Articles 2 and 3 of the
Constitution, with the result that s 6(1) of the (amended) 1956 Act stated that
"Every person born in Ireland is an Irish citizen from birth." The recent
amendment of Article 9 removes the constitutional guarantee of citizenship
and restores the approach that such matters are to be the subject of legislative
determination. Consequently, the broad citizenship rights granted by Article 2
must now be read in the restrictive light of Article 9(2) of the Constitution,
which now reads:

1. Notwithstanding any other provision of this Constitution, a person born in
   the island of Ireland, which includes its islands and seas, who does not have,
   at the time of the birth of that person, at least one parent who is an Irish citizen or entitled to be an Irish citizen is not entitled to Irish citizenship or
   nationality, unless *provided for by law*. [emphasis added]
2. This section shall not apply to persons born before the date of the enactment
   of this section.

The provisions of Article 9(1) have been given legislative effect by the Irish
Nationality and Citizenship Act 2004, which amends the provisions of s 6A of
the 1956 Act.[52] In short, the amending legislation provides that a child of two
non-national parents can only become an Irish citizen if at least one parent has
lived for three out of the previous four years in Ireland.[53] However, the amending legislation does not apply to a person born before the commencement of
the Irish Nationality and Citizenship Act 2004.[54] The consequence of such legislation is that there will be two categories of children born in Ireland, those
with citizenship and those without. The concern is that such categorisation

---

[51] Article 2, *Bunreacht na hEireann*, Government Stationery Office, Dublin. The current wording of Article 2 itself is relatively new and arose out of the 19th Amendment to the Constitution
which replaced the wording of Articles 2 and 3 as required by the Good Friday Agreement,
negotiated to end the conflict in the North.
[52] Section 3.
[53] Section 4.
[54] Section 6A(2)(a) Nationality and Citizenship Act 1956.

will form the basis of discrimination as between these children with the basis of such discrimination deriving from the level of protection accorded to rights by the Irish Constitution. Of particular concern are the rights of the child that are currently protected by Article 40.3.1, which enshrines the State's obligation to respect and, as far as practicable by its laws, to defend and vindicate the personal rights of the citizen and Article 40.3.2's requirement to protect these rights as best it can from unjust attack. In terms of the Irish-born children of asylum seekers born before the Constitutional amendment and ensuing legislation, the level of protection afforded to such families remains unclear.

In general terms, the Constitutional protection afforded to the family is to be found in Article 41.1.1, which provides that:

> The State recognises the Family as the natural primary and fundamental unit group of society, and as a moral institution possessing inalienable and imprescriptible rights antecedent and superior to all positive law.

The Constitutional protection accorded to family is further strengthened by the provisions of Article 41.2 which provides that:

> The State, therefore, guarantees to protect the Family in its constitution and authority, as the necessary basis of social order and as indispensable to the welfare of the Nation and the State.

The rights of the child are derived from Article 42, in particular. On the one hand, the rights of the child are inextricably linked to the rights of the family, and in endorsing the principle of non-interventionism, Article 42.1 states:

> The State acknowledges that the primary natural educator of the child is the family and guarantees to respect the inalienable right and duty of parents to provide, according to their means, for the religious and moral, intellectual, physical and social education of their children.

Nevertheless, the rights accorded to parents are not absolute and Article 42.5 allows the State to intervene to secure the rights of the child:

> In exceptional cases, where the parents for physical or moral reasons fail in their duty towards their children, the State, as guardian of the common good, by appropriate means shall endeavour to supply the place of the parents, but always with due regard to the natural and imprescriptible rights of the child.[55]

As such, the State may only interfere in family life when parents fail to care adequately for their children, with such intervention being governed by the principle of securing the rights of the child. The lack of clarity as to the extent of the rights of the child to family life stems from that fact that Articles 41 and 42 make no reference as to whether they are rights accorded to citizens only.

---

[55] Ibid, Article 42.

However, Art. 4.1.1's statement regarding the family as an institution possessing inalienable and imprescriptible rights antecedent and superior to all positive law, such as any legislation passed by the Oireachtas, should mean that the legal protection accorded to the family unit should not make any distinction between citizens and non-citizens and their families.

The nature of the balance that has to be struck between rights of the family, the rights of the child and the rights of the State to intervene has been explored by the courts particularly in relation to child custody proceedings. To that end, in *Re article 26 and the Adoption Bill (No. 2) 1987*,[56] Finlay CJ observed that the balance of welfare, as defined in s 3 of the Guardianship of Infants Act 1964, had to be the sole criterion for the determination of the issue of custody in a contest between married parents and third parties. In the event of such a dispute he noted that:

> [Section] 3 of the Act of 1964 must be construed as involving a constitutional presumption that the welfare of the child, which is defined in Section 2 of the Act in terms identical to those contained in Article 42, S.1, is to be found within the family, unless the Court is satisfied on the evidence that there are compelling reasons why this cannot be achieved, or unless the court is satisfied that the evidence establishes an exceptional case where the parents have failed to provide education for the child and continue to fail to provide education for the child for moral or physical reasons.[57]

The Supreme Court continued with an exploration of what constitutes 'compelling reasons' in the context of custody disputes. With regard to Article 42.5, which was referred to in the Bill, the Court noted that it was not to be construed as being confined to the duty of parents to educate their children. According to the Court, this provision should be interpreted as a parental duty to cater for the other personal needs of the child.[58] It noted that:

> The guarantees afforded to the institution of the family by the Constitution, with their consequent benefit to the children of a family, should not be construed so that upon the failure of that benefit it cannot be replaced where the circumstances demand it, by incorporation of the child into an alternative family.[59]

---

[56] [1989] IR 656; [1989] ILRM 266. This case related to the constitutionality of the Adoption Bill (No. 2) which was unsuccessfully attacked on the ground that it violated the 'inalienable and imprescriptible rights' of the original family. Both Houses of the Oireachtas passed the Adoption Bill (No. 2) in June 1988. The President of Ireland referred the Bill to the Supreme Court pursuant to Article 26.1 of the Constitution for a decision on the question of whether any part of the Bill could be construed as being repugnant to the Constitution. The Bill provided for the adoption of any child under certain circumstances whether born in wedlock or not, and whether one or more of the parents survived or not. It also provided for the adoption of children without the consent of their parents or guardian.

[57] Ibid, at 397.
[58] Ibid, at 663.
[59] Ibid.

The Court also referred to the fact that the State had a duty, both under Article 42.5 and Article 40.3, to protect the rights of the child, noting that:

> The Court accepts the submission made on behalf of the Attorney General that the right and duty of the State to intervene upon the failure of parents to discharge their duty to a child can be considered under both Article 42, s 5 and Article 40, s 3. By the express provisions of Article 42, s 5, the State in endeavouring to supply the place of the parents is obliged to have due regard for the natural and imprescriptible rights of the child. Any action by the State pursuant to Article 40, s 3 endeavouring to vindicate the personal rights of the child would . . . be subject to the same limitation.[60]

Thus, the Court seems to have drawn a distinction between the personal rights arising from one's status as citizen, on the one hand, and the natural and imprescriptible rights accorded to the family unit and the child on the other. The Court came to the conclusion that the obligation to have due regard for all persons concerned was firmly enjoined in the context of ascertaining the best interests of the child and that the verification of the child's best interests would necessarily:

> be adjudged against the background of the child's constitutional rights. The phrase 'best interests of the child' . . . would necessarily involve some proper consideration of all the consequences, from the point of view of the child, of bringing it by adoption out of the family.[61]

This point was reiterated two years later in *M.F. v Superintendent, Ballymun Garda Station*.[62] In the High Court, O'Flaherty J recognised that "cases concerning the care and custody of children and the protection of their rights are in a special and possibly unique category".[63] He noted the decision that had been reached in *The Adoption (No. 2) Bill 1987*[64] concerning the regard that must always be had to the natural and imprescriptible rights of the child. To that end, O'Flaherty J noted that:

> Even prior to the setting up of the State in 1922 it was recognised by the courts in this country when they came to deal with the custody of the child that the paramount consideration was the welfare of the child in the widest sense of the term . . .[65]

---

[60] Ibid.

[61] Ibid.

[62] [1991] 1 IR 189; [1990] ILRM 767. The case concerned an invocation of s 20 of the Children Act 1908, which resulted in the applicant's children being taken into care. An application was subsequently made to the High Court pursuant to Article 40 of the Constitution regarding the legality of the children's detention.

[63] Ibid, at 200.

[64] *The Adoption (No. 2) Bill 1987*, supra note 56.

[65] *M.F. v Superintendent, Ballymun Garda Station*, supra note 62, at 201.

Both cases support a contention that there is adequate constitutional justification for a judicial approach to custody disputes which prioritises the rights and interests of the child. Similarly, in *P.W. v A.W.*, Ellis J followed the approach traditionally adopted by the Irish courts that the best place for a child was with its family.[66] Nevertheless, he also stated that:

> . . . in my view, the only way the 'inalienable and imprescriptible' rights of the child can be protected is by the Courts treating the welfare of the child as the paramount consideration in all disputes as to its custody . . . I take the view also that the child has the personal right to have its welfare regarded as the paramount consideration in any such dispute as to its custody. . . .[67]

Such an interpretation of the Constitution not only allows for greater emphasis to be placed upon the rights and interests of the child, which are more protective of the important psychological relationships between the child and the adult, it also prioritises the inalienable and imprescriptible rights of the child. This argument may have particular significance in instances where attempts may be made to roll back the rights of a child of non-nationals regarding family life on the basis that such constitutional protection applies to citizens only. This argument should also be considered in light of the State's obligation to ensure that the best interests of the child underpin any intervention by the State with regard to parents' custody over their children. These cases should be considered as being relevant to cases concerning the deportation of asylum seekers with Irish-born children on the basis that Deportation Orders will inevitably interfere with asylum-seekers' custody of their Irish-born children.

4.2. Legislative Protection

The constitutional rights, if not the judicial interpretation accorded to these rights, govern the manner in which the legislative framework regarding children born of asylum seekers is to be interpreted and implemented. These rights are fleshed out by such legislative provisions as the Guardianship of Infants Act 1964, s 2 of which defines the term 'welfare', in terms taken from the Constitution, as " 'Welfare', in relation to an infant, comprises the religious and moral, intellectual, physical and social welfare of the infant". In addition, s 3 of the Act states:

> Where in any proceedings before any court the custody, guardianship or upbringing of an infant, or the administration of any property belonging to or held on trust for an infant, or the application of the income thereof, is in question, the court, in deciding that question, shall regard the welfare of the infant as the first and paramount consideration.

[66] High Court, 21 April 1980.
[67] Ibid.

The law regarding guardianship and custody of, and access to, children was subsequently updated by the Children Act 1997. Section 11 of the Act provides specifically that the wishes of the child are to be taken into account where the court deems it to be appropriate and practical having regard to the age and understanding of the child. Similarly, s 24 of the Child Care Act 1991 states:

> In any proceedings before a court under this Act in relation to the care and protection of a child, the court, having regard to the rights and duties of parents, whether under the Constitution or otherwise, shall—
> (a) regard the welfare of the child as the first and paramount consideration,. . . .

In terms of asylum seekers, at a general level, s 2 of the Refugee Act 1996 reiterates the definition accorded by Article 1 of the Refugee Convention 1951.[68] In addition, s 5(1) of the Refugee Act 1996, regarding the prohibition of *refoulement*, provides that:

> A person shall not be expelled from the State or returned in any manner whatsoever to the frontiers of territories where, in the opinion of the Minister the life or freedom of that person would be threatened on account of his or her race, religion, nationality, membership of a particular social group or political opinion.[69]

This principle is further explored in s 3 of the Immigration Act 1999. Section 3(1) states:

> Subject to the provisions of section 5 (prohibition of refoulement) of the Refugee Act, 1996, and the subsequent provisions of this section, the Minister may by order (in this Act referred to as 'a deportation order') require any non-national specified in the order to leave the State within such period as may be specified in the order and to remain thereafter out of the State.[70]

The section makes some provision taking into account the relationship between a child born in Ireland and his or her asylum-seeking parents, as s 3(6) of the Immigration Act provides, inter alia, that:

> In determining whether to make a deportation order in relation to a person, the Minister shall have regard to- . . .
> (c) the family and domestic circumstances of the person;
> (d) the nature of the person's connection with the State, if any;
>
> and
>
> . . .
>
> (j) the common good; . . .
> so far as they appear or are known to the Minister.[71]

---

[68] Supra note 3.
[69] Section 5 Refugee Act 1996.
[70] Section 3(1) Immigration Act 1999.
[71] Ibid, s 3(6).

Finally, Ireland's obligations to other Member States of the European Union are incorporated into domestic law by virtue of the Dublin Convention (Implementation) Order 2000.[72]

5. Judicial Interpretation of the Rights of Irish-Born Children of Asylum Seekers: Lobe, Osayande and Others v Minister for Justice, Equality and Law Reform

In spite of the level of protection from State intervention that may be accorded to the right to respect for family life by the European Convention, on the one hand, and the Irish Constitution, on the other, the Supreme Court decision of *Lobe, Osayande and Others v Minister for Justice*[73] is indicative the actual level of protection currently afforded to children born in Ireland whose parents are the subject of Deportation Orders. Mr and Mrs Lobe and their three children arrived in Ireland on 31 March 2001 from the UK. Mrs Lobe was pregnant at this time. The Lobe family were Czech nationals. They applied for asylum in Ireland but were unsuccessful, with a subsequent appeal to the Refugee Appeals Tribunal also being unsuccessful, and they were due to be deported from Ireland in October 2001. Kevin Lobe was born on 2 November 2001. The Lobes submitted to the Minister that they should not be deported in the light of the birth of Kevin Lobe in Ireland. The Minister refused their application for a number of reasons; the Lobe family had only been in the State for nine months, they could adapt to their return to the UK and the Czech Republic and their lives or well-being would not be endangered, the need to apply the Dublin Convention to which Ireland is a party, and the overriding need to preserve respect for and the integrity of the asylum and immigration systems.[74] With regard to the Osayande family, Mr and Mrs Osayande were Nigerian nationals who arrived in Ireland with their daughter 6 May 2001. Mr Osayande applied for refugee status on 15 May after having unsuccessfully applied for asylum in the UK. The Irish Refugee Appeals Commissioner sought to return Mr Osayande to the UK. Mr Osayande unsuccessfully appealed the decision and he was due to be deported in October 2001. On 4 October 2001, Mrs Osyande gave birth to a son, Osaze. Similarly to the Lobes, the Osyande family made an application to the Minister which was refused for identical reasons, except that relating to return to the Czech Republic.[75] The bases of the Minister's decision are to be found in a memorandum prepared by the Immigration Division of the

---

[72] Dublin Convention (Implementation) Order 2000 (SI 343/2000).
[73] Supra note 1.
[74] Ibid, at paras 1–4.
[75] Ibid, at paras 5–7.

Ministry of Justice, Equality and Law Reform – the Lohan Memorandum – which largely formed the basis for the ensuing cases in the High Court and Supreme Court. The Supreme Court, by a five-two majority, subsequently upheld the decision of the High Court in deciding that non-national parents of Irish-born children and their non-national siblings were not entitled to live in Ireland by virtue of having an Irish-born child.

The views of the majority are echoed in Keane CJ's judgment. The Chief Justice dismissed the appeal on a number of grounds, some of which had particular resonance for children's rights and age discrimination. Firstly, with regard to the citizenship of the child applicants, Keane CJ referred to s 6 of the Nationality and Citizenship Act 1956 and Article 2 of the Constitution, and accepted that the children in question were Irish citizens and were entitled to their constitutional rights, including the right not to be expelled from Ireland. However, he added that, in general, this right was not absolute and cited extradition as an example of a restriction.[76] Chief Justice Keane drew a distinction between the citizenship rights held by adults and those held by children, on the basis that newly-born infants were incapable of making, still less articulating, any decisions as to where they would reside and that the decision as to where such children would reside was normally made by their parents. According to the Chief Justice, this distinction was of paramount importance in the case at hand. He stated that, in general, adult Irish citizens could exercise a choice as to whether they wished to reside in Ireland or some other country unless they were under a legal constraint which effectively prevented them from exercising that right, an example being where they were in prison. Chief Justice Keane stated that the position of children of the age of the minor applicants was significantly weaker than that of adult citizens who were in prison or otherwise constrained from exercising a choice of residence, since these children had never been capable in law of exercising the right. He further stated that in practical terms, as distinct from legal theory, such a right may reasonably be regarded as one which does not vest in them until they reach an age at which they are capable of exercising it.[77] With regard to the constitutional right of the children to be in the care and company of the other members of their families, Keane CJ accepted this right but rejected the claim that they had the constitutional right to that care and company in Ireland simply by virtue of their having been born in Ireland in circumstances where their parents had no legal right to reside in the State and could lawfully be expelled from the State. The Chief Justice was of the opinion that the parents of the children in

---

[76] Ibid, at paras 28–33.
[77] Ibid, at para 35.

question could not assert a choice to reside in the State on behalf of their children even if such a decision was in the interest of those children. The making of such a choice would presuppose that the minor applicants were, in law, entitled to choose where they resided. However, according to Keane CJ, these children were both factually and legally incapable of making such a choice. He stated that if the parents were lawfully entitled to choose to reside in Ireland – which they were not – the right of the minor citizens to reside with them in Ireland would accordingly derive, not from the fact that they were Irish citizens, but rather from their constitutional right to be in the care and custody of their parents.

The second ground for Keane CJ's dismissal was based on Ireland's sovereign right to expel or deport non-nationals, a right which had been affirmed by the High Court in *Pok Sun Shun v Ireland*.[78] In *Pok Sun Shun* it was argued, *inter alia*, that the statutory framework to control non-nationals that was in place at the time[79] violated the constitutional protection accorded to the family unit. Chief Justice Keane referred to the response made by Costello J to the contention that the mechanisms in place to control the movement of non-nationals violated the constitutional rights afforded to the family and subsequent refusal to uphold the declaration sought in *Pok Sun Shun*:

> I do not think that the rights given to the 'family' are absolute, in the sense that they are not subject to some restrictions by the State and, as counsel for the State has pointed out, restrictions are, in fact, permitted by law, when husbands are imprisoned and parents of families are imprisoned and, undoubtedly, whilst protected under the Constitution, these are restrictions permitted for the common good on the exercise of its rights.[80]

Keane CJ also noted that this statement of the law had been reaffirmed in the Supreme Court in *Laurentiu v Minister for Justice*.[81]

This approach to the balance of statutory rights conferred on the Minister of Justice to control immigration against the constitutional rights of the family was reiterated by Gannon J in *Osheku & Others v Ireland*, a case where the plaintiff was unemployed and it was uncertain whether he had any intention of gaining employment.[82] The State's right to control non-nationals was outlined by Gannon J:

> That it is in the interest of the common good of a State that it should have control of the entry of aliens, their departure and their activities and duration of stay within the State is and has been recognised universally and from earliest times.

---

[78] [1986] ILRM 593.
[79] Aliens Act 1935.
[80] *Lobe*, supra note 1, at para 60.
[81] Ibid, at para 65. *Laurentiu v Minister for Justice* [1999] 4 IR 27.
[82] [1986] IR 733.

> There are fundamental rights of the State itself as well as fundamental rights of the individual citizen, and the protection of the former may involve restrictions in circumstances of necessity on the latter.[83]

Thus, according to Keane CJ in *Lobe*, there was precedent for the argument that the statutory provisions arising from the inherent right of the State to control immigration superseded any constitutional right to protection of the family unit. The third basis for his decision to dismiss the appeal related to the earlier Supreme Court decision of *Fajujonu v Minister of Justice*,[84] a case in which the balance of rights between immigration control and family rights was considered more fully in both the High Court and the Supreme Court. Chief Justice Keane drew upon the High Court decision of Barrington J in *Fajujonu* in which the High Court judge stated the issues as:

> The present case appears to me to raise much more complex issues. I am prepared to accept that the child has, generally speaking, a right, as an Irish citizen, to be in the State. I am also prepared to accept as a general proposition that the child has the right to the society of its parents. But does it follow from this that the child has the right to the society of its parents in the State?[85]

In response to this question, Barrington J concluded:

> In the present case the parents never had a right to live or to work in Ireland. The child clearly has a certain right to be in Ireland. She also has the right to the society of her parents. But it does not follow from this that she has a right to the society of her parents in Ireland. I do not think that the parents can by positing on their child a wish to remain in Ireland in their society confer upon themselves a right to remain in Ireland, such as could be invoked to override legislation passed by the Irish parliament to achieve its concept of what the common good of Irish citizens generally requires. I think this distinguishes the present case from *The State (M) -v- The Attorney General.* There the paramount issue was what the welfare of the child required. *But the present case does not turn merely upon the rights of the child, it also raises the powers of the Oireachtas to control the immigration of aliens into the country.*[86] [emphasis added]

Chief Justice Keane referred to Barrington J's reiteration of the statement of law regarding immigration control made in *Pok Sun Shun* and in *Osheku* and his dismissal of the appeal, a decision that was subsequently appealed to the Supreme Court. Chief Justice Keane continued by referring to Finlay CJ's summation of the *Fajujonu* issue before the Supreme Court. According to Finlay CJ, the law:

> was not an assertion of the absolute right incapable of being affected by the provisions of the Act of 1935, but rather the assertion of a constitutional right of

---

[83] Ibid, at 746.
[84] [1990] 2 IR 151.
[85] *Lobe*, supra note 1, at para 72.
[86] Ibid, at para 73.

great importance which could only be restricted or infringed for very compelling reasons.[87]

Chief Justice Finlay was of the opinion that the deportation of the Fajujonu family from the State, where the parents were non-nationals but three children of the family were Irish-born and thus citizens of Ireland, would have to be for a grave and substantial reason associated with the common good.[88] However, Finlay CJ also said that the determination of this question would have to made by the Minister who would have to be satisfied the deportation and its attendant consequences for the citizens of that family was for good and sufficient reason the common good.[89]

Chief Justice Keane also referred to Walsh J's judgment in *Fajujonu* where Walsh J, having said that it was abundantly clear that Irish citizens could not be deported, continued by saying:

> In view of the fact that these are children of tender age who require the society of their parents and when the parents have not been shown to have been in any way unfit or guilty of any matter which makes them unsuitable custodians to their children, to move to expel the parents in the particular circumstances of this case, would, in my view, be inconsistent with the provisions of Article 41 of the Constitution guaranteeing the integrity of the family.[90]

Having expressed his agreement with the opinion of Finlay CJ, that the matter would have to be reconsidered by the Minister, bearing in mind the constitutional rights involved, Walsh J added:

> In my view, he would have to be satisfied, for stated reasons, that the interests of the common good of the people of Ireland and of the protection of the State and its society are so predominant and so overwhelming in the circumstances of the case, that an action which can have the effect of breaking up this family is not so disproportionate to the aim sought to be achieved as to be unsustainable.[91]

In seeking to rely on the judgments of Finlay CJ and Walsh J in *Fajujonu*, Keane CJ noted that that they contained no expression of disapproval of the statement of the law by Gannon J in *Osheku* and *Pok Sun Shun*.[92] This observation allowed the Chief Justice to conclude that applicants in *Lobe* had no basis for their argument that the claimed right of the minor applicant(s) to enjoy the society of their parents in Ireland would be infringed by the deportation of the other members of the families, unless there were specific reasons arising in

[87] Ibid, at para 78.
[88] Ibid, at para 81, per Keane CJ.
[89] Ibid, at para 84.
[90] Ibid, at para 87.
[91] Ibid, at para 88.
[92] Ibid, at para 96.

their particular cases which would render the continued residence of the other members of the family in the State inimical to the common good.[93] The Chief Justice distinguished *Fajujonu* on the ground that there were specific circumstances to which the Court thought the Minister should have regard in *Fajujonu*, together with the constitutional rights of the family and any other matters relevant to their continued stay in the State which might come to the Minister's attention, such as:

(1) the "appreciable time" (approximately eight years at the date of the hearing in this court) for which they had resided as a family in Ireland;
(2) the fact that the family had made its "home and residence" in Ireland;
(3) the fact that the first plaintiff had been offered employment, that the relevant authority was prepared to issue him a work permit and that the only ground on which a permit would not be issued was that the Minister in that case had refused to grant him permission to stay in Ireland.[94]

According to Keane CJ, not one of those three factors was present in the circumstances of the applicants in *Lobe*.[95] Chief Justice Keane was also satisfied that *Fajujonu* was distinguishable on another ground, namely that the factual and statutory context in which the Minister was required to decide whether a deportation order should be made had altered radically since that case was decided. In particular, he was of the opinion that the Executive was entitled to take the view that the orderly system in place for dealing with immigration and asylum applications should not be undermined by persons seeking to take advantage of the period of time which necessarily elapses between their arrival in the State and the complete processing of their applications for asylum by relying on the birth of a child to one of them during that period as a reason for permitting them to reside in the State indefinitely. This was the background against which the Chief Justice said that the test for determining whether the Minister was entitled to make the orders of deportation was whether the decision was so manifestly contrary to reason and common sense that it had to be set aside by the High Court and he was satisfied in both cases that it was not.[96]

In her dissenting judgment, McGuinness J said that in light of the High Court's decision that the circumstances giving rise to the deportation orders for the Lobe and Osayande families met the *Fajujonu* standards,[97] and that it was "therefore necessary for this Court to consider the nature, importance and weight of the rights of the child citizens, of their families, and of the State,

---

[93] Ibid, at paras 97–98.
[94] Ibid, at paras 99–100.
[95] Ibid, at para 101.
[96] Ibid, at para 103.
[97] Ibid, at para 217, per McGuinness J.

in the context of the *Fajujonu* judgment".[98] After tracing through the case law relevant to the rights of citizenship of the applicant children and their rights under Articles 41 and 42 of the Constitution,[99] McGuinness J concluded that the *Fajujonu* decision had to be regarded in a broader context where:

> The origin, importance and weight of the rights of the family are all stressed in this powerful line of decisions both of the High Court and of this court. They are not absolute rights, but they are not readily displaced and compelling reasons are required to displace them.[100]

After an in-depth analysis of the *Fajujonu* case and the law behind that case, McGuinness J observed that although the Supreme Court had dismissed the appeal in that case, nevertheless rigorous standards were set in both the High Court and the Supreme Court with regard to the reasons which might justify the Minister in deporting the Fajujonu family. She noted both Finlay CJ and Walsh J's test for deportation and acknowledged that the personal rights of the child, or the rights of the family, could, for proper and proportionate reasons, yield to the requirements of the common good.[101] With regard to such rights McGuinness J referred to Finlay CJ's finding that the Fajujonu parents were entitled to assert a choice of residence on behalf of their infant children, in the interests of those infant children. According to McGuinness J, Finlay CJ had made it clear:

> that the parents cannot claim any constitutional right of their own to remain in Ireland. Any right of the parents to remain must therefore in the terms of the judgment arise from the right of the children to remain. While, as citizens, the children may not be deported, it is not suggested that they are compelled to remain here because they are citizens. As citizens they may choose to remain here or to leave; as infants they are incapable of making that choice for themselves. It therefore, as seen by Finlay C.J., falls to their parents to assert their choice for them.
>
> It is only as a result of that choice that the parents may assert as part of the rights of a family under Articles 41 and 42 that they, too, have a right, albeit not an absolute right, to reside with the children in this country. The issue of the parents' right to remain and the findings of the Court in that respect are built on the assertion of the child's choice, which must therefore in my view be an inherent part of the ratio of the decision. In the absence of any direct challenge to the *Fajujonu* decision, therefore, it must be assumed to be binding on this Court.[102]

---

[98] Ibid, at para 219.
[99] Ibid, at paras 220–249.
[100] Ibid, at para 250.
[101] Ibid, at paras 264–265.
[102] Ibid, at paras 270–271.

This analysis allowed McGuinness J to state that if the Supreme Court's decision was to distinguish these cases from *Fajujonu* on length of residence and number of Irish-born children, it would create a situation where future cases must be pleaded and decided on a "sympathy" basis, on the varying circumstances, carrying with it the danger of inconsistency and arbitrariness. She then referred to the commentary on the *Fajujonu* case by the authors of *Kelly on the Constitution*[103] who remarked:

> There is evidence in the passages quoted from both judgments that the judges were influenced by the fact that the Plaintiffs had resided in Ireland for quite some time and that the family had made its home here. An obvious implication is that an alien family, one of whose children is fortuitously born in the country, thereby acquiring citizenship, might not be in the same fortunate position as the *Fajujonus* when it comes to the matter of deportation. However it is submitted that, as the rights of the child derive from its citizenship, the length of time which the family as a unit has resided in the State would appear to be irrelevant in this context. For once the child, as a citizen, is entitled to reside in the State it is difficult to see how its right to the company, care and parentage of its parents, derived from Articles 41 and 42, can depend on the length of this period of residence. Furthermore, in policy terms, the desirability of promoting and protecting the psychological bond between parent and child must also call into question any linkage between the child's rights to the company of its parents and the length of time which the family has resided in the State.

With regard to the Minister's reasoning that the families must be deported in order to preserve respect for and the integrity of the asylum and immigration systems, described as an "overriding" need in the Lohan memorandum, McGuinness J questioned whether this particular reason was sufficient to meet the standards set by the Supreme Court in *Fajujonu*, and whether it was sufficient to outweigh both the family's and the child's constitutional rights. McGuinness J reiterated the standards set in *Fajujonu* by Finlay CJ and Walsh J. According to McGuinness J, these standards required the Minister to have some specific evidence of the danger to the common good arising from the illegal immigrant parents concerned, whether as individuals or as members of a class or group. She noted that the Fajujonu parents were at all times illegal immigrants but that it was clear from the Supreme Court decision that their illegal presence in the country was not in itself sufficient reason to outweigh the constitutional rights of the child and the family. In that respect, McGuinness J referred again to Walsh J's requirement of reasons that were so predominant and overwhelming *in the circumstances of the case*. This requirement allowed McGuinness J to conclude that it would surely envisage some reason more specific to the individuals in the family concerned than a general statement as

---

[103] G Hogan and G Whyte, *Kelly on the Constitution* (3rd ed), Dublin, Butterworths, 1993, at 1002.

to the maintenance of the integrity of the asylum and immigration system. She then referred to Gannon J's judgment in *Osheku*[104] when he spoke of the protection of the fundamental rights of the State that could involve restrictions in circumstances of necessity on the fundamental rights of individual citizens. Thus, according to McGuinness J, if the State sought to rely successfully on the *Osheku* dictum the circumstances of necessity which would permit it to restrict not only the rights of the individual citizen but also the rights of the family had to be set out fully, explicitly and in detail.[105]

She identified a further difficulty with the Minister's reasoning that the integrity of the asylum system had to be maintained. The generality of such reasoning could give rise to the potential dangers that phrases such as 'respect for the integrity of the immigration and asylum system' or 'preserving the integrity of the immigration and asylum system' could become too widely used. In McGuinness J's opinion, it was questionable whether such a general and undefined reason could be sufficient in a case where the constitutional rights of an Irish citizen and his or her family were at stake. Rather, she stated, reasons that were grave and substantial or were predominant and overwhelming had to be defined reasons that were justified by evidence as to their actual impact on the common good of the people of Ireland.[106]

Justice McGuinness' judgment continued with an analysis of the issue of proportionality. She referred to Walsh J's dictum in *Fajujonu* regarding the proportionality of a deportation order that could have the effect breaking up that family. She continued by referring extensively to Costello J's statement of the principle in *Heaney v Ireland*[107] that the objective of the impugned provision had to be of sufficient importance to warrant overriding a constitutionally-protected right. It had to relate to concerns pressing and substantial in a free and democratic society and the means chosen had to pass the following proportionality test where the means had to:

(a) be rationally connected to the objective and not be arbitrary, unfair or based on irrational considerations;
(b) impair the right as little as possible; and
(c) be such that their effects on rights are proportional to the objective.[108]

Justice Costello's judgment in *Heaney* also made reference to the case of *Cox v Ireland*[109] as an example of an Irish case in which disproportionate means to

---

[104] Supra note 82.
[105] Ibid, at para 281.
[106] Ibid, at para 282.
[107] [1994] 3 IR 593.
[108] Ibid, at 607.
[109] [1992] 2 IR 503.

obtain a legitimate object rendered invalid a statutory provision. According to the Court in *Cox*, in pursuing the statutory objectives in question:

> the State must continue to protect as far as is practicable the constitutional rights of the citizen. Having examined the operation of the section it concluded that because the State had not as far as was practicable protected the citizens' constitutional rights, notwithstanding the fundamental interests of the State which the section sought to protect, the provisions of this section were impermissibly wide and indiscriminate.[110]

With regard to the appellant's submission in *Lobe*, McGuinness J was of the opinion that the interference with the constitutional rights of the family amounted to a denial of fundamental constitutional rights and that the Minister's justification for that denial fell far short of the objectives involved in the *Cox* decision and that the overriding reason for maintaining the deportation orders as framed by the Minister was not proportionate to the effect that these orders would have on the Lobe and Osayande families.[111]

In conclusion, McGuinness J stated that given the repeated emphasis by the Supreme Court in its decisions over the years to the nature, weight and importance of the rights of the family set out in Articles 41 and 42 of the Constitution – rights which the Minister had accepted were rights possessed by the Lobe and Osayande children and their families – she was not satisfied that respect for the maintenance of the immigration and asylum system was sufficiently grave and substantial a reason or so predominant and overwhelming a reason in the circumstances of the cases and in the context of the common good to justify the denial of the constitutional rights of these children and their families. She therefore allowed the appeal.

Justice Fennelly provided the second dissenting judgment which rested on a number of points, the first of which was the relationship between the Supreme Court's decision in *Fajujonu* and the case at hand. He referred to Finlay CJ's statement that in spite of the fact that the Fajujonu parents, being aliens and not citizens, could not claim any constitutional right to remain in the State, they were nonetheless entitled to assert a choice of residence on behalf of their infant children, in the interests of those infant children. Fennelly J also referred to Walsh J's statement to the same effect that it was abundantly clear that Irish citizens could not be deported.[112] Thus, according to Fennelly J:

> The State cannot expel an adult Irish citizen from the national territory. Nor can it expel a child citizen who has validly elected through his parents, to remain in the State. . . . From the words of Finlay C.J., it is clear that it was for the parents

---

[110] *Lobe*, supra note 1, at para 287.
[111] Ibid, at paras 288–289.
[112] Ibid, at paras 498–499.

to decide what was in the best interests of their child. It was perfectly rational for the parents, considering, in particular, the terms of Article 2 of the Constitution, to decide that the child remaining in Ireland would best serve those interests.[113]

According to Fennelly J, there was no justification for the State seeking to substitute its views, in reality its wishes, so as to justify the de facto deportation of the child especially as "the 'birthright . . . of the child . . . to be part of the Irish nation' could not, on any realistic view, survive such de facto deportation".[114]

With regard to the issue of the rights of the family and the rights of the State, Fennelly J referred to the uniqueness of the case in that the State sought to assert that its own sovereign rights were so urgent and compelling that they should prevail and be accorded precedence over the constitutional rights of the child. This description of the issue led Fennelly J to the decision of the Supreme Court in *Fajujonu* and his acceptance of Finlay CJ's statements that any disruption to the primacy of the family unit had to be based on compelling reasons or had to be for grave and substantial reasons. Justice Fennelly referred to a further significant Supreme Court case, *North Western Health Board v H.W. and CW*[115] and highlighted Keane CJ's narrative on the relationship in the Irish constitutional scheme between the family and the State as follows:

> Article 41 speaks, not of the authority of parents, but of the authority of the family . . . which is endowed with an authority which the Constitution recognises as being superior even to the authority of the State itself. While there may inevitably be tensions between laws enacted by the State for the common good of society as a whole and the unique status of the family within that society, the Constitution firmly outlaws any attempt by the State in its laws or its executive actions to usurp the exclusive and privileged role of the family in the social order.[116]

Justice Fennelly described the present case as one which pitted the claims of the State itself against the constitutional rights of an Irish-born citizen child to be raised as a member of his family in the State, and stated that it was impossible to improve on the "compendious explication" of Articles 41, 42 and 43 as contained in the judgment of Walsh J in *McGee v Attorney General*:

> The individual has natural and human rights over which the State has no authority; and the family, as the natural primary and fundamental unit group of society, has rights as such which the State cannot control. However, at the same time it is true, as the Constitution acknowledges and claims, that the State is the guardian of the common good and that the individual, as a member of society, and the family, as a unit of society, have duties and obligations to consider and respect the common good of that society.[117]

---

[113] Ibid, at para 501.
[114] Ibid, at para 502.
[115] [2001] 3 IR 622.
[116] *Lobe*, supra note 1, at para 512.
[117] [1974] IR 284, 310.

It was against this background of the constitutional protection to be afforded to the Lobe family that Fennelly J considered the sovereign power of the State. According to the Judge, the Minister's case was essentially encapsulated in the proposition as enunciated by Gannon J in *Osheku*.[118] The *Lobe* case was governed by s 3(1)(e) of the Immigration Act 1999 which states that each subject of a deportation order is "a person whose application for asylum has been transferred to a convention country for examination pursuant to section 22 of the Refugee Act, 1996". According to the Minister, the need to give effect to that order should prevail over the rights of the child.[119] This observation led Fennelly J to the question of whether *Fajujonu* should be distinguished and he noted that the material part of the judgment where the Chief Justice stated:

> I have come to the conclusion that where, as occurs in this case, an alien has in fact resided for an appreciable time in the State and has become a member of a family unit within the State containing children who are citizens, that there can be no question but that those children, as citizens, have got a constitutional right to the company, care and parentage of their parents within a family unit. I am also satisfied that prima facie and subject to the exigencies of the common good that that is a right which these citizens would be entitled to exercise within the State.[120]

In response to the Minister's contention that the principle underlying *Fajujonu* was restricted to cases of "appreciable residence" in the State and/or cases where there was more than one child, Fennelly J stated that he could not discover any legal reasoning in the material part of Finlay CJ's judgment that would suggest that the constitutional rights of an Irish-born child depended on the length of time during which his parents had resided in the State and that there could be no such a principle. According to Fennelly J, it was rightly conceded that the applicant minors in the present cases were Irish citizens and it followed that these children enjoyed constitutional rights, as a member of their families, rights that were guaranteed by the Constitution and had been described in case law. To that end, Fennelly J stated "Indeed, the younger a child is, in many respects, the more pressing and urgent is its need for the nurture and care of its parents, particularly its mother."[121] Fennelly J also rejected the argument regarding the number of children in the family on the basis that the child was a citizen with the resulting right to the society, care and nurture of its parents in the State, and that consequently there could be no constitutional principle making those rights of an Irish-born citizen depend on the number of other Irish-born citizens in the family. According to Fennelly J, *Fajujonu*

---

[118] *Lobe*, supra note 1, at para 522.
[119] Ibid, at para 528.
[120] Ibid, at para 532.
[121] Ibid, at para 537.

could not be distinguished in any meaningful way as it had simply laid down the standards to be considered by the Minister and these standards had to be based upon grave and substantial reasons or reasons that were predominant and overwhelming to justify a negative decision.[122]

Justice Fennelly's final reason related to the Minister's decision relating to the integrity of the asylum and immigration systems which the judge regarded as being the most important. With regard to State interference with the constitutional rights afforded to the family, he referred to the dicta of Finlay CJ in *In re J. H.*,[123] which established a standard of compelling reasons, Finlay CJ's dicta in *Fajujonu* where grave and substantial reasons was the standard applied, and Walsh J's dicta in *Fajujonu* where the standard was reasons that were so predominant and overwhelming.[124] These dicta provided the basis for the possibility of such interference. According to Fennelly J, these passages were unanimous in requiring reasons of a very high and compelling order to justify the invasion of family rights of the sort that were at issue in this case and that these standards had not been reached in the case at hand.[125] In Fennelly J's opinion, the need to preserve the asylum and immigration system was an abstract, open-ended administrative reason that could not satisfy the test propounded in *Fajujonu* and that any changes to the statutory circumstances since *Fajujonu* was decided did not give any added force to the Minister's reliance on the need to preserve respect for the system.[126]

Justice Fennelly concluded his judgment by reiterating that he did not consider that the first reason given, relating to the length of time each family had resided in the State (or, in the Lobe's situation, the possibility of the Irish-born child adapting to another country than Ireland) could prevail over the constitutional rights of the child which he said had been the issue at all times in these cases. He acknowledged that the fact that the parents may have resided in the State for a longer or shorter period could be relevant to the consideration of their rights and interests but he was of the opinion that the State had throughout present cases approached the matter on the assumption that they were concerned with the rights of the parents. Justice Fennelly disagreed with this emphasis on the rights of parents and, in allowing the appeal, he stated:

> I do not accept that the State has shown, in any respect, that there exists sufficiently powerful reasons for the State's rights to prevail over those of the child.[127]

---

[122] Ibid, at paras 538–540.
[123] [1985] IR 375.
[124] *Lobe*, supra note 1, at para 558.
[125] Ibid, at para 559.
[126] Ibid, at paras 560–562.
[127] Ibid, at para 576.

5.1. *Lobe: Disregarding the Rights of the Child-Citizen, Discriminating against the Rights of the Child*

The requirement for proportionality, indicated particularly in the dissenting judgments of *Lobe*, has strong echoes of the test employed by the European Court of Human Rights in relation to Article 8(2) of the Convention. Inasmuch as the judges of the European Court acknowledged a State's right in international law to control its borders, McGuinness J and Fennelly J recognised that Ireland, as a sovereign state, had a Constitutional and statutory right to control the entry of all immigrants, asylum seekers or otherwise, into the State. Similarly, both Courts noted the special position accorded to the family in society as well as the rights that flowed from this position, rights which were not absolute. However, it is from this point forward that the similarities in the analyses of both Courts cease.

Chief Justice Keane's analysis recognises the conflict of rights between the State and the individual. However, the conflict is resolved in a manner which favours the rights of the State with little to no analysis of the extent to which the rights of the Irish-born child are circumscribed. At the level of domestic law, the question is whether the object of the deportation orders as issued by the Minister for Justice was sufficiently important to warrant overriding the constitutionally-protected rights that are attached to the child both as a member of a family unit and an autonomous rights-holder. Whilst it is acknowledged that the issue of asylum seekers may be a pressing concern, the question remains as to whether the means chosen to deal with this issue actually passes the proportionality test as determined by the domestic courts and the European Court of Human Rights. The deportation orders may be materially concerned with Ireland's desire to preserve the respect for and the integrity of its asylum and immigration systems, as well as its obligations under the Dublin Convention and, to that end, the orders are not based upon irrational considerations. Nevertheless, the question remains as to whether, in terms of the rights of the child, they are unconstitutional, arbitrary or unfair. The arbitrary nature of the decision as well as its (un)fairness should be called into account given that the Minister, in his recommendation to the Lobes, pointed out that the interests of the child were not only best served by him remaining within the family unit but that any decision by them to abandon their child in the Ireland would have consequences under the provisions of the Child Care Act 1991.[128] Whilst the family remains responsible primarily for the welfare of the child, the State also bears some responsibility to support the family in such an endeavour, a responsibility overlooked by the Minister. Moreover, the Minister paid scant

---

[128] Ibid, at para 468.

regard to the Constitutional rights of the child to remain in the State, with such failure serving to undermine any claims that such a decision was either balanced or fair.

Justice McGuinness' close attention to the *Heaney* test for proportionality reveals that the means chosen to meet the ends of the decision must impair any rights affected as little as possible. Very simply, the rights of the child are wholly and completely impaired by the deportation orders. For the child, the effect is one of a State-sanctioned choice between being either deprived of the right to remain in the country of his or her birth and enjoyment of such rights that may ensue, or being deprived of the right to the care and comfort of his or her family. This portion of the test has unequivocally failed. The question remains as to whether the effect of such deportation orders are proportional to the objective, which according to the Executive and the Judiciary, is the internationally-recognised right to border control in asylum and immigration matters. Whilst some attention is paid to the need to preserve the family unit and the prerogative of the State to intervene into and limit the rights of the family, not only do the majority of the Supreme Court fail to explore appropriately the extent of such State interference into family life in such situations, they do not adequately analyse the degree of harm likely to be caused by such intervention, let alone consider the rights and interests of the child as a part of the equation.

Whilst Keane CJ was content to refer to the necessity of supporting the obligations undertaken by Ireland with regard to the provisions of the Dublin Convention, he made no reference to the necessity of supporting Ireland's international obligations under the European Convention, nor did he consider the cases decided by the European Court with regard to the effect of deportation orders on the right to respect for family life. Given the previous judicial recognition accorded to the persuasive nature of the judgments of the European Court of Human Rights, it is strongly arguable that the notion of the 'common good' should be interpreted in line with the broader test adopted by the European Court regarding what is 'necessary in a democratic society'. The facts of the *Berrehab* case would appear to be broadly similar to the *Lobe* case, in the sense that the deportation of a non-resident parent would have compromised the family ties that existed between him and his daughter and, according to the Court, the Deportation Order was not legitimate with regard to the aim pursued and were, therefore, unnecessary in a democratic society. Moreover, in the *Mehemi* case, the fact that the applicant had been convicted of drug offences did not outweigh, in the Court's opinion, the impact that such deportation would have on his right to respect for family life. Chief Justice Keane could even have considered the decision of the European Court to deport the applicant in the *Dalia* case irrespective of her having a child of French nationality. However, a distinction should be drawn between that case and the case before the Supreme Court as the applicant was deported on the basis that her son was born whilst she was in France illegally and that her conviction for drug-dealing posed a threat to public order in France. In *Lobe,* the applicants were not in Ireland illegally and the response of the Minister and the majority of the Supreme Court was that that their mere presence in Ireland constitutes a threat to public order. The failure of the majority of the Supreme Court to look beyond the rights of the State to control immigration and the entry of asylum seekers allowed them to ignore the rights of the children involved, rights that are derived from international human rights law and from the Irish Constitution, the latter rights having been expressly recognised by the Supreme Court in *Fajujonu.*

The issue of discrimination was highlighted by Walsh J in *Fajujonu,* when he noted that the State was intervening into the family life of the Fajajonus for reasons other than those mandated by the Constitution. The plaintiff parents were not in any way unfit to maintain the guardianship and custody of their children and there was no ground upon which the State could lawfully interfere to separate the parents from the children either temporarily or permanently.[129] Rather, the basis for the Minister's decision to deport the non-Irish members of the Fajujonu family was simply that Mr Fajujonu was unable to support his family without assistance from the State irrespective of the fact that the reason why Mr Fajujonu was unable to support his family was because the State refused to him permission to work. According to Walsh J:

> Such a position could not arise in respect of the support of his family if the parents were citizens and therefore to that extent the members of the Irish family who were Irish citizens were suffering discrimination by virtue of the fact that their parents were aliens.[130]

From the perspective of the provisions of the Irish Constitution, therefore, the Irish-born children of asylum seekers were being discriminated against. For Walsh J the question which then arose was:

> whether a family, the majority of whose members are Irish citizens, can effectively be put out of the country on the grounds of poverty. The dilemma posed for the parents by this attitude is that they must choose to withdraw their children, who are Irish citizens, from the benefits and protection of Irish law under the Constitution or alternatively, to effectively abandon them within this State, which would then be obliged to support them.[131]

As such, Keane CJ's determination that Irish-born children, such as those of the Osayande and Lobe families, could accompany their parents upon deportation

---

[129] *Fajujonu,* supra note 84, at 165.
[130] Ibid, at 166.
[131] Ibid.

is discriminatory on two grounds. Firstly, it effectively allows the State to deport a certain category of Irish citizen and thereby denies them their constitutional rights to be part of the Irish nation and the personal rights that derive from such a status. Secondly, the level of protection from State intervention accorded to the family unit made up of asylum seekers and their Irish-born children is less than that afforded to those families constituted solely of Irish citizens, a discrimination compounded by the refusal of the Irish State to grant Irish residency to the parents of such children. The drawing of such a distinction between the rights afforded to different categories of Irish children violates the principles of non-discrimination and equality, principles that not only underpin the Irish Constitution but which form the cornerstone of international human rights law.

The decision of the Supreme Court is also problematic with the judgment of the Chief Justice having serious implications for the protection of rights in Ireland in general and for the protection of children's rights in particular. Chief Justice Keane's statement that the Court's function was "to ensure that the constitutional and legal rights of all persons affected by the legislation were protected and vindicated"[132] runs somewhat contrary to his interpretation of the extent to which the Constitution accords rights to Irish-born children. His interpretation of such rights as being less than absolute because of the lack of capacity on the part of the child right-holders is itself a misconception of the nature of children's rights. It is agreed that rights, whether they be derived from the Constitution or human rights treaties, are not absolute. However, the conditional nature of such rights is based upon the extent to which the exercise of these rights would encroach upon or violate the rights of other individuals. To argue that rights are only granted to and may be exercised by those who are capable, either legally or factually, of exercising such rights is not only alarming, but it runs contrary to the fundamental premise upon which rights are based as both Chapter 1 and the opening sections of this chapter indicate.

6. *Conclusion*

The need to protect the 'integrity' of the Irish asylum and immigration system has been advanced as the basis for deciding that the non-resident parents of Irish-born children are not entitled to remain in the State. However, as this chapter has sought to highlight, the rights and best interests of certain Irish children constitute little to no part of the decision-making process on the part of the Irish Executive and Judiciary when deciding to deport the parents of

---

[132] *Lobe,* supra note 1, at para 56.

such children. In so doing, the Supreme Court not only disregards the rights accorded to certain categories of Irish-born children, it also (re)inforces the notion that the effective protection and implementation of the citizen rights of Irish-born children will depend on the nationality of their parents, a notion which runs contrary to the non-discrimination provisions of national and international law regarding the rights of the child and the protection to be accorded to the family unit.

CONCLUSION

In this book children are regarded as rights-holders and, consequently, a framework of equality based on rights is the most appropriate mechanism for securing the exercise of the rights of children and young persons. As the previous chapters indicate, the obligation to protect and provide for young persons can be regarded as an important and significant objective for limiting the rights of young persons but only where such limits are rational and proportionate and amount to no more than legitimate differential treatment which serves to secure equality of treatment and non-discrimination. Age may serve as the point of departure for such differential treatment but it should not be the sole consideration. Rather, it should be considered to be a general indicator of the capacity of the young person to exercise his or her rights. In addition, the impact of the differential treatment needs to be assessed. In broader human rights language, a balance as between rights has to be struck, in addition to the striking of a balance as between individual rights-holders. In terms of children's rights, the justification of such treatment should also incorporate reference to the Guiding Principles of the Convention on the Rights of the Child in order to determine whether the differential treatment satisfies the requirement that it constitutes the important and significant objective of protecting and providing for the child. Such an approach underpins the role of equality law, both national and international, which enshrines the notion that dignity and equality is to be accorded to *all* human beings. Equality legislation also provides a means for examining any departures from the requirement for non-discrimination especially where such a departure constituted an age-based limitation of the rights of the child in order to determine whether such a departure is justified or, alternatively, amounts to discrimination.

In Chapter 2, we saw that the courts have been governed by the rule that some children are legally competent to refuse to consent to medical treatment. Where such competency is lacking, the courts have acknowledged the rights of parents to make decisions regarding medical treatment that is in the best interests of their child. Moreover, the courts are equally empowered to constrain such parental rights where they conflict with the best interests of the child. Such power to impose limitations on the rights of the young person to refuse medical treatment stemmed from the courts' determination that the young persons in question were lacking the appropriate levels of capacity to exercise their rights. In the context of age-based discrimination, such limitations were justifiable as they attempted to serve the important and significant objective of preserving the life of the child. In terms of the effects of such measures upon the rights of the child, Chapter 2 concludes that the effects on the right of the child to refuse medical treatment were also rational and proportionate as impairing this right allowed the child to avoid death or severe and permanent injury. Thus, Chapter 2 demonstrates that children, parents and the courts need to ensure that the exercise of the right to medical treatment, including the right to refuse such treatment is as a result of differential treatment which is legitimate and, therefore, reflective of a course of action that is necessary to avoid discrimination.

The consideration in Chapter 3 of the rights of New Zealand children born of AHR demonstrates that the balance of rights as between parents and children remains very much in favour of the former who are under no legal obligation to inform their children of the true nature of their genetic identity. Chapter 3 focuses upon the manner in which the current adult-orientated AHR regime discriminates against children in two ways in particular: the age-based distinctions that form the basis for access to either non-identifying or identifying information regarding genetic heritage and the non-retroactive nature of the legislation that differentiates between the ability of children born before and after the HART Act to access information regarding their genetic identity. The question that is considered in Chapter 3 is whether this balance of rights as between parent and child, that favours the former and limits the right to identity of the latter, may be justified. The basis for the current legislative regime in New Zealand fails to do this as no clear argument is advanced to support the assertion that the embargo on information that may be accessed by donor-conceived children is aimed at meeting the important and significant objective of providing for and protecting the child aged under 16 years because of his or her immaturity. Moreover, the severity of the consequences that may flow from such an embargo are not fully explored and thus, in terms of rationality and proportionality, the use of the distinction remains to be justified. Similarly, the non-retrospective nature of the HART Act also gives rise to discrimination-related concerns. These concerns could be met with greater harmonisation of rights as between pre-Act donors and their donor off-spring under the terms of the Privacy Act 1993 and the Health Information Privacy Code, whereby each party could obtain such information with regard to each other as the merits of each case would warrant. Consequently, Chapter 3 concludes with the assertion that the current AHR legislation needs to be amended to avoid discrimination by ensuring the right of the donor-conceived child to access information regarding his or her genetic identity.

Chapter 4 analyses parental corporal punishment and contends that the statutory defence of domestic discipline amounts to age-based discrimination because the sole focus of current legislation is upon whether the punishment was excessive. The legislation does not allow for any discussions as to whether the difference in the level of protection from any assault and violence as between children and adults is justifiable. At a general level, Chapter 4 considers the question of whether the express prioritisation of the right of parents to inflict corporal punishment upon their children over the right of such children to be free from such punishment can be justified, that is, whether it serves an important and significant objective which is rational and proportionate. The chapter concludes that the protection to be accorded to the family unit and the importance of the role of parents within this unit is of sufficient importance within a free and democratic society to override some of the rights of children within that family unit. However, in the context corporal punishment, the ensuing limitations on children's rights fail to satisfy the proportionality test, as no rational connection is made between the legislative provisions and their underlying objective. Furthermore, some of the cases referred to in this chapter demonstrate that the measures adopted and their effects, even if rationally connected to the objective, fail the requirement of minimally impairing the rights or freedoms of children. Thus, Chapter 4 concludes that any defence to corporal punishment that results in different levels of protection from violence as between adults and children cannot be justified and, accordingly, should be regarded as discriminatory.

Chapter 5 considers the rights of the non-offending, at-risk child in Ireland that derive both from national and international law. A reasonably coherent framework of legal protection for such children does exist and it has been relied upon by both the Irish courts and the European Court of Human Rights in their determinations that the rights of the at-risk child in Ireland have been violated by the slow pace of the Government's provision of alternate care and confinement facilities. The issue of age discrimination arises from judicial recognition of the fact that the Constitutional rights of the child are to be interpreted with reference to differences of capacity based upon age, differences that are also to take account of the welfare of the child. However, the State's Constitutional obligation to defend and vindicate the personal rights of its child citizens who have been deemed to be 'at risk' remains. The courts have determined that this obligation requires the State to provide care and confinement facilities. The State's response to this requirement has been to confine such children in penal institutions, a limitation on the rights of the child that Chapter 5 reveals cannot be justified. The courts ordered the young people in question to be detained in penal institutions despite the fact that such an order was not in response to a criminal offence. The Irish courts sought to justify such orders on the basis that they were according preference to securing the welfare of the child over the right to liberty of the child in an attempt to justify such detention as serving an important and significant objective. However, Chapter 5 notes that the adoption of such measures and their effects were not fully considered by the Irish Supreme Court *D.G. v The Eastern Health Board*,[1] in order to determine whether they were rationally and proportionally connected to the stated objective. Consequently, any determinations that such differential treatment was justifiable did not serve as a satisfactory justification for the detention of at-risk children in penal institutions. This chapter also highlights that at-risk children have been subject to further discrimination that has derived from the limited extent, practically speaking, to which the courts, operating as an organ of the State, were going to able to vindicate the personal rights of a certain portion of its citizens. Thus, this chapter highlights the fact that the age discrimination issues may not always derive directly from gaps in the law but rather they may also derive from the discriminatory conduct of the State in failing to give such legal protection a practical application. Chapter 5 concludes that unjustifiably different levels of protection have been accorded to that subset of Irish at-risk children that were most in need of a much higher level of protection.

Chapter 6 considers the balance that is to be struck between a State's rights to preserve the respect for and the integrity of its asylum and immigration systems and the rights of the child as a citizen and a member of a family unit that is subject to a deportation order, with particular reference to the jurisprudence of the European Court of Human Rights. Chapter 6 also focuses upon recent determinations by the Irish Supreme Court as to whether such concerns were sufficiently important to warrant overriding the constitutionally protected rights that are accorded to the Irish child. The chapter concludes that the decision of the majority of the Supreme Court in *Lobe*[2] was discriminatory because it failed to explore adequately the extent of such State interference into family life in such situations. It did not analyse adequately the degree of harm likely to be caused by such intervention, nor did it give due consideration to the rights and interests of the child in question. The failure of the majority of the Supreme Court to look beyond the general rights of the State to control immigration and the entry of asylum seekers allowed them to ignore the rights of the children involved. Thus, the Supreme Court decision was discriminatory on two grounds: it amounted to the *de facto* deportation of Irish children who are dependent on their parents to exercise their Constitutional rights; and it accorded a lesser level of protection to the family unit made up of asylum seekers and their Irish-born children than is afforded to those families constituted solely of Irish citizens. The drawing of such a distinction between

---

[1] [1997] 3 IR 511.
[2] *Lobe v Minister for Justice, Equality and Law Reform* [2003] IESC 3 (23 January 2003) http://www.bailii.org.ezproxy.waikato.ac.nz:2048/ie/cases/IESC/2003/3.html, as viewed 27 April 2005.

the rights afforded to different categories of Irish children violates the principles of non-discrimination and equality. It amounts to discrimination on the basis of age as it suggests that the extension of rights to certain Irish children may be less than absolute because of the lack of capacity on the part of the child right-holders to exercise those rights. Chapter 6 concludes that any argument that rights are only granted to and may be exercised by those who are capable, either legally or factually, of exercising such rights runs contrary to the fundamental premise upon which rights are based as both Chapter 1 and the ensuing chapters of this book indicate.

It is recognised throughout this book that rights, whether they be derived from national law or international human rights treaties, are not absolute. Thus, any conditionalities or limitations that may be attached to these rights are based upon the extent to which an individual is capable of exercising those rights or where they relate to instances where the exercise of these rights would encroach upon or violate the rights of other individuals. However, national and international law requires that, in order to avoid discrimination, such limitations must serve an important and significant objective and that, accordingly, the limiting measures employed and their effects must have a rational and proportionate connection to the objective. The chapters of this book demonstrate that although many limits on the rights of the child can be justified, primarily by reference to the best interests and welfare of the child, these limitations must be more fully explored in order to determine whether they fulfil the criteria for age-based differential treatment. With the exception of Chapter 2 where the differential treatment was justifiable, the previous chapters highlight situations where further explorations revealed that the limitations on the rights of the children in question could not satisfy the test for legitimate differential treatment and thus, the young people in question had been subjected to age-based discrimination.

BIBLIOGRAPHY

Primary Materials

A v United Kingdom (1998) 27 EHRR 611.
(A Minor) (Wardship: Medical Treatment) [1997] 1 WLR 242; EWCA Civ 805.
Ausage v Ausage [1998] NZFLR 72.
African Charter on the Rights and Welfare of the Child OAU Doc. CAB/LEG/24.9/49 (1990).
African [Banjul] Charter on Human and Peoples' Rights OAU Doc. CAB/LEG/67/3 (1981).
American Convention on Human Rights, O.A.S. Treaty Series No. 36.
Auckland Healthcare Services v L (1998) 17 FRNZ 376; [1998] NZFLR 998.
Auckland Healthcare Services v Liu (1996), Judge Tompkins, HC Auckland M81/96.
Auckland Healthcare Services v T [1996] NZFLR 670.
B v F, alt cit Bonnar v Fischbach (2001) 20 FRNZ 593; [2001] NZFLR 925.
Belgian Linguistic Case (No.2) Series A No. 6 (1968) 1 EHRR 252.
Body of Principles for the Protection of All Persons under Any Form of Detention or Imprisonment, General Assembly Resolution 43/173 of 9 December 1988.
Bouamar v Belgium, Judgment of 29 February 1988, Series A No. 129.
Bunreacht na hEireann, Dublin, Government Stationery Office.
Campbell and Cosans v United Kingdom (1982) 4 EHRR 293.
Care of Children Act 2004 (NZ).
Charter of Fundamental Rights of the European Union, 2000/c 364/01 (2000).
Chen v Secretary of State for the Home Department, Case C-200/02, 19 October 2004.
Child Care Act 1991 (Ireland).
Children, Young Persons and Their Families Act 1989 (NZ).
Committee Against Torture (2002), Third Periodic Reports of States Parties Due in 1999: New Zealand, CAT/C/49/Add.3.
Committee of Experts on Family Law (2002), "White Paper" on Principles Concerning the Establishment and Legal Consequences of Parentage, CJ-FA (2001) 16 rev.
Committee of Experts on Family Law (2001), Draft Report on Principles Concerning the Establishment and Legal Consequences of Parentage (the Legal Status of Children) 2001, Draft No.1 Council of Europe (02/08/01).
Committee on the Rights of the Child, (2003), General Comment No. 5: *General Measures of Implementation for the Convention on the Rights of the Child*.
Committee on the Rights of the Child (2003), Concluding Observations of the Committee on the Rights of the Child: New Zealand, CRC/C/15/Add.216.
Committee on the Rights of the Child (2003), Second Periodic Report of New Zealand (continued) CRC/C/SR.897.
Committee on the Rights of the Child (1998), Concluding Observations Regarding Ireland, CRC/C/15/Add.85.
Committee on the Rights of the Child (1997), Summary Record of the 364th meeting: New Zealand, CRC/C/SR.364.
Committee on the Rights of the Child (1997), Summary Record of the 365th meeting: New Zealand, CRC/C/SR.365.
Committee on the Rights of the Child (1997), Concluding Observations of the Committee on the Rights of the Child: New Zealand, CRC/C/15/Add.71.

Committee on the Rights of the Child (1996), Concluding Observations with Regard to Zimbabwe, CRC/C/15/Add.55.

Committee on the Rights of the Child (1996), *General Guidelines for Periodic Reports*, CRC/C/58.

Committee on the Rights of the Child, (1995), Summary Record of the 205th Meeting, U.N. GAOR, Comm. on the Rts. of the Child, 8th Sess., 205th mtg., U.N. Doc. CRC/C/SR.205.

Committee on the Rights of the Child (1995), Concluding Observations Regarding the United Kingdom, CRC/C/15 Add.34.

Committee on the Rights of the Child (1995), Concluding Observations Regarding Sri Lanka, CRC/C/15/Add.40.

Committee on the Rights of the Child (1995), Consideration of Reports Submitted by States Parties under Article 44 of the Convention: New Zealand, CRC/C/28/Add.3.

Convention for the Protection of Human Rights and Dignity of the Human Being with regard to the Application of Biology and Medicine: Convention on Human Rights and Biomedicine (the Oviedo Convention), ETS No. 164 (1996).

Costello-Roberts v United Kingdom (1993) 19 EHRR 112.

Crimes Act 1961 (NZ).

D.B. v The Minister for Justice [1999] 1 IR 29.

D.G. v The Eastern Health Board and Others [1997] 3 IR 511.

D.(T.) v Minister for Education [2000] IEHC 21; [2000] 3 IR 62; [2000] 2 ILRM 321.

Director-General of Social Welfare v M (1991) 8 FLRNZ 498.

Doyle v The Commissioner of An Garda Siochana [1999] 1 IR 249.

E v Attorney-General [2000] 3 NZLR 257.

Equal Status Act 2000 (Ireland).

Erick v Police 7/3/85, Heron J, HC Auckland M1734/84.

European Convention for the Protection of Human Rights and Fundamental Freedoms, 213 U.N.T.S., p. 221, no. 2889; Council of Europe, ETS No. 5 (1950).

European Convention for the Prevention of Torture and Inhuman or Degrading Treatment or Punishment ETS No. 126 (1987).

European Convention on the Exercise of Children's Rights ETS No. 160 (1996).

European Social Charter CETS No. 163 (1996).

F.N. v Minister for Education [1995] 1 IR 409.

Fogelberg v Association of University Staff of New Zealand Inc (2000) 6 HRNZ 206; [2000] 2 ERNZ 196.

G. v An Bord Uchtala [1980] IR 32.

Gaskin v United Kingdom, Judgment of 7 July 1989, Series A, No. 160, (1989).

Gillick v West Norfolk and Wisbech Area Health Authority [1986] AC 112.

Gosselin v Quebec (Attorney-General) [2002] 4 SCR 429; (2002) SCC 84.

Health Select Committee, *Human Assisted Reproductive Technology Bill (195–2)*, Wellington, House of Representatives, 2004.

Healthcare Otago Limited v Brendon Williams Holloway and Trena Williams Holloway, Unreported Judgment, Family Court Dunedin, FP 012/23/99, 6 May 1999.

Healthcare Otago Limited v Brendon Williams Holloway and Trena Williams Holloway 18/3/99, Judge Blaikie, FC Dunedin FP 012/23/99.

Healthcare Otago Limited v Brendon Williams Holloway and Trena Williams Holloway 4/3/99, Judge Blaikie, FC Dunedin FP 012/23/99.

Healthcare Otago Limited v Brendon Williams Holloway and Trena Williams Holloway 25/2/99, Judge Blaikie, FC Dunedin.

Hemmes v Young 8 March 2005, CA33/04 (NZ).

Human Assisted Reproductive Technology Act 2004 (NZ).

Human Fertilisation and Embroyology Act 1990 (UK).

Human Fertilisation and Embryology Authority (Disclosure of Donor Information) Regulations 2004 (SI 2004/1511).

Human Reproductive Technology Act 1991 (WA).

Human Rights Act 1991 (NZ).

Human Rights Committee (2000), General Comment 28: *Equality of Rights Between Men and Women (Article 3)*, CCPR/C/21/Rev.1/Add.10.

Human Rights Committee (1992), General Comment 20, *Replaces General Comment 7 Concerning Prohibition of Torture and Cruel Treatment or Punishment (Article 7)*.

Human Rights Committee (1992), General Comment 27: *Freedom of Movement (Article 12)* CCPR/C/21/Rev.1/Add.9.

Human Rights Committee (1989), General Comment 17: *Rights of the Child (Article 24)*.

Human Rights Committee (1989), General Comment 18: *Non-discrimination*.

Human Rights Committee (1986), General Comment 15: *The Position of Aliens under the Covenant*.

Human Rights Committee (1984), General Comment 13: *Equality before the Courts and the Right to a Fair and Public Hearing by an Independent Court Established by Law (Article 14)*.

Human Rights Committee (1982), General Comment 8: *Right to Liberty and Security of Persons (Article 9)*.

Human Rights Committee (1981), General Comment 3: *Implementation at the National Level (Article 2)*.

Human Rights Committee (1981), General Comment 4: *Equality between the Sexes (Article 3)*.

In Re A (Male Sterilisation) [2000] 1 FLR 549.

In Re B (A Minor) (Wardship: Medical Treatment) [1981] 1 WLR 1421.

In Re F (Mental Patient: Sterilisation) [1990] AC 1.

In Re I, T, M & J [2000] NZFLR 1089.

In Re M.B. (Medical Treatment) [1997] 2 FLR 426.

In Re T (A Minor) (Wardship: Medical Treatment) [1997] 1 WLR 242.

In Re Z (A Minor) (Identification: Restrictions on Publication) [1996] 2 WLR 88.

International Convention on the Elimination of All Forms of Racial Discrimination 660 U.N.T.S. 195 (1965).

International Covenant on Civil and Political Rights, U.N. G.A. Res. 2200 (XXI), 21 UN GAOR, Supp. (No. 16) 52, U.N. Doc. A16316 (1966).

International Covenant on Economic, Social and Cultural Rights, G.A. Res. (XXI), U.N. GAOR 21st SESS., (Supp. No. 16), at 49, U.N. Doc. A/6316 (1966).

Kelly v O'Neill [1999] IESC 81; [2000] 1 IR 354; [2000] 1 ILRM 507.

Kendall v Director of Social Welfare (1986) 3 FRNZ 1.

Law v Canada (Minister of Employment and Immigration) [1999] 1 SCR 497.

M.F. v Superintendent Ballymun Garda Station [1991] 1 IR 189.

Marckx v Belgium Series A No. 31 (1979) 2 EHRR 330.

Mikulić v Croatia, Judgment of 04/09/2002, http://cmiskp.echr.coe.int/tkp197/view.asp?item= 1&portal=hbkm&action=html&highlight=Mikuli%u0107%20%7C%20v.%20%7C%20 Croatia&sessionid=1298569&skin=hudoc-en

Minors Contracts Act 1969 (NZ).

Moonen v Film and Literature Board of Review [2000] 2 NZLR 9.

Moonen v Film and Literature Board of Review [2002] 2 NZLR 754.

Morrow & Benjamin Ltd v Whittington [1989] 3 NZLR 122.

National Bank of New Zealand v Ram (1992) 2 NZBLC 102.

New Zealand Bill of Rights Act 1990.

NZPD, Vol. 620, 6 October 2004.

O'C. (J.) v D.P.P. [2000] IESC 58.

Police v Bannin [1991] 2 NZLR 237.

Police v Raponi (1989) 5 CRNZ 291.

R v Drake (1902) 22 NZLR 478.

R v Oakes [1986] 1 SCR 103, 1986 CanLII 46.

Race Relations Act 1976 (UK).

Re A (Children) [2000] EWCA Civ 254.

Re C (Detention) (Medical Treatment) [1997] 2 FLR 180.

Re E [1993] 1 FLR 386.

Re J (A Minor) (Wardship: Medical Treatment) [1991] Fam 33.

Re J: B and B v Director-General of Social Welfare [1995] 3 NZLR 73; [1996] 2 NZLR 134.

Re K and Public Trustee (1985) 19 DLR 4th 255.

Re K, W and H (Minors) (Medical Treatment) [1993] 1 FLR 854.

Re L (Medical Treatment: Gillick Competence) [1998] 2 FLR 810.

Re M (child: refusal of medical treatment) [1999] 2 FCR 577; (1999) 52 BMLR 124.

Re R (A Minor) [1992] Fam 11; [1991] 4 All ER 177; [1991] 3 WLR 592; [1992] 1 FLR 190.

Re S (A Minor) (Consent To Medical Treatment) [1995] 1 FCR 604.

Re the Five M Children [2004] NZFLR 337.

Re W (a minor) (medical treatment) [1992] 4 All ER 627.

Re X [1991] NZFLR 49.

Reproductive Technology (Clinical Practices) Act 1988 (SA).

Rose & Another v Secretary of State for Health [2002] EWHC 1593.

Ryan v The Attorney-General [1965] IR 294.

Sex Discrimination Act 1975 (UK).

Sharma v Police [2003] 2 NZLR 473; [2003] NZFLR 852.

Spence v Spence [2001] NZFLR 275.

Status of Children Amendment Act 2004 (NZ).

Steyn v Brett [1997] NZFLR 312.

T (A minor) (Wardship: Medical Treatment) [1997] 1 WLR 242.

T v T 9/7/99, FC Auckland FP004/919/90.

T.D. v Minister of Education, Judgment of the Irish Supreme Court of 17 December 2001, http://www.ucc.ie/law/irlii/cases/203–00_g.htm.

Tavita v Minister of Immigration [1994] 2 NZLR 257.

The Adoption (No 2) Bill, 1987 [1989] IR 656.

Tyrer v United Kingdom (1978) 2 EHRR 1.

United Nations Convention on the Rights of the Child, UN Doc. A/44/736, (1989), UNGA Doc. A/Res/44/25 of 5 December, (1989) 28 I.L.M., 1448, (1989).

Universal Declaration of Human Rights, G.A. Res. 217A, (III) U.N. Doc. A1810 (1948).

Wellington District Legal Services Committee v Tangiora [1998] 1 NZLR 129.

X, Y and Z v United Kingdom, Judgment of 22 April, Reports II, (1997).

Secondary Material

Abbot, M, *Family Ties: English Families 1540–1920*, London, Routledge, 1993.

ACYA Youth Video Working Group (2003), *Whakarongo Mai/Listen Up* (video) Wellington, ACYA.

Ahdar, R and Allan, J, "Taking Smacking Seriously: The Case for Retaining the Legality of Parental Smacking in New Zealand" [2000] 1 NZ Law Review, 1.

Aquinas, *Summa Theologiae*, Part II, Book II, Question 57, Article 4, reprinted in W Baumgarth and R Regan (eds), *St. Thomas Aquinas: On Law, Morality, and Politics*, Indianapolis, Hackett Publishing, 1988.

Archard, D, *Children: Rights and Childhood*, London, Routledge, 1993.

Atkin, B "Medico-Legal Implications of HART" (1994) 1(5) Butterworths Family Law Journal 90.

Attorney-General's Department, *Information Paper: Proposals for Commonwealth Age Discrimination Legislation*, Commonwealth of Australia, 2002.

Augustine, *The City of God*, Book XIX, Chapter 15. Reprinted in M Tkacz and D Kries (trans), *Augustine: Political Writings*, Indianapolis, Hackett Publishing, 1994.

Austin, G, "The UN Convention on the Rights of the Child – and Domestic Law" (1994) 1(4) Butterworths Family Law Journal 63.

Austin, G, "Children's Rights in New Zealand Law and Society" (1995) 25 Victoria University of Wellington Law Review 249.

Australian Human Rights and Equal Opportunity Commission, *Age Matters? A Discussion Paper on Age Discrimination*, Sydney, HREOC, 1999.

Barwick, H and Gray, A, *Analysis of submissions by children and young people to the Agenda for Children: Children's Discussion Pack*, Wellington, Ministry of Social Development, 2001.

Baumrind, D, "A Blanket Injunction Against Disciplinary Use of Spanking is Not Warranted by the Data" (1996) 98(4) Pediatrics 828.

Bedggood, M, Breen, C, Elliot, S, Harrington, J, Hancock, J, Harvey, N, Ludbrook, R, Taylor, N, Trainor, C and Wood, B, Action for Children and Youth Aotearoa, *Report to the United Nations Committee on Torture: Some Aspects of New Zealand's Compliance with the United Nations Convention Against Torture and Other Cruel, Inhuman or Degrading Treatment or Punishment*, Auckland, ACYA, 2004.

Benatar D, "Corporal Punishment" (1998) 24 Social Theory and Practice 237.

Beyleveld, D and Brownsword, R, "Human Dignity, Human Rights, and Human Genetics" (1998) 61(5) Modern Law Review 840.

Bitensky, S, "Spare the Rod, Embrace Our Humanity: Toward a New Legal Regime Prohibiting Corporal Punishment of Children" (1998) 31 Uni of Michigan Journal of Law Reform 353.

Boon, M, *Age of Electoral Majority*, London, The Electoral Commission, 2003.

Breen, C (ed), *Children's Needs, Rights and Welfare: Developing Strategies for the "Whole Child" in the 21st Century*, Victoria, Australia, Thompson-Dunmore Press, 2004.

Breen, C, "Refugee Law in Ireland: Disregarding the Rights of the Child-Citizen, Discriminating against the Rights of the Child" (2004) 15(4) International Journal of Refugee Law 750.

Breen, C, "Protecting the Rights of the Non-Offending Child in Ireland: Balancing State Rights with State Obligations" (2004) 12(4) International Journal of Children's Rights 379.

Breen C, *Age Based Distinctions and the New Zealand Bill of Rights Act: Commissioned Report for the Ministry of Justice*, 2004.

Breen, C, *The Right to Identity of Donor Conceived Children – Responses to Some Issues Raised in Chapter 5 of 'New Issues in Legal Parenthood'*, Submission Prepared for Action for Children and Youth Aotearoa, Auckland, ACYA, 2004.

Breen, C, *Children's Rights Issues Arising New Issues in Legal Parenthood'*, Background Paper to *The Right to Identity of Donor Conceived Children – Responses to Some Issues Raised in Chapter 5 of 'New Issues in Legal Parenthood'*, prepared for Action for Children and Youth Aotearoa, Auckland, ACYA, 2004.

Breen, C, "The Right to Education of Persons with Disabilities: Disabled in Interpretation and Application" (2003) 21(1) Netherlands Quarterly of Human Rights 7.

Breen, C, *The Standard of the Best Interests of the Child: A Western Tradition in International and Comparative Law*, Dordrecht, Martinus Nijhoff, 2002.

Breen, C, "The Corporal Punishment of Children in New Zealand: The Case for Abolition" [2002] 4 NZ Law Review 359.

Breen, C, "Poles Apart? The Best Interests of the Child and Assisted Reproduction in the Antipodes and Europe" (2001) 9(2) International Journal of Children's Rights 157.

Burrows, J, *Statute Law in New Zealand*, Wellington, Butterworths, 1992.

Callus, T, "Tempered Hope? A Qualified Right to Know One's Genetic Origin: *Odièvre v France*" (2004) 67(4) Modern Law Review 658.

Committee to Consider the Social, Ethical and Legal Issues Arising from In Vitro Fertilisation (CCSELIAIVF), *Report on Donor Gametes In IVF*, Victoria, CCSELIAIVF, 1983.

Council of Europe, *The Draft Report on Principles Concerning the Establishment and Legal Consequences of Parentage (the Legal Status of Children), Draft No. 1,* Council of Europe, 2001.

Cretney, S, "'What Will the Women Want Next?' The Struggle for Power within the Family 1925–1975" (1996) 112 Law Quarterly Review 110.

Crown Law Office, *Consistency with the New Zealand Bill of Rights Act 1990: Civil Union Bill,* Wellington, Crown Law Office, 2004.

Department of Child, Youth and Family Services, *Parenting Without Hitting/Smack-Free Zone/Wahi Patu Kore,* Information from Department of Child, Youth and Family Services, "Alternatives to Smacking" Campaign, Wellington, CYPS, 1997.

Department of Justice, *Assisted Human Reproduction: A Commentary on the Report of the Ministerial Committee on Assisted Reproductive Technologies,* Wellington, Department of Justice, 1995.

Detrick, S (1999), *A Commentary on the United Nations Convention of the Child,* Dordrecht, Martinus Nijhoff, 1999.

Dixon, S, *The Roman Family,* London, Johns Hopkins University Press, 1992.

Dworkin, R, *Taking Rights Seriously,* London, Duckworth, 1997.

Dworkin, G, "Paternalism" in R Wasserstrom (ed), *Morality and the Law,* California, Wadsworth Publishing, 1971.

Eekelaar, J, "The Interests of the Child and the Child's Wishes: the Role of Dynamic Self-Determinism" (1994) 8 International Journal of Law and the Family 42.

Eekelaar, J, "The Emergence of Children's Rights" (1986) 6 Oxford Journal of Legal Studies 161.

Elster, J, *Solomonic Judgements: Studies in the Limitations of Rationality,* Cambridge, CUP, 1989.

Elster, J, "Solomonic Judgements: Against the Best Interests of the Child" (1987) 54 University of Chicago Law Review 1.

Eisler, R, "Human Rights: Towards An Integrated Theory for Action" (1987) 9 Human Rights Quarterly 287.

Electoral Commission, Minimum Age Limits and Maturity in *Age of Electoral Majority: Report and Recommendations,* London, Electoral Commission, 2004.

Enright, M, "'Mature' Minors & The Medical Law; Safety First?" (2003) VII Cork On-Line Review.

Explanatory Report, European Convention for the Prevention of Torture and Inhuman or Degrading Treatment or Punishment (ETS no. 126).

Farson, R, *Birthrights,* London and New York, Macmillan, 1974.

Feinberg, J, "The Nature and Value of Rights" in J Feinberg (ed), *Rights, Justice and the Bounds of Liberty: Essays in Social Philosophy,* Princeton, Princeton University Press, 1980.

Fergusson, D and Lynskey, M, "Physical Punishment/Maltreatment During Childhood and Adjustment in Young Adulthood" (1997) 21(7) Child Abuse and Neglect 617.

Fortin, J, *Children's Rights and the Developing Law,* London, Butterworths, 2003.

Foster, H and Freed, D, "A Bill of Rights for Children" (1972) 6 Family Law Quarterly 343.

Fox Harding, L, *Perspectives in Child Care Policy,* London, Longman, 1997.

Franklin, R, "The Case For Children's Rights: A Progress Report" in R Franklin (ed), *The Handbook of Children's Rights: Comparative Policy and Practice,* London, Routledge, 1995.

Fredman, S, The Age of Equality, in S Fredman and S Spencer (eds), *Age as an Equality Issue: Legal and Policy Perspectives,* Oxford, Hart Publishing, 2003.

Freeman, M, *Rights and Wrongs of Children,* London, Pinter, 1983.

Freeman, M, "The New Birth Right? Identity and the Child of the Reproduction Revolution" (1996) 4 International Journal of Children's Rights 273.

Frith, L, "Beneath the Rhetoric: The Role of Rights in the Practice of Non-Anonymous Gamete Donation" (2001) 5–6 Bioethics 473.

Gerven, P, *The Religious Roots of Physical Punishment and the Psychological Impact of Physical Abuse*, New York, Alfred A Knopf, 1991.

Gies, F and Gies, J, *Marriage and the Family in the Middle Ages*, New York, Harper & Row, 1987.

Goldstein, J, Freud, A and Solnit, A, *Beyond the Best Interests of the Child*, London, Burnett Books, 1980; New York, The Free Press, 1973.

Hall, C, "Child Abuse v Domestic Discipline" (1998) Youth Law Review (November) 10.

Harris, C, *The Family and Industrial Society*, NSW, Allen & Unwin, 1983.

Harris, J, "The Political Status of Children" in K Graham (ed), *Contemporary Political Philosophy*, Cambridge, CUP, 1982.

Hassall, I, *Hitting Children — Unjust, Unwise and Unnecessary*, Wellington, OCC, 1993.

Health and Disability Commissioner, *Code of Health and Disability Services Consumer's Rights*, Auckland, Health and Disability Commissioner, 1996.

Henaghan, M and Atkin, B (eds), *Family Law Policy in New Zealand*, Auckland, OUP, 1992.

Holt, J, *Escape from Childhood: The Needs and Rights of Children*, Harmondsworth, Penguin, 1975.

Human Fertilisation and Embryology Authority, *Code of Practice: Explanation*, London, HFEA, 1993.

Interim National Ethics Committee on Assisted Reproductive Technologies (INECHART), *Non-Commercial Surrogacy by Means of In-Vitro Fertilisation: Report of the Interim National Ethics Committee on Assisted Reproductive Technologies*, Wellington, Ministry of Health, 1995.

Irish Human Rights Commission, *Preliminary Observations on the Proposed Referendum on Citizenship and on the 27th Amendment to the Constitution Bill*, Dublin, IHRC, 2004.

Irish Human Rights Commission, *Observations on the Proposed Draft Irish Nationality and Citizenship (Amendment) Bill*, Dublin, IHRC, 2004.

Joseph, S, Schulz, J and Castan, M, *The International Covenant on Civil and Political Rights: Cases, Material and Commentary*, Oxford, OUP, 2000.

Kleinig, J, *Paternalism*, Totowa, Rowman & Allenheld, 1942.

Locke, J, *Two Treatises of Government*, in P Laslett (ed), Cambridge, CUP, 1949.

Locke, J, "Some Thoughts Concerning Education" in J Adamson (ed), *The Educational Writings of John Locke*, London, Edward Arnold, 1912.

Ludbrook, R, *Youthism: Age Discrimination and Young People*, 1995.

Maclean, S and Maclean, M, "Keeping Secrets in Assisted Reproduction – the Tension between Donor Anonymity and the Need of the Child for Information" (1996) 8(3) Child and Family Law Quarterly 243.

Mason, A, Skolnick, A and Sugarman, A (eds), *All Our Families: New Policies for a New Century*, New York, OUP, 1998.

Maxwell, G, *Physical Punishment in the New Zealand Home, Occasional Paper No 3*, Wellington, OCC, 1994.

Maxwell, G and Carroll-Lind, J, *The Impact of Bullying on Children*, Wellington, OCC, 1997.

Maxwell, G and Carroll-Lind, J, *Children's Experiences of Violence*, Wellington, OCC, 1996.

Mental Health (Compulsory Assessment and Treatment) Act 1992 (NZ).

Ministerial Committee on Assisted Reproductive Technologies (MCHART), *Assisted Human Reproduction: Navigating Our Future: Report of the Ministerial Committee on Assisted Reproductive Technologies*, Wellington, Department of Justice: Wellington, 1994.

Ministry of Justice, *Report of the Attorney-General Under The New Zealand Bill Of Rights Act 1990 on the Care of Children Bill*, Wellington, Department of Justice, 2005.

Ministry of Justice (2003), *Consistency with the New Zealand Bill of Rights Act 1990: Identity (Citizenship and Travel Documents) Bill*, Wellington, Department of Justice, 2003.

Ministry of Youth Affairs, *Children in New Zealand: United Nations Convention on the Rights of the Child: Second Periodic Report of New Zealand*, Wellington, Ministry of Youth Affairs, 2000.

Ministry of Youth Affairs, *Does Your Policy Need An Age Limit? A Guide to Youth Ages from the Ministry of Youth Affairs*, Wellington, Ministry of Youth Affairs.

Mnookin, R and Szwed, E, "The Best Interests Syndrome and the Allocation of Power in Child Care" in H Geach and E Szwed (eds), *Providing Civil Justice for Children*, London, Edward Arnold, 1983.

National Health and Medical Research Council (NHMRC), *Ethical Guidelines on Assisted Reproductive Technology*, Canberra, Australian Government Publishing Services, 1996.

New Zealand Human Rights Commission, "Generic Issues" in *Consistency 2000*, Wellington, Human Rights Commission, 1998.

New Zealand Human Rights Commission, *Submission of the Human Rights Commission to the Ministerial Committee on Assisted Reproductive Technologies*, Auckland, Human Rights Commission, 1994.

New Zealand Law Commission, *New Issues in Legal Parenthood* – NZLC PP54, Wellington, NZLC, 2004.

Nowak, M (1990), "The Covenant on Civil and Political Rights" in R Hanski and M Suksi (eds), *An Introduction to the International Protection of Human Rights: A Textbook* (2nd ed), Turku/Abo: Institute for Human Rights, Abo Akademi University, 1999.

O'Donovan, K, "What Shall We Tell the Children?" in R Lee and D Morgan, *Birthrights, Law and Ethics at the Beginnings of Life*, New York, Routledge, 1989.

O'Neill, O, "Children's Rights and Children's Lives" in P Alston, S Parker and J Seymour (eds), *Children, Rights and the Law*, Oxford, Clarendon Press, 1992.

Office for the Commissioner for Children, *Think About it: is Hitting Your Child Really a Good Idea?* Wellington, OCC, 2001.

Office for the Commissioner for Children, *Hitting Children is Unjust*, Wellington, OCC, 2001.

Office of the Privacy Commissioner, *Assisted Human Reproduction Bill, Report by the Privacy Commissioner to the Minister of Justice in Relation to Part 3 of the Assisted Human Reproduction Bill*, 1999: http://www.privacy.org.nz/people/assisted.html

Plato, *The Symposium* (W Hamilton (trans)) London, Penguin Classics, 1959.

Rawls, J, *A Theory of Justice*, Massachusetts, Harvard University Press, 1971.

Roberts, M, "A Right to Know for Children by Donation – Any Assistance from Down Under" (2000) 12(4) Child and Family Law Quarterly 371.

Robertson, R, Adams, F, Finn, J and Mahoney, R, *Adams on Criminal Law*, Wellington, Brookers, 2001.

Royal Commission on New Reproductive Technologies, *Proceed with Care: Final Report on New Reproductive Technologies*, Ottowa, Canada Communications Group, 1993.

Saller, R, *Patriarchy, Property and Death in the Roman Family*, Cambridge, CUP, 1994.

Sants, H, "Genealogical Bewilderment in Children with Substitute Parents" in P Bean (ed), *Adoption: Essays in Social Policy, Law, and Psychology*, London, Tavistock, 1994.

Sartorius, R, *Paternalism*, Minneapolis, University of Minnesota Press, 1983.

South Australian Council on Reproductive Technology (2000) *Discussion Paper of the South Australian Council on Reproductive Technology, Conception by Donation, Access to Identifying Information in the Use of Donated Sperm, Eggs and Embryos in South Australia*, South Australia, SACRT, 2000.

Straus, M, "Corporal Punishment and Primary Prevention of Child Abuse" (2000) 24(9) Child Abuse and Neglect 1109.

Tefft Stanton, K (ed), *Secrecy: A Cross-Cultural Perspective*, New York, Human Sciences Press, 1980.

ter Haar, C, "A Fight to the Death? The Needs, Rights and Welfare of the Child in Need of Life-Saving Medical Treatment" in C Breen (ed), *Children's Needs, Rights and Welfare: Developing Strategies for the 'Whole Child' in the 21st Century*, Victoria, Thompson-Dunmore Press, 2004.

Van Bueren, G, "Children's Access to Adoption Records – State Discretion or an Enforceable Right" (1995) 58(1) Modern Law Review 37.

Warnock, M, *A Question of Life: the Warnock Report on Human Fertilisation and Embryology*, Oxford, OUP, 1985.

Web, P and Treadwell, P, *Family Law in New Zealand* (11th ed), Wellington, LexisNexis, 2003.

Wolfson, S, "Children's Rights: The Theoretical Underpinning of the 'Best Interests of the Child'" in M Freeman and P Veerman (eds), *The Ideologies of Children's Rights*, Dordrecht, Martinus Nijhoff, 1992.

Wood, B, *Children are People Too – Facilitating Social Change about Physical Punishment*, Auckland, Public Health Association Conference, 2001.

Wood, B, *Submission to the Minister of Justice, Minister of Social Services and Minister of Youth Affairs from EPOCH New Zealand on Repeal or Amendment of Section 59 Crimes Act 1961*, Wellington, EPOCH, 2001.

Wood, B, *Hey! We Don't Hit Anybody Here*, Wellington, OCC, 1996.

Wood, B, *Living in a No-Hitting Family: Children are Family Members Too: a Teaching Resource Kit*, Wellington, OCC, 1994.

Youth Law, *Action for Children in Aotearoa 1996: The Non-Governmental Organisation Report to the United Nations Committee on the Rights of the Child*, Auckland, Youth Law Project/Tino Rangatiratanga Taitamariki, 1996.

INDEX

1. Bertrand G. Ramcharan: *Humanitarian Good Offices in International Law.* The Good Offices of the United Nations Secretary General in the Field of Human Rights. 1983
ISBN 90-247-2805-3

2. Bertrand G. Ramcharan: *International Law and Fact-Finding in the Field of Human Rights.* 1983
ISBN 90-247-3042-2

3. Bertrand G. Ramcharan: *The Right to Life in International Law.* 1985
ISBN 90-247-3074-0

4. Katarina Tomaševski and Philip Alston: *Right to Food.* 1984   ISBN 90-247-3087-2

5. Arie Bloed, Pieter van Dijk: *Essays on Human Rights in the Helsinki Process.* 1985
ISBN 90-247-3211-5

6. K. Tornudd: *Finland and the International Norms of Human Rights.* 1986
ISBN 90-247-3257-3

7. Berth Verstappen and Hans Thoolen: *Human Rights Missions. A Study of the Fact-Finding Practice of Non-Governmental Organizations.* 1986   ISBN 90-247-3364-2

8. Hurst Hannum: *The Right to Leave and Return in International Law and Practice.* 1987
ISBN 90-247-3445-2

9. H. Danelius and Herman Burgers: *The United Nations Convention Against Torture. A Handbook on the Convention Against Torture and Other Cruel, Inhuman or Degrading Treatment or Punishment.* 1988   ISBN 90-247-3609-9

10. David A. Martin: *The New Asylum Seekers: Refugee Law in the 1980's.* The Ninth Sokol Colloquium on International Law. 1988   ISBN 90-247-3730-3

11. Cecilia Medina: *The Battle of Human Rights. Gross, Systematic Violations and the Inter-American System.* 1988   ISBN 90-247-3687-0

12. Claus Gulmann, Lars Adam Rehof: *Human Rights in Domestic Law and Development.* Assistance Policies of the Nordic Countries. 1989   ISBN 90-247-3743-5

13. Bertrand G. Ramcharan: *The Concept and Present Status of the International Protection of Human Rights. Forty Years After the Universal Declaration.* 1989   ISBN 90-247-3759-1

14. Angela D. Byre: *International Human Rights Law in the Commonwealth Caribbean.* 1991
ISBN 90-247-3785-0

15. Natan Lerner: *Group Rights and Discrimination in International Law.* 1990
ISBN 0-79230-853-0

16. Shimon Shetreet: *Free Speech and National Security.* 1991   ISBN 0-79231-030-6

17. Geoff Gilbert: *Aspects of Extradition Law*. 1991   ISBN 0-79231-162-0

18. Philip E. Veerman: *The Rights of the Child and the Changing Image of Childhood*. 1992
                                                                    ISBN 0-79231-250-3

19. Mireille Delmas-Marty: *The European Convention for the Protection of Human Rights*. International Protection versus National Restrictions. 1992   ISBN 0-79231-283-X

20. Arie Bloed and Pieter van Dijk: *The Human Dimension of the Helsinki Process*. The Vienna Follow-up Meeting and its Aftermath. 1991   ISBN 0-79231-337-2

21. Lyal S. Sunga: *Individual Responsibility in International Law for Serious Human Rights Violations*. 1992   ISBN 0-79231-453-0

22. Dinah Shelton and Stanislaw J. Frankowski: *Preventive Detention*. A Comparative and International Law Perspective. 1992   ISBN 0-79231-465-4

23. Michael Freeman and Philip E. Veerman: *Ideologies of Children's Rights*. 1992
                                                                    ISBN 0-79231-800-5

24. Stephanos Stavros: *The Guarantees for Accused Persons Under Article 6 of the European Convention on Human Rights*. An Analysis of the Application of the Convention and a Comparison with Other Instruments. 1993   ISBN 0-79231-897-8

25. Allan Rosas, Diane Goodman and Jan Helgesen: *Strength of Diversity*. Human Rights and Pluralist Democracy. 1992   ISBN 0-79231-987-7

26. Andrew Clapham and Kees Waaldijk: *Homosexuality: A European Community Issue*. Essays on Lesbian and Gay Rights in European Law and Policy. 1993
                                                                    ISBN 0-79232-038-7

28. Howard Charles Yourow: *The Margin of Appreciation Doctrine in the Dynamics of European Human Rights Jurisprudence*. 1995   ISBN 0-79233-338-1

29. Lars Adam Rehof: *Guide to the Travaux Préparatoires of the United Nations Convention on the Elimination of all Forms of Discrimination against Women*. 1993.   ISBN 0-79232-222-3

30. Allan Rosas, Arie Bloed, Liselotte Leicht and Manfred Nowak: *Monitoring Human Rights in Europe*. Comparing International Procedures and Mechanisms. 1993
                                                                    ISBN 0-79232-383-1

31. Andrew Harding and John Hatchard: *Preventive Detention and Security Law: A Comparative Survey*. 1993   ISBN 0-79232-432-3

32. Yves Beigbeder: *International Monitoring of Plebiscites, Referenda and National Elections*. Self-Determination and Transition to Democracy. 1994   ISBN 0-79232-563-X

33. Thomas David Jones: *Human Rights: Group Defamation, Freedom of Expression and the Law of Nations.* 1997   ISBN 90-411-0265-5

34. David M. Beatty: *Human Rights and Judicial Review: A Comparative Perspective.* 1994
                                         ISBN 0-79232-968-6
35. Geraldine Van Bueren: *The International Law on the Rights of the Child.* 1995
                                         ISBN 0-79232-687-3

36. Tom Zwart: *The Admissibility of Human Rights Petitions.* The Case Law of the European Commission of Human Rights and the Human Rights Committee. 1994
                                         ISBN 0-79233-146-X

37. Helene Lambert: *Seeking Asylum.* Comparative Law and Practice in Selected European Countries. 1995   0-79233-152-4

38. E. Lijnzaad: *Reservations to UN-Human Rights Treaties.* Ratify and Ruin? 1994
                                         ISBN 0-7923-3256-3

39. L.G. Loucaides: *Essays on the Developing Law of Human Rights.* 1995
                                         ISBN 0-7923-3276-8

40. T. Degener and Y. Koster-Dreese (eds.): *Human Rights and Disabled Persons.* Essays and Relevant Human Rights Instruments. 1995   ISBN 0-7923-3298-9

41. J.-M. Henckaerts: *Mass Expulsion in Modern International Union and Human Rights.* 1995
                                         ISBN 90-411-0072-5

42. N.A. Neuwahl and A. Rosas (eds.): *The European Union and Human Rights.* 1995
                                         ISBN 90-411-0124-1

43. H. Hey: *Gross Human Rights Violations: A Search for Causes.* A Study of Guatemala and Costa Rica. 1995   ISBN 90-411-0146-2

44. B.G. Tahzib: *Freedom of Religion or Belief.* Ensuring Effective International Legal Protection. 1996   ISBN 90-411-0159-4

45. F. de Varennes: *Language, Minorities and Human Rights.* 1996   ISBN 90-411-0206-X

46. J. Raikka (ed.): *Do We Need Minority Rights?* Conceptual Issues. 1996
                                         ISBN 90-411-0309-0

47. J. Brohmer: *State Immunity and the Violation of Human Rights.* 1997
                                         ISBN 90-411-0322-8

48. C.A. Gearty (ed.): *European Civil Liberties and the European Convention on Human Rights.* A Comparative Study. 1997   ISBN 90-411-0253-1

49. B. Conforti and F. Francioni (eds.): *Enforcing International Human Rights in Domestic Courts.* 1997   ISBN 90-411-0393-7

65. C. Tiburcio: *The Human Rights of Aliens under International and Comparative Law*. 2001
ISBN 90-411-1550-1

66. E. Brems: Human Rights: *Universality and Diversity*. 2001   ISBN 90-411-1618-4

67. C. Bourloyannis-Vrailas and L.-A. Sicilianos: *The Prevention of Human Rights Violations*.
2001   ISBN 90-411-1672-9

68. G. Ulrich and K. Hastrup: *Discrimination and Toleration*. New Perspectives. 2001
ISBN 90-411-1711-3

69. V.O. Orlu Nmehielle: *African Human Rights System*. Its Laws, Practice and Institutions.
2001   ISBN 90-411-1731-8

70. B.G. Ramcharan: *Human Rights and Human Security*. 2002   ISBN 90-411-818-7

71. B.G. Ramcharan: *The United Nations High Commissioner for Human Rights*. The Challenges
of International Protection. 2002   ISBN 90-411-1832-2

72. C. Breen: *The Standard of the Best Interests of the Child*. A Western Tradition in International and Comparative Law. 2002   ISBN 90-411-1851-9

73. M. Katayanagi: *Human Rights Functions of United Nations Peacekeeping Operations*. 2002
ISBN 90-411-1910-8

74. O.M. Arnadottir: *Equality and Non-Discrimination under the European Convention on Human
Rights*. 2002   ISBN 90-411-1912-4

75. B.G. Ramcharan: *The Security Council and the Protection of Human Rights*. 2002
ISBN 90-411-1878-0

76. E. Fierro: *The EU's Approach to Human Rights Conditionality in Practice*. 2002
ISBN 90-411-1936-1

77. Natan Lerner: *Group Rights and Discrimination in International Law*. Second Edition. 2002
ISBN 90-411-1982-5

78. S. Leckie (ed.): *National Perspectives on Housing Rights*. 2003   ISBN 90-411-2013-0

79. L.C. Rcif: *The Ombudsman, Good Governance and the International Human Rights System*. 2004
ISBN 90-04-13903-6

80. Mary Dowell-Jones: *Contextualising the International Covenant on Economic, Social and Cultural Rights: Assessing the Economic Deficit*. 2004   ISBN 90-04-13908-7

81. Li-ann Thio: *Managing Babel: The International Legal Protection of Minorities in the Twentieth
Century*   ISBN 90-04-14198-7

INTERNATIONAL STUDIES IN HUMAN RIGHTS

82. K.D. Beiter: *The Protection of the Right to Education by International Law.* 2006
ISBN 90 04 14704 7

83. J.H. Gerards: *Judicial Review in Equal Treatment Cases.* 2005   ISBN 90 04 14379 3

84. V.A.Leary and D. Warner: *Social Issues, Globalization and International Institutions. Labour Rights and the EU, ILO, OECD and WTO.* 2005   ISBN 90 04 14579 6

85. J.K.M. Gevers, E.H. Hondius and J.H. Hubben (eds.): *Health Law, Human Rights and the Biomedicine Convention.* Essays in Honour of Henriette Roscam Abbing. 2005
ISBN 90 04 14822 1

86. C. Breen: *Age Discrimination and Children's Rights.* Ensuring Equality and Acknowledging Difference. 2006   ISBN 90 04 14827 2

87. B.G. Ramcharan (ed.): *Human Rights Protection in the Field.* 2006   ISBN 90 04 14847 7

This series is designed to shed light on current legal and political aspects of process and organization in the field of human rights

MARTINUS NIJHOFF PUBLISHERS – LEIDEN • BOSTON